MORTAL REMAINS

MORTAL REMAINS

//

A TRUE STORY OF RITUAL MURDER

HENRY SCAMMELL

Edward Burlingame Books
An Imprint of HarperCollinsPublishers

To

my wife Caroline
and our children

and our friends
Joe & Carolyn Basso
Bill & Celia Calhoun

with love

FIRST EDITION

Designed by Helene Berinsky

Library of Congress Cataloging-in-Publication Data

Scammell, Henry
   Mortal remains: a true story of ritual murder/Henry Scammell. —1st ed.
      p.   cm.
   ISBN 0-06-016327-5
   1. Murder—Massachusetts—Fall River—Case studies.   I. Title.
HV6534. F2S28   1991   9055556
364.1 ' 523' 0974485—dc20

91 92 93 94 95 MAC/RRD 10 9 8 7 6 5 4 3 2 1

CONTENTS

PREFACE: HOW THIS BOOK WAS WRITTEN

A ll of the events described in this book are drawn from evidence supplied by eyewitnesses and participants.

By far the largest part of that evidence was created by the legal process, starting with the police investigations into the three murders and ending eight years later with the disposition of the final appeal. Between these two brackets are over one hundred reports by local and state police and the FBI, plus verbatim transcripts of dozens of interrogations of witnesses and suspects, testimony at two murder trials, and the documentation of years of appeals. Collectively this written record comprises more than six thousand pages.

The heart of that documentary evidence was impounded at the time of the final trial described in this book. Without it, I would not have been able to tell the complete story. I am very grateful to Bristol County District Attorney Ronald Pina, who supported my motion to the Bristol Superior Court to vacate the order of impoundment.

The truth behind a great crime, however, inevitably lies deeper than the facts contained in any public record. For the perspective, relevance, and telling details that must combine in order for the events to come back to life, I interviewed many of the participants. Most notably, these included Detectives Alan Silvia, Tom Joaquim, and Paul Carey of the Fall River Police Department Major Crimes Division; State Police Detectives Paul Fitzgerald and Dan Lowney of Bristol County CPAC; Dr. Douglas Ubelaker of the National Museum of Natural History; Alan Robillard of the FBI; Rhode Island Medical Examiner Dr. William Sturner; George Dean; Assistant District Attorney David Waxler; defense attorney John Birknes; Carl Drew; and the former Carol Fletcher.

One witness spoke with me long enough to say she had never told a lie. A week later her attorney told me she had decided against a lengthier interview.

The dialogue in this book comes from two sources. The more obvious of the two is the verbatim record of the events themselves, where such records were made: stenographic transcripts of interrogations by the police and various attorneys, hearings and depositions, and testimony at the trials. Except for the need to edit for brevity, that dialogue is offered here as it was given.

Where I have offered conversations for which no verbatim record exists, I have relied on the memories of those who heard them and on official written reports filed by police officers who were involved in the conversations, supported by my own inferences from the tone and speech patterns as I was able to determine them from my interviews and verbatim records.

If everyone's versions of the facts agreed, there would be no need for a trial. In resolving disparities for the purposes of telling the story as accurately and fairly as possible, I have relied first on the findings of the court, then on the record, and finally on my own best judgment of what the witnesses told me ten years after the events took place. Where a witness repeatedly revised testimony as the case unfolded— in one notable instance, apparently without once telling a lie—I have had to rely on the collective opinion of the police, the prosecutors, and the expert witnesses in selecting the most plausible version from among those attested to.

I would also like to thank Detective Kenneth Martin of the Bristol County CPAC; Marcel Gantreau and Marc Santos of Bristol Superior Court; Deodato Arruda of the Massachusetts Department of Corrections; Steve Marquart and Chet Blythe of the FBI; Special Agent Paul Brown of the Narcotics Task Force; Margaret Charig, James Ragsdale, Maurice Lauzon, and Marguerite Habicht of New Bedford's *Standard Times;* Dave Grey of the *Providence Journal-Bulletin;* Dr. Robert Courey of St. Anne's Hospital; James Lyons and Robert Murray, formerly of St. Anne's; Jean Gavin of Taunton Superior Court; and Jim Martin of the Bristol County DA's office.

Henry Scammell

See, I have set before you this day
life and good,
and death and evil.

Deuteronomy 30:15

You can't believe in God
without believing in the Devil.
They go together.

Convicted murderer Carl Drew

PART ONE

//

PART ONE

ONE / **POINT OF IMPACT**

In early February of 1978, a great winter storm was predicted for southern Rhode Island and eastern Massachusetts. Forecasts are usually tentative in the northeast, where the ocean creates its own climate and can change everything at the last minute. But from all indications, this one was a sure thing: the same blizzard had already paralyzed the entire coast from the Carolinas through New York City and, despite the time of year, the satellite image on the television screen showed the classic whirling cartwheel of a hurricane.

Carl Drew loved storms, and at noon on the day it was to hit, when Channel 6 in nearby New Bedford displayed the radar pattern and described the approaching event as a juggernaut, he switched off the television set, got out of bed, and peered out at the lowering, leaden clouds over the city of Fall River. It looked good. There was very little traffic. The parking lots at the muffler shop across the street and the gay bar a couple of doors to the left of it were empty. Above this familiar panorama, a malignant, alien sky was flowing steadily, like cold lava, toward the northeast. There was still no snow, but when Drew raised one of the three sooty bay windows and inhaled the air, he was sure. It was going to be a big one.

He dressed without bothering to shower or shave, added a sweater and his black leather Sidewinders motorcycle jacket, slid into his stompers, and slammed the door behind him. Skimming down the dark flight of stairs, he bounded through the entryway and out onto the sidewalk, then headed up Pleasant Street at an easy lope, throwing back his head and delighting in the steam in his breath as he ran. Carl Drew wanted to be at Pier 14, in the middle of things, when the first flakes began to fall.

Pier 14 was a bar in the city's combat zone. Nowhere near the water, it stood less than a block away from its coaxis at the blighted urban center, the headquarters of the Fall River Police Department. The two buildings, on opposite sides of Bedford Street, were within sight of each other. The bar was a gray, decayed, wooden firetrap with empty, uninhabitable apartments on the second and third floors; a row of six bleak and weathered dormers in the front of its mansard roof stared out over the street traffic—dopers, pimps, prostitutes, and the circling army of tricks—like the eyes of a giant spider. The police department building, by contrast, seemed sightless: slightly newer but still badly decayed, it was a cubic, grimy, sand-colored bastion, sheltering and separating its occupants from the streets it was ostensibly designed to protect.

Carl Drew usually started his workday at the Pier just about suppertime, an hour or two ahead of the other pimps, most of whom wheeled their women in from Boston and Providence in their spotless, heavily chromed and whitewalled Lincolns and Cadillacs. It was a way of anchoring his territory—not because he was afraid of the competition or the out-of-towners or that he even discouraged them, but because he recognized that there are hierarchies even in apparent anarchy, and whoever gets somewhere first usually winds up in charge.

This time, despite the fact that it was only twelve-thirty in the afternoon and the day had barely started, Drew realized that he had not gotten there first. As he walked into Pier 14, he saw that someone had already taken up his position, filling his customary space: he appeared to be about the same age—in his middle twenties—but an easy three inches taller than Drew's six feet and, under his long cashmere overcoat, perhaps ninety or one hundred pounds heavier. Except for the bartender, there was no one else in the place. The big man was leaning against the bar, looking up at the television and pouring a Bud against the side of his glass, his back to the door. Unseen, Drew crossed over to an empty table on the side farthest from the bar and noiselessly took a seat.

"I love these weather jerks," the guy was saying, shaking his head contemptuously at the TV over the bar and glancing toward the bartender for a reaction. The bartender had not seen Drew either: he was bent down behind the row of beer handles, testing the hose on a keg; it was early, and he was still setting up.

The customer didn't seem to mind that he was being ignored; while the bartender's back was turned, he reached across and stole a maraschino cherry and two pimento olives from the service tray, popping them all into his mouth at once. He chewed three or four times, swallowed, then looked at himself in the mirror, drawing back his lips to check out his teeth, adjusting the lapels of his coat, admiring his reflection as he continued to blow off. "How can anyone say what it's gonna do in Fall River, Massachusetts, just because it's snowing in Washington, D.C., for Chrissake?"

Drew looked beyond him at the TV above the street end of the bar. A reporter from Channel 4 in Boston was running National Weather Service pictures like the ones he had seen in his apartment a half hour earlier on Channel 6, only now the cartwheel had overspread all of Long Island and was reaching across Providence, New Bedford, Fall River, Block Island, Martha's Vineyard, Nantucket, even the southern side of Cape Cod. "The storm is following the same path as the great hurricane of nineteen thirty-eight, picking up moisture and momentum from the ocean, building in volume and intensity," the forecaster was saying. "And just as forty years ago, this area on the southeast coast"—he pointed to Providence, Fall River, New Bedford—"is about to receive the full impact as it roars in for a landfall."

The man in the cashmere coat bent down and peered toward the window, then turned and squinted at the glass panels at the top of the door. As he did, his eyes stopped for just the briefest moment as he took in Drew for the first time, sitting twenty feet away at the table, his hands in his jeans pockets, stretching out his legs, looking back at him under his lids. The man turned back to the bartender, who had straightened up behind the taps. "That'd be about the last time anyone bothered to clean these windows," he said, and when the bartender still didn't respond he decided to explain it. "Nineteen thirty-eight."

The bartender continued to ignore him. He had seen Drew at the same moment the customer did, and he smiled over at him and elaborately pantomimed a double take on his bare wrist. "What? Are you early, or did my watch stop?"

"Who's been in?" Drew asked.

He glanced at the customer, then back at Drew, shaking his head. "Nobody. Not inside, anyway."

The bartender knew that he was asking about women, in particular the women who worked for Drew on the streets, and he was carefully leaving open the possibility that one or more of them might be working the sidewalk outside the bar, as some of them occasionally did at lunchtime. Drew accepted the information without comment and looked back up to the TV.

The bartender said, "This storm is going to kill tonight, from the looks of it."

Without moving his eyes from the screen, Drew shrugged, as though to say he didn't know or it didn't matter.

The man at the bar had been studying Drew in the mirror. Now he put down his beer glass and said to the bartender, "C'mon, what storm? There's no storm out there."

Drew continued to watch the screen, but out of the corner of his eye he could see the bartender looking back at the guy and shrugging. "Yeah, well," he said, and turned away to dust off the cash register with his towel.

Drew turned back pointedly toward the mirror, and when he caught the customer's eye, he held it. The guy looked surprised by the challenge. He was still not finished sizing Drew up and was uncertain what risks were involved if he should choose to take offense at the stare. Drew decided to make it easier for him. "You looking for something?" he asked quietly.

The customer turned from the mirror and stared back at Carl Drew across the room. Drew still had his legs stretched out in front of him and one hand in the pocket of his jeans; with the other, he was brushing lightly at the feathery goatee on his chin, smiling almost invisibly as he waited for an answer.

The man glanced behind himself at the bartender for an instant, then back at Drew. "Who are you talking to? Me?" When Drew continued to look at him, still waiting, he added, "Looking for what?" He still had not made up his mind how to deal with this.

Drew stopped stroking the beard, motioning toward the other chair at his table. "Have a seat."

The man hesitated. He turned back to the bartender and said, "Gimme another Bud."

The bartender reached into the ice and pulled out a bottle and capped it on the side of the chest. But instead of putting it on the bar, he raised the service gate, walked over to where Drew was sitting, and placed it in front of the proffered second chair. The man in the cashmere coat hesitated, then dropped a dollar bill on the bar and crossed to the chair and sat down. "Looking for what?" he asked Drew again, only this time more out of curiosity than belligerence.

Just as coolly, Drew regarded him thoughtfully from across the small table. "For the same as everyone else. For a little comfort, right?"

The big man looked carefully neutral, but his eyes narrowed and

Drew knew that he had guessed right: the guy was a trick, and he had come into the Pier because it was still early and there was nothing out on the street. He watched Drew a moment longer without answering, then picked up the bottle the bartender had left on the table.

"Right?" Drew asked again.

The guy tilted his head noncommittally, pouring the beer against the side of his glass. It seemed for a moment as though he were not going to answer at all, but when he finished pouring he set down the bottle and glanced up at Drew. "You a pimp?"

This time it was Drew who did not answer; instead, he leaned back in the chair and resumed stroking his thin goatee idly with his left hand, then looked slowly around the bar as though taking possession of the room. When his eyes returned to the man in front of him, Drew saw that the trick was straining to read the message written on that hand. Tattooed in blue ink, with one letter on the base of each finger, was the word HATE.

"The problem I have with pimps—*one* of the problems—" the guy said, sipping at the foam and looking back up at Drew across the rim of the glass, his eyes still narrowed, "is that I kind of like to see what I'm getting."

Drew couldn't have cared less what else bothered him about pimps; he shrugged, ignoring the bait. "What I've got is a lot better than what you're going to find on the streets—at this time of day, anyway. And if you wait any longer, with the weather coming, you'll be lucky to wind up with a tall dog."

The guy continued watching him and sipped some more beer, weighing his options and perhaps deciding whether it was all worth it.

"Seventeen," Drew continued. "Pretty face. Good body. Still in high school."

The guy grinned, not in amusement but sneering and openly incredulous. "What do I do, pick her up at the playground?"

Drew did not grin back. He stood up and impatiently juggled a dime in his hand in front of the man's face. "What's it going to be? I'll call her and set it up. Now or never. Thirty bucks. Make up your mind."

"Fuck this," the guy said, more to himself than to Drew. He stood up as well, looking angry, and walked across the barroom to open the front door. His coat billowed out and from behind him, Drew could see the first fine flakes of the storm sifting horizontally along Bedford Street. The man shook his head in frustration, turning back to the table. "Fuck this," he said again, then added, "How far is she from here?"

"Not far," Drew said. "Less than a block."

The guy looked out the window. "Go ahead."

Drew stopped juggling the dime and closed his fist. He held out the other hand to the trick, palm up.

"Call her first."

"Thirty bucks," Drew insisted. "I'm like you—I like to see what I'm getting."

The trick reached into his pocket and pulled out three tens. He laid them on the table, but then he placed his hand on top of them. He leaned his weight on the hand, staring at the pimp with stubborn defiance and saying nothing.

Drew took it in, making up his mind. Then he went to the wall telephone next to the rest rooms, dropped in the dime, and punched in seven digits.

He spoke so quietly, the trick could hear nothing of the conversation. Drew was back at the table in less than thirty seconds. Without a word, he reached down and grasped the smallest finger of the hand on the money, and he bent it up until the big man shifted his weight defensively and pulled back in pain. Still using the finger as a lever, Drew then easily lifted the hand from the table, removed the three bills, and placed them in his pocket.

"Okay, Hard-on," he said, relaxing the pressure on the hand and crooking his own index finger in the trick's face. "Let's go."

Before the customer could respond, Drew was across the room and out the door. Rubbing his hand, his expression a combination of surprise and anger, the trick followed him into Bedford Street.

Once outside, Drew was surprised as well, at how much the weather had changed in the short time since he had entered the Pier. The street was already covered with a rippling, shifting carpet of snow, and it was coming down so quickly, the black clouds that carried it were no longer visible through the swirling white. He flipped up the collar of his Sidewinders jacket, and when he was satisfied the trick was behind him, he lowered his head, leaned into the wind, and pushed up toward the corner.

The apartment Drew had called was in the tenement directly behind Pier 14, less than seventy yards from the barroom. Drew jogged briskly up the front steps. There were no buzzers, no lock on the front door, and no names on the rusted, broken mailboxes. He shook the snow from his hair, climbed quickly to the second floor, and opened one of the doors without knocking. The big man followed several steps behind; by the time he caught up, Drew saw that a fine layer of snow was imbedded like a skim of plaster in the front of his cashmere coat. The trick was winded from the cold and the climb, and he still looked mad.

The room they had entered was so sparsely furnished, it looked almost abandoned. There was a bed against the far wall, a night table with a lamp and a phone beside it, and a straight-backed wooden chair next to the door. The floor was a collage of tattered linoleum, and there was no rug or carpet.

A young woman in blue jeans and a man's plaid jacket was at the far side of the room, one foot on the windowsill, looking out through the dirty glass at the snow whipping between the buildings; across the alley, some of the flakes were starting to cling to the asbestos shingles on the rear of the derelict apartments above Pier 14. The girl turned toward the door when Drew entered, regarding him with obvious recognition but no greeting, then turned away again when the trick walked in behind him. She ran her fingers through her stringy brown hair as she looked out at the snow. "Is this weather supposed to amount to anything?" She sounded dreamy and abstracted.

Drew stared angrily at her, then quickly scanned the room for any sign of what she was using; the instant he had seen her eyes, he was sure she was on something. This girl had been trouble before, and he kept a watch on her for signs of heroin. This time, it was probably beans—uppers or maybe mescaline—and he decided he would deal with her later.

He turned back to the business at hand. "We got a rule," he told the trick, "like in a store: you break it, you buy it."

The man brushed the snow from his coat and gave Drew a dark, sidewise look of dismissal. "Fuck your rules. What are you talking about?"

Drew's hand shot out and touched the man under the chin, barely making contact, but the trick pulled quickly back as though he had been hit, holding up an arm to defend himself. Drew said, "You got it wrong, Hard-on. This is what you fuck, over there," gesturing over his shoulder with his thumb toward the girl. "My rules you don't fuck."

The man watched him warily, then glanced over at the girl and slowly dropped the arm.

"What I'm saying is, you're a big guy," Drew went on. "What do you go, three hundred pounds?"

It was clear the trick had not yet made up his mind about how to react to what had happened a moment earlier back in the Pier—or whether to react at all. But Drew could see that he was angry, and he knew that pushing him further was making it worse. The big man avoided looking at him, glowering at the girl instead, and said, "Hey, c'mon, what is this? I gotta pass some kinda physical?"

"Three ten?" Drew asked, persisting.

The guy still wouldn't look at Drew. He hesitated, visibly swallowed his rage, then shifted his eyes from the girl as well. "Two seventy-seven," he muttered, almost inaudible.

"Okay, two seventy-seven," Drew said, smiling derisively as though he didn't believe it. "That's between two and three times our prom queen here. So what I'm saying is, be careful."

The big guy had picked a place on the wall between Drew and the girl at the window and now was staring at it—a neutral midpoint between the source of threat and the witness to his unwillingness to accept the challenge. Drew could see that the man was starting to sweat. Like the matador who so perfectly understands the moment of conquest that he dares to lean over the horns, Drew reached out his hand again and touched the man's face a second time; with the thumb on one side of his mouth and his fingers on the other, he pressed his cheeks in a chubby-baby squeeze, puckering the man's lips. "Atta boy," he said quietly, almost with affection, before letting go.

As Drew started from the room, he stopped in the doorway and looked back at the girl. Whatever it was she had taken, he could see it again in her oblique, excited eyes, at once clouded and acute, detached and feral. "If I'm not at the Pier, I'll be over at Charlie's," he told her. "As soon as you're finished, don't hang in here."

Her eyes flicked apprehensively at the man between them, then back at Drew; the trick still was not looking at either of them but he was beginning to shake, and the girl obviously had doubts about what might happen when they were alone. Drew ignored the look. He pulled the door shut behind him, strode quickly down the hallway, and descended the stairs.

But he did not go back out into the street. He stood at the bottom of the flight, raising the collar of his leather jacket once more against the cold and the snow that was blowing into the hallway through the open entrance. After a moment, he rapped on the door of the first-floor apartment. Inside, someone turned off the radio that had been playing a talk station from Boston, and after another few seconds, a high-pitched boy's voice asked from behind the door, "Who is it?"

Drew didn't answer. All he had wanted was for the radio to be turned off so he could hear what was going on in the apartment above. He could tell that the kid was listening on the other side of the door, waiting for a response, before asking again, louder, "Who's there?"

At the same time, Drew heard something else. It was a muted gasp, and then the sound of something falling, like the small table or the wooden chair, on the linoleum floor above. He put one foot on the second step, listening intently. There was another thud, this time softer, and the girl screamed, a terrified howl, one that could have been heard a block away. Drew took the stairs four at a time, holding onto the newel post at the top as he swung around the corner, and in two more strides he threw his weight against the door without even bothering to try the handle. The panels cracked, the frame splintered at the latch, and the flimsy door flew inward, smashing against the wall.

The girl was sitting on the floor, facing the doorway. The trick was behind her, still wearing his cashmere coat, sitting on the edge of the bed, pulling her hair in his large fist to hold her head immobile against his bare thigh and covering the lower half of her face with his other hand to stop her from screaming again. There was blood coming from both her nostrils, and the left side of her face was flushed from where he had struck her.

When the man saw Drew coming at him, he pushed the girl aside and attempted to stand to meet the attack. But the girl was still in his way, and he was clutching at her for support and pushing his weight forward to rise from the low bed when Drew landed on him. Drew kicked him in the chest with his right foot, regained his balance as the big man fell forward in response, then brought up the same foot again and caught him in the face with the heel of his black motorcycle boot.

The second blow broke several of the man's upper front teeth, driving them through his heavy lower lip, and a torrent of blood poured down his shirt and onto his bare thighs. Drew then hit him several times in the face with his fists, but the big man raised his arms in defense and, driven by the sudden realization that he was fighting for his life, pushed his attacker back until he was finally able to stand.

The trick's trousers and shorts were around his ankles, and because he still had on his shoes, he discovered in a panic there was no way he could kick them free. "Ftop, ftop!" he said, tears of pain and terror swimming in his eyes, trying to keep his balance despite the hobbles and at the same time holding out his hands in desperation to fend off Drew's fists. "Pleeeze! Pleeeeze!"

As suddenly as Drew had started the attack, he stopped. He dropped his hands and let his arms hang limp at his sides. After a moment, when the man still did not dare to move, Drew backed away, spreading his hands palms up before him to show that they were no longer fists. "Pull up your pants," he said in a surprisingly soft voice, in the same tone an adult might use with an errant child.

Still cowering, the big man hesitated, then bent down and grabbed at his shorts and jeans together, pulling them hastily up over his legs. He fumbled with the belt buckle, then dabbed cautiously at his torn mouth with the back of one hand. The blood was still streaming, and now it glistened in vivid, ornamental spangles on both lapels and all down the front of his coat like crimson filigree. One of the broken pieces of tooth the size of a Chiclet dislodged from his lower lip and fell audibly to the linoleum at his feet. He sobbed in disbelief.

Drew, by contrast, was composed to the point of serenity. He surveyed the beaten man without the slightest hint of emotion, either of anger or of empathy. And when Drew turned his attention to the girl, he looked her over with the interested detachment of an insurance appraiser after a minor collision, assessing the damage to someone else's automobile. He made a gesture with his hand, telling her to get up. "C'mon, we're leaving."

She put one hand on the end of the bed and the other on the windowsill and awkwardly gained her feet. Drew did nothing to help. Her plaid jacket was on the floor behind her, fallen from where she had apparently laid it on the night table when Drew had left the room a few minutes earlier. Her shirt was unbuttoned, and her brassiere had been hiked up to reveal her breasts—not as a result of what the trick had done to her, Drew assumed, but as a normal part of her preparation for work. Her hands were shaking so badly that at first she simply clasped the shirt together to cover herself, but then she reached inside and pulled the bra down again to its proper position. Still trembling, she struggled into the jacket, all the while eyeing the beaten, bleeding man with residual fear and a vengeful, nearly manic delight at her deliverance.

Drew placed a hand on her shoulder to guide her toward the door. "Wait outside," he told her, "on the street."

She hurried along the hallway and down the stairs.

Turning back to the trick, Drew said, "All set?"

The big man nodded, not trying to speak, and pointed helplessly at the blood that was still cascading from his mouth.

"Yeah, I know," Drew said. "We gotta do something about that." He gestured toward the door, and the man walked painfully out into the hallway.

At the top of the stairs, Drew stopped him with a hand on the shoulder. The man turned, a pleading look on his face, and said, "I god do go do a hofital."

Drew reached around for a lapel of the man's coat and used it to turn him gently but firmly until his back was to the stairway. "That's what I'm going to do," he assured him. "I owe you, and I'm going to put you in the hospital."

The man knew instantly what Drew meant, and he threw his arms around him, clasping him in a bear hug to avoid being hit again. But Drew made no attempt to resist; instead, he allowed himself to be drawn in, and then he lifted a knee like a piston into the trick's crotch. The big man sucked in his breath in agony. As Drew pulled himself free, the trick vomited bloody beer onto the steps, then lurched backward and tumbled thunderously down the stairs.

By the time Drew trotted down after him and stepped over his unconscious body and out onto the stoop, a patrol car from the Fall River Police Department was pulling up to the curb in front of the tenement. The girl was waiting on the sidewalk as she had been told, and she started yelling at the two cops before they could get out of the cruiser. "This is none of your business," she shouted. "Keep the fuck out of it." The pills, or whatever she had taken earlier, were back at work. The cops grabbed the girl, held her down against the snow-covered hood of the car while they cuffed her hands behind her back, then trundled her into the caged rear seat of the cruiser.

Drew, by contrast, made no attempt to get away. He descended the few steps to the street and walked over to the police car. Both the officers were in uniform, and he addressed the one with the sergeant's stripes on his sleeve. "She's upset because this guy just attacked her," he said.

"Run, Carl!" the girl yelled from the backseat, kicking noisily against the iron grille separating the front seat from the back. "Run!"

By contrast, Drew was the picture of reasonableness and self-control. He watched her curiously, even aloofly, before turning back to the sergeant. "She's still afraid of him. He's in the house, and she thinks he's going to hurt her."

The sergeant and the other officer looked up at the entrance to the tenement. The outside door was still ajar, and there was some motion on the floor behind it. Drew added, "He was beating up on her, and when she broke away, he fell down the stairs."

"No kidding," the sergeant said. He looked at Drew. "Who are you?"

"A friend." He indicated the girl in the patrol car. "Of hers."

The sergeant peered up toward the vestibule, then told the other officer to call for Rescue. He asked Drew, "Did you happen to have anything to do with him falling?"

Drew considered for a moment. "Not with the falling."

The cop looked at him skeptically, and Drew added, "I did tune him up a little, I admit it—but the reason he fell was because he was trying to chase her out onto the street."

"You're her pimp," the sergeant said. It was a question, but he was asking as though he already knew the answer.

Drew looked away and shook his head, not by way of a reply but to indicate disappointment. "What's this about? I'm trying to be a citizen—a good Samaritan. Aren't you guys always telling people to get involved? All of a sudden I'm a pimp." He smiled in pain at the irony, and the sergeant looked at him uncertainly.

Meanwhile, the second policeman had reemerged from the patrol car and walked up the steps to the entry. He pushed the door against the heavy body lying behind it, then peered around to look down at the man on the floor. After a moment, he called back to the sergeant. "This guy's taken more than a fall. He looks like he's been through a woodchipper."

The sergeant asked Drew, "That's your tune-up?"

Drew's face returned to neutral, and he shrugged and looked away.

The sergeant opened the rear door of the cruiser and told the girl to push over. Drew entered the car voluntarily. Unlike the girl, his hands were not cuffed.

Ten minutes later, after the Rescue Squad had arrived and taken away the trick on a stretcher, the two cops got back in and drove around the corner to the station house. By now the snow had accumulated in small dunes on the street, and the patrol car slewed as they turned into the parking garage in the basement.

The sergeant got out and opened the rear door on the other side of the car from Drew. He reached in and took the girl by the arm, protecting her head from the door frame with his other hand and looking over at Drew. "Ladies first. We'll be back for you in a minute."

"Sure," Drew said, nodding agreeably. "Ladies first."

As soon as they were gone, he looked quickly around the cruiser. There were no inside handles or window cranks on the rear doors, so there was no way he could open them. Looking quickly out the side and rear windows, he checked to see if there were any other people in the garage. It appeared to be empty, although he knew there was a glass booth at the entrance where a cop monitored arrivals and departures. Drew only had a few seconds to make his move.

Leaning forward, he laced his fingers through the metal mesh of the screen over the back of the front seat and tested how firmly it was welded to the side posts. It didn't budge.

He considered kicking out one of the windows, but he dismissed that possibility as too noisy: even if he succeeded, the glass would land on the cement floor and the cop in the booth would look around the corner to see what was going on.

Drew dropped one hand from the screen and placed it just below the divider, on the top of the front seat back. He concentrated for a moment, then pulled with one powerful arm against the screen as he pushed with the other against the seat back. And although the screen remained absolutely unyielding, the seat back below it moved—just a fraction of an inch, but it moved.

Drew quickly slid down and braced his shoulders against the back of the rear seat, placing his feet at the top of the seat ahead of him. He knew from his work in a body shop that there were only two posts anchoring the front seat to its track on the car floor. Although they were designed to withstand the impact of a collision, Drew knew as well that he had tremendous power in his legs—maybe enough power, given the right leverage, to bend the posts or break the tracks that held the seat in place. Closing his eyes, clenching his jaw, focusing all his energy into his back and legs, applying more and more pressure to the seat, he began slowly to uncoil his body.

The front seat moved forward another two inches, squeaking sorrowfully with the strain, and then stopped. Drew let up the pressure and leaned forward to measure his progress. It was obvious that he lacked the necessary purchase, and this approach was not going to work.

Drew surveyed the garage again to make sure it was still empty. Then he turned and knelt on the rear seat, facing the back window. He lowered his head. Bracing himself with his head and shoulders, he lifted the lower half of his body like a bucking horse and kicked violently backward against the front seat. The entire cruiser rocked on its springs, and he glanced apprehensively out the window to see if the noise had attracted any attention. The garage was still empty. When he turned to check the result of his efforts, he saw that the original gap between the seat and the iron grille had widened to six inches.

He lowered his head, braced himself, and kicked again four times in a row, each kick reaching further than the last. When he stopped, the seat back had been collapsed into a wedge, like the bow of a ship, with the apex resting against the dashboard. Looking quickly around the garage one last time, Drew crawled under the wire screen, opened the front door on the passenger side, and slid out of the cruiser.

He used both hands to wipe the sweat from his face before starting across the garage. As Drew passed by the glass booth on his way out of the garage, the cop at the desk looked up and waved at him. The cop was an old man, and it was a bye-bye wave, a wriggling of the fingers, the kind that women use with babies and children. Carl Drew cupped his own hand, the one with HATE written on it, and waved back in the same way, grinning, fighting the impulse to laugh outright. Then he once more turned up the collar of his Sidewinders jacket, pushed open the pedestrian door against the pressure of the wind, and stepped out into the blinding whiteness.

TWO / NIGHTERS

In the Major Crimes Division (MCD) of the Fall River Police Department, the first detectives ever assigned to regular night duty were a couple of young newcomers named Alan Silvia and Tom Joaquim. To outsiders, including Silvia and Joaquim, the logic of a night shift was obvious: at least two of the division's detectives would be working the same hours as most of the people they were hired to catch.

But the older detectives in the division smiled at the choice: like their captain, most of them looked down on the newcomers, both on the force only a couple of years, both college educated and still in their middle twenties, before they even met them. The captain and the old-timers saw the nighttime assignment as a way to insulate these two different and potentially troublesome kids from a relatively comfortable status quo, the real life of the division.

Their first day on the new job, two incidents occurred that seemed to both Joaquim and Silvia to be intended to set the tone for their shared future.

The first was within a few minutes of their arrival, as they stood more or less at attention in Captain Reis's office. The captain looked them over, each in turn, apparently confirming his worst doubts, then nodded slowly and announced, in a controlled, nearly conversational voice, "I didn't ask for you, I don't want you here, and as far as I'm concerned, you can each shove your education up your ass."

Joaquim winced. Silvia nodded affably and gave a big smile, holding the captain's eye. Reis appeared to recognize that Silvia was the more dangerous of the two, and he studied him for a moment longer, not in a friendly manner.

A few minutes later, Silvia and Joaquim were standing in the hallway, trying to figure out how to get organized on their new jobs without an office or even a desk of their own. One of the other detectives, an old-timer who wore the kind of porkpie hat Eddie Egan had made famous a few years earlier in *The French Connection,* watched them for a while and then strolled over. He gripped Silvia's elbow in the time-honored way of street detectives when they are about to invite a felon into the patrol car for a trip to the county line. "Hey, kid," he said. "You've got an education. What are you doing hanging around here anyway?"

Silvia looked at him without knowing what to say, then decided to say nothing. Again, he smiled.

The old-timer smiled back, released his grip, and patted Silvia on the shoulder. Unlike the scene with the captain, Silvia decided, this wasn't a challenge; it was a friendly warning.

Silvia and Joaquim found themselves outside the system that employed them, but they were both intimately familiar with the larger system of the city, with the streets where they would be working, with the people who lived on them. Each had been born in the tough South End of Fall River, each had gone to school there—Silvia through the public schools and Durfee High, Joaquim through the Catholic parochial schools—and each had come back to Fall River after a term in the military.

Alan Silvia, three years older than his partner, graduated from Durfee High in 1970 and enlisted in the marines. Up to then he had been a street kid, tough, wise, experienced in the local arts: hanging around corners, sometimes getting into fights, and, while still a juvenile, occasionally breaking into houses. One of the reasons he had picked the Marine Corps was because he recognized that it could be a turning point, and it was; he spent two years overseas, shuttling back and forth as a message courier to Vietnam, and when he came out he was ready for a different life. At the time of his assignment with the Major Crimes Division, he was enrolled at Salve Regina College in nearby Newport, Rhode Island, working on a master's degree in human services and management.

Tom Joaquim joined the army as soon as he graduated from high school, served three years, and got out in 1974. He was in his second year of college when he joined the police department on the same day as Alan Silvia in April 1976.

Once on the force, Silvia served as a uniformed patrolman for six months and then became a detective. Joaquim was on the streets for two years as a patrolman and didn't become a detective until this assignment to the Major Crimes Division.

In their first few days on the job, almost no one called the two new men by their names. To their faces they remained Hey, Kid. When the other detectives, the old-timers, were talking among themselves, they referred to them simply as the Nighters.

Even if the day force viewed the new shift as a form of exile, Silvia and Joaquim didn't. From the very first, they looked on it as the necessary next step in their careers as detectives, part of the dues to be paid in continuing up a somewhat indefinite ladder. But within just a few days, they both realized the night work was the doorway to something far better: it was the rabbit hole that led to opportunities they would find nowhere else on the police force, not just for advancement but for great adventure.

More important, they began to get results. While the combined activity of the nine daytime detectives in the Major Crimes Division might average some four or five arrests in an entire week, there were times when Silvia and Joaquim would do several times that number in a single night.

One morning Captain Reis arrived at work to find every available room on the second floor of the station house filled with stolen property recovered in a raid the night before. Following a procedure that by then had become routine, he called across the squad room, "Silvia, come into my office." The daytime crew enjoyed the ritual; it was not uncommon for the sliding windows in the captain's office to rattle with his rage. "Get your ass in here," Reis sputtered, as Silvia got nearer, "and shut the goddamned door."

Silvia obeyed. Through the glass, he looked across the room with exaggerated seriousness at Joaquim before turning to face the captain.

"Where did all this stuff come from, and how the hell did you get it into the station?"

"It's stolen property," Silvia answered. "We ran a raid last night. I tried to reach you. I left messages at the station. I called your house."

"You're going to make me sick. You're driving me crazy," the captain said.

"Gee, we thought you'd be pleased," Silvia lied. "There's over a quarter million worth of loot here; this is a major—"

"Goddamnit, I asked you how you got it all into the station!"

"Well," Silvia said, shrugging diffidently, "we rented a U-Haul. That was all we could do."

"Oh, shit," the captain said, sitting down as though Silvia had pushed him. "I can't believe this shit. Where are we getting the money to go around renting U-Hauls?" It wasn't a question that Silvia could answer because the division was famous for spending almost nothing for outside expenses. The captain got up from his chair and slapped the flat of his hand on the top of his desk. "Where"—bang— "are we getting the money"—bang, bang—"to rent goddamned U-Hauls?" Bang. Bang. Bang.

Silvia looked behind the captain out into the squad room. The windows were shaking more than usual this morning, and Tom Joaquim was pretending to busy himself at a file cabinet, grinning broadly; the captain's shows of outrage were the nearest thing they ever got to praise. Three daytime detectives were standing together nearby, and although they were not as open in showing their amusement, they too were taking in the morning show.

Silvia looked thoughtful, pondering the captain's question. "Well," he said after a moment, "one thing we could do—how about a tag sale?"

As the two young detectives became more and more successful on the job, their accomplishments began to attract the attention of the news media, a development that further aggravated their relationship with the captain. Reis had always had an attitude toward the press that tended to be adversarial, and now it became commonplace for him to arrive with a newspaper under his arm in the morning, shout for Silvia to get his goddamned ass into the office, and start berating him about whatever he had heard Silvia saying on the radio on his way into work. "I read about you in the paper, and now I have to listen to you on that goddamned radio—" Sputter, sputter.

Silvia would wait for a break, then try to explain to the captain what he and Joaquim had managed to accomplish during their latest shift—during the hours when the captain and all the other detectives in the Major Crimes Division were at home with their wives and families, having dinner, watching television, sleeping through the night.

Even when there were no particular surprises awaiting Reis on his arrival at the station in the morning during those first months, he seemed determined that the briefings would be less than cordial. On slow days, he developed a habit of circling in red pencil the typos and spelling errors on their reports, especially Silvia's, and confronting them, often noisily and at length, with their intellectual failings. Silvia made an effort at first to be more careful at the typewriter, but after a few weeks he began thinking of these sessions as a relatively benign safety valve for the captain's anger, and there were times when he would plant a deliberate, trivial error, knowing it would explode harmlessly the following morning, a window-rattling sneeze that cleared the captain's head and helped them both get on with their work.

Almost at the beginning, Silvia and Joaquim noticed a pattern to their difficult relationship with the captain and, more generally, with the day shift: the better the Nighters became at what they did, the greater the problems it often created for them back at headquarters. Part of it was that they were rocking the boat, and they knew it.

But as Joaquim and Silvia talked with each other, they also came to recognize that the nature of their cases was very different from those that occupied the detectives in the daytime. During regular business hours, the typical arrest in the Major Crimes Division was for such relatively civilized offenses as larceny by check or money order and perhaps the odd housebreak. But the Nighters got the bright lights and the heavy action, dealing with people who weren't even awake during the day shift. And when some of those night people decided to rob a bar or a convenience store, Silvia and Joaquim were as likely as the patrolman on the beat to arrive on the scene while the crime was still in progress, while the threats were being made and violence was being committed by people who used fists, clubs, knives, and guns.

But it went beyond the fact that their work was more exciting. The really big distinction was that at night the rules were different.

For example, at about five o'clock one evening in their second winter on the job, Silvia and Joaquim were just about to leave for a night on the streets when the dispatcher got a call from a travel agency on North Main; a man was attempting to negotiate a forged traveler's check. The call was close to the station house, and the Nighters set out at a dead run.

When they came within sight of the travel agency, they saw a heavyset man of about forty in a tweed overcoat just coming out the door, looking furtively up and down the street and apparently deciding on which way to make his escape. The two detectives didn't wear uniforms, but it was obvious that the person in the doorway immediately recognized them as police. Rather than running off, he hesitated, then in an elaborate display of innocence he ambled slowly in the other direction, frantically stuffing a piece of paper into his mouth and chewing vigorously.

The detectives caught up and each grabbed him by an arm. Silvia held his elbow with one hand and clamped his face with the other, trying to force open the jaws. The man wriggled and lowered his head, gagging and gasping for breath, but still chomping as fast as he was able on the wad of paper. "You swallow that, you son of a bitch, and you're in a lot of trouble," Silvia said.

The big man nodded as though in agreement, his eyes wide with fear and the strain of gagging, but he kept on wriggling and chewing, despite Silvia's pressure on his face. Finally, he swallowed. "Ah, shit!" Silvia said. He could see the muscles in the man's neck stretch tight and the blood vessels bulge as the wad slid down his throat, like a snake enveloping a rat, and then the struggle stopped. "Shit!"

The suspect's expression was a combination of apology and relief. He grinned sheepishly at the two policemen, then said, "What's the matter, huh? Whadda you guys want, anyway?"

They cuffed his hands behind his back, Joaquim recited the suspect's rights, and Silvia spoke briefly with the manager of the travel agency. Then the two detectives, one on each elbow, walked their truculent prisoner back to the station house. During the short trip, Silvia glowered but said nothing. Halfway to their destination, Joaquim leaned over and said, confidentially and almost in a whisper near the suspect's ear, "I've never seen him so pissed."

The prisoner looked at Joaquim in alarm and puzzlement, then furtively toward Silvia on his right, as though assessing him in a new light. In the same low voice, Joaquim added, "Just don't make things worse, okay?" He gripped the suspect's elbow more firmly for emphasis. "Okay?" he repeated.

Obviously on his guard, the suspect made a grudging nod. Nothing more was said until they got to the station house.

After the formalities at the desk, the detectives took the man to an interview room. There were three straight-backed wooden chairs and a gray Steelcase table in the room, and on the table was a heavy ashtray of black Lucite. Joaquim indicated where the suspect was to sit, on the chair in the middle, and then he pointedly moved the ashtray to the other end of the table, away from Silvia. "I don't want you repeating any mistakes," he said.

When Silvia didn't reply, Joaquim explained the remark as he unlocked the prisoner's handcuffs. "My partner here nearly killed a guy with one of these about a month ago. Smashed his face with it, knocked one of his eyes loose. Right where you're sitting." He was telling a story about an errant friend, a boys-will-be-boys kind of thing, good for laughs; clearly he was more concerned with keeping his psycho partner out of trouble than he was with the suspect's health or well-being.

The man muttered, "Yeah, bullshit," but he avoided eye contact with either of them, keeping his gaze fixed on the ashtray at the end of the table.

Silvia leaned forward, spreading his hands on the cool tabletop, and craned around to put his face in the suspect's line of sight. "The manager of the travel agency says you tried to pass a forged traveler's check for a hundred bucks. We don't want to waste any more of our time with you. We want a statement right now so we can lock you up and get on with the night's work."

The suspect leaned back in the chair and shifted his gaze upward, toward the ceiling. "I didn't try to pass no fucking check in no fucking travel agency. I went in to get a brochure. Period. He doesn't know what he's fucking talking about."

Joaquim put his hand out protectively, as though to ward off the explosion he feared from Silvia. "Hey!" he said. "Hey, hey, hey!"

But the attack didn't come. Silvia remained in the same position, watching the subject like an unblinking, meat-eating bird, not moving a muscle. The man in the overcoat seemed more like a big bad boy than a felon. He slid down in the chair, still looking at the ceiling, and despite the pressures on either side it was clear that he was trying hard to appear composed or even indifferent as he evaluated his position. No doubt by then he could feel his digestive juices attacking the wad of evidence in his stomach, breaking it down into unreadable pulp. And after a moment more, he smiled the faintest possible smile. "So, what about this check, huh? Where the fuck is it?"

The tableau remained unchanged for a moment longer, then Silvia stood up so abruptly the prisoner flinched. The detective left the room, slamming the door behind him.

The suspect was uncertain how to interpret what was happening, and he looked to Joaquim for a clue. Joaquim just looked back, then shook his head slowly in resignation and regret. Clearly, matters were now out of his hands.

A moment later the door opened again and Silvia reappeared. He was carrying a large metal plate, a length of filthy red hose, and a bucket. Some of the offices in the back of the building were being renovated, and when Joaquim looked more closely he recognized the items in his partner's hands as parts of a wallpaper steamer. Silvia set the paraphernalia noisily on the metal table. "There's an easy way to do this and a hard way," he said. "Your choice."

The big man didn't want to give up any of his earlier advantage, but it was obvious he had no idea what he was looking at, and it made him nervous. Finally, he glanced edgewise at Joaquim and asked, "Do what?"

As before, Joaquim just shook his head, perhaps with even more resignation than a moment earlier. "Your choice," he said, imitating his partner. Joaquim had no idea what Silvia had in mind, and he was worried that this might get out of hand.

"Pump your stomach, asshole," Silvia said.

"No, no, you're not!" the suspect said. "You can't!" The smug smile had vanished, and he was in a panic. He struggled to sit upright, but his weight was against him and his rump kept slipping back down across the seat of the chair. Joaquim placed a restraining hand on his shoulder, which appeared to be offered in sympathy but had the effect of holding him in the awkward, slumped position.

"I'll have a warrant here in five minutes," Silvia said.

"It's against the law!" The prisoner turned to Joaquim for affirmation, but all he got was the hand on the shoulder and more of the same expression he had seen before, the look that said, "Now you've done it." Quaking with fear, he turned back to Silvia. "You're not going to stick that thing down my throat!"

"Okay," Silvia said, with just enough affability to convey, for a moment, a hint of reprieve. Then he added, "Down your throat, up the other end, all the same to me. Either way, we get the check."

The suspect blanched and slumped back with resignation. By six o'clock they had his signed confession, the wallpaper steamer had been returned to where Silvia had found it, and the two detectives were back on the street.

As time passed, their relationship with Captain Reis gradually improved, at least to the point where the early strain began to ease and both sides grudgingly accepted the fact that their fortunes were connected. The more the two night detectives continued to accumulate results, the more credit their efforts brought to the Major Crimes Division and its captain. When things went well, Captain Reis generally left them alone, although the relationship never reached a point that could be called cordial. When things didn't go well, however, it was a very different story. The best they could hope for, they felt, was a kind of grudging neutrality and the benign neglect that seemed to follow their successes.

In fairness, both Silvia and Joaquim recognized that the problem was not all one-sided, and if the captain regarded them as upstarts and troublemakers, the two Nighters seldom went out of their way to prove him wrong. And the more Captain Reis criticized them for what they considered to be their strengths, the more they resented what they came to view as his corresponding deficiencies. They knew they were proving themselves to be extremely effective investigators, and as their triumphs increased, their shared opinion of their captain's police skills correspondingly declined.

Once, at the end of their shift, after Silvia was interviewed on radio in connection with an important case he and Joaquim had helped to solve, Reis called them both into his office. Never mentioning their success, he berated them for a minor procedural omission related to the paperwork on the case. "Our captain sure knows the book," Joaquim said on the way out of the station house.

"Yeah, that makes up for a lot," Silvia said. "Never mind that he couldn't find a skunk in a phone booth."

"Not on a leash," Joaquim agreed.

Perhaps one reason the tension relaxed somewhat between the captain and his two troublesome detectives was that stresses on Reis were building from another quarter. In part, that new pressure began with the murder of a young girl.

THREE / ON THE TOWN

T he body was found by a couple of women jogging on the outdoor track at Fall River's Diman Regional Vocational Technical High School, at seven-thirty on the morning of October 13, 1979. It was under the steel-frame bleachers, lying in its own blood. Because it was so small—barely five feet tall and weighing less than ninety pounds—the victim appeared to have been little more than a child.

Also at first glance, the crime looked like a case of rape-murder. All the girl's clothing had been removed except for her blouse. The skull had been crushed by multiple blows with a blunt object—probably only two or three hours earlier that same morning. But the wrists and ankles were bound with twine and fishing line, which implied far more premeditation than goes into a typical sex crime, and a closer examination of the body and clothes recovered nearby showed signs of a deliberate effort to hide the victim's identity.

The autopsy produced no medical evidence of sexual assault. Police recovered several blood-spattered rocks from the murder site, and in addition to the multiple skull fractures, the medical examiner found stab wounds at the back of the head. She had not been bludgeoned by a single instrument.

Captain Reis assigned a senior detective named Paul Carey to run the investigation, and under Carey he assigned Alan Silvia and Tom Joaquim. The Massachusetts State Police were also in on the investigation from the beginning, along with an assistant DA from the office of Bristol County District Attorney Ron Pina.

Reis released a composite picture of the victim to the media in the hope of discovering her identity, but he did not release all the details to the press, nor did he release any of the conclusions drawn by the medical examiner from the evidence gathered at the site.

It was an important assignment for Silvia and Joaquim, and they were pleased with the new chain of command. Paul Carey had in common with the Nighters that he was something of an outsider—he had not grown up in Fall River, but in Boston. Besides that, he gave the impression of being a loner by nature. He belonged to a local motorcycle club. He did not look or act particularly like a policeman. Most important of all, they liked him; beneath his cynical but easy personality, they recognized the doggedness and slightly warped imagination that comprise a natural instinct for the street.

The body was not identified for another twenty-four hours, after the victim's father saw the composite portrait and read a description of the clothing in New Bedford's Sunday *Standard Times*. Her name was Doreen Ann Levesque. She was seventeen.

One of the reasons it took so long to identify Doreen was that she did not belong in Fall River; she had lived in New Bedford with her parents and six younger siblings. Her father told police she sometimes stayed out overnight with friends, and he had assumed that was why she had not returned on Friday night. Raising children is difficult in any circumstance, and both Fall River and New Bedford are cities of large families; it was the kind of situation that people could readily understand and sympathize with.

On Tuesday, three days after her death, the newspapers revealed that Doreen had been in the state's program for Children in Need of Services and had received counseling for a year under the supervision of the court. In cases of violent crime and mystery, the news media sometimes treat that kind of information as a bellwether, the vanguard of a still unseen army of damning facts that can be expected to follow. But there was no sense of that in the *Standard Times*, and the new revelation was not offered in a way that suggested the victim had somehow invited her fate. "Today's world is tough," her father was quoted. "It's not the same world that my wife and I grew up in."

Reporters showed up at the funeral two days later. Paul Fitzgerald, one of the state troopers on the case, told them there were still no real clues to the killing, adding that the area around the Diman playing field was a popular parking spot for teenagers. The high point of the service was the reading of Doreen's poetry and a letter she had written some months before to Jesus. "Dear Jesus," it said, "I hope I spelled your name right. Thank you for everything you've done for me and anything you might do. . . . Someday I would like to be with you in heaven. . . . If I have trouble following you, I'd like for you to help me." She was buried in a white casket in the Mother Seton section of St. John's Cemetery.

But the early image of the victim that had taken root in the press and budded in the public imagination began to wither badly the following Sunday, when the *Standard Times* published a front-page report on Doreen Levesque's brief life. "My daughter went the whole route," her mother was quoted as saying. "Drugs, alcohol, whatever went on in the streets she was aware of, because she was a part of it." She had been in trouble almost steadily since the age of twelve. She was arrested for shoplifting, ran away from home, twice dropped out of school, and lived with a succession of friends who had taken her in to keep her off the streets. There was a strong implication that she was a prostitute.

Prostitution was not just a casual embarrassment in New Bedford and Fall River; it was a major industry that drew on a labor pool extending as far away as New York, New Jersey, and even Florida. Some 40 percent of the population of both cities is Portuguese, either by descent or direct immigration, and a quarter are of French ancestry. Those populations, like every other, vary widely, but on balance they have their own particular levels of cultural tolerance. Prostitution was not something either city was proud of, but it could be abided. When it involved their own children, however, there were other things the public wanted to read about.

The newspaper gave that to them as well. There was more about the letter to Jesus, and the article revealed that Doreen had been bothered by the notion that God had allowed His Son to suffer on the cross; she had removed the small figure of Jesus from her crucifix, placing it in a little box under a small blanket, and she slept with a statue of Christ beside her bed. She also wrote poetry—about the pain of growing up, about disappointed love, about separation and death and "screwed-up lives." The article described her terrible self-consciousness about being short, revealing that she wore high heels and developed a compensating strut. She was quoted by friends as saying she was not long for this world and that probably she'd be happier when she died. The mother of a friend said Doreen would do almost anything for affection. This was still reassuring, familiar ground, filled with the same icons of faith, the same hopes, uncertainties, pains, and failures that marked the lives of most of the readers of that story. Even in describing her as different, the article maintained Doreen's position as one of their own.

However she had lived, her place in the mainstream of another major local tradition was virtually assured by the manner of her death. That was the tradition of bizarre murders involving women.

What Reis had held back when he spoke with the press was the fact that Paul DeVillers, the county medical examiner, had determined that Doreen's murder had probably been committed by more than one killer. He also suspected that the mutilation of the body was more than an attempt to hide the girl's identity; it appeared to have involved elements of ritual. Instead of a lethal beating in the wake of a rape, the evidence pointed to the possibility of torture and death by stoning.

The first Fall River murder to attain national prominence occurred nearly a century and a half earlier, in 1832, when the body of a local factory worker named Sarah Cornell was discovered one December morning next to a haystack on the Durfee farm, in what has since become the south side of the city. She was hanging from a pole, and the body had been arranged in a manner suggesting suicide. After the funeral, however, Williams Durfee, who had gone to sea as a young man, examined the knot in the rope which had choked her. It was a clove hitch, he announced, and even with the weight of her body it could not have been pulled tight with both ends held together as they were when the rope was found around her neck; she had been strangled, and then her body was placed on the pole. The corpse was exhumed, and a medical examiner confirmed that she had first been beaten, then murdered.

The autopsy also determined that Sarah was pregnant, a condition that had been assumed at the time of the funeral and which now became as persuasive a motive for murder as it had been earlier in support of the assumed suicide. The suspected father—and therefore her likely killer—was a Methodist minister named Avery.

It was a time of great cultural change in Fall River, and there was a lot at stake in the outcome of the case. The local textile industry dominated the economy, and it depended on the availability of cheap labor. The region was making a transition from an agrarian to an industrial economy, and women like Sarah had been lured into the mills with the promise that the workplace was as safe as their own homes. The mill owners wanted to see Avery convicted in order to deliver on as much of that promise as they could still keep. The fact that the mill owners were themselves Calvinist Congregationalists, ideological opposites to Methodists, lent added zeal to a crusade which was otherwise entirely economic in nature.

Their efforts failed. Even though Avery's own reputation and career were destroyed in the process, his defense was a classic attack on the character of the dead victim, and it succeeded. In effect, it was the lowborn temptress Sarah Cornell, not the elegant adulterer who almost certainly killed her, who stood condemned by the judgment of the jury. But in a broader sense, the mill system stood convicted as well, both for exploiting Sarah's life while she still had it and then for exploiting her death as shamelessly.

Far and away the most famous case in the distinguished annals of Fall River murder took place on August 4, 1892, when an unpleasant, roundheaded, slightly exophthalmic Sunday school teacher named Lizbeth was accused of killing her father, a prominent banker named Andrew Jackson Borden, and her stepmother, Abby Durfee Gray Borden. The crime gave rise to an epic piece of doggerel—Lizzie Borden took an ax and gave her father forty whacks; when she saw what she had done, she gave her mother forty-one—as well as thousands of articles, at least eight books, several stage plays, a ballet, two movies, and an apparently endless stream of speculation on her guilt with which rabid partisans on either side have titillated themselves for a century.

In one of those films, actress Elizabeth Montgomery stripped down to the buff for the bloodbath, ostensibly to avoid soiling her frock and undies and certainly to build viewership. In another, Lizzie took the rap for her allegedly demented sister, Emma. Public attention was so formidable at the time that the venue for the trial was shifted to New Bedford. If she were to be tried again today, it would be hard to raise an unprejudiced jury on Sri Lanka.

The panel that finally sat in judgment at her trial consisted of one blacksmith and eleven farmers or country tradesmen. (Women were not allowed to sit on juries until the following century, although that prejudice in no way diminished their popularity as victims.) In part because of the persistence and ubiquity of the jingle, it is easy to forget that Lizzie was found innocent. It probably didn't hurt her case that she came from one of the city's first families, and it certainly helped that she was a single woman, now alone in the world.

Plain, old-fashioned luck also played a major role in her trial. Just five days before she was to appear in court for killing her father and stepmother, as she languished in the Taunton jail, another ax murder occurred in Fall River. The body of Bertha Manchester, a farmer's wife, was found chopped up in her kitchen; the press reported that a total of twenty-three distinct ax marks had been counted in the vicinity of the head and shoulders. In short order, a Portuguese immigrant named José Manuel Correira was arrested for the crime. José had worked a few days for Bertha's husband. Among other things, he apparently resented the low wages and a steady diet of codfish three times a day, and he took his objections to Bertha.

Public hysteria at the notion the ax murderer was still at large was only slightly diminished by Correira's arrest and the subsequent revelation that he was nowhere in the vicinity of Fall River at the time of the Borden killings. Ax murders are relatively rare, and this latest development seemed to exceed the reasonable probability of an unrelated coincidence. It was still not generally recognized that in cases of great notoriety—and by then the Borden tragedy had achieved the status of Crime of the Century—deliberate copycat crimes are relatively commonplace. In the course of murdering an innocent woman, Correira may have helped set a guilty one free.

Lizzie Borden lived for another three and a half decades, variously despised and admired, pitied and feared, but almost universally tolerated even by those convinced of her guilt. Due process had been observed, and even if the result was wrong, it must be abided. In fact, the only open social censure she really encountered—at least from within her own class—was in her later years when she entered what was probably a sexual relationship with another woman. She died seven years after the enactment of the Nineteenth Amendment to the Constitution. Even today, her partisans believe she was borne innocently aloft on the wings of angels, and others are equally certain she went straight to hell. Officially, the crime is still unsolved. T-shirts with Lizzie Borden's picture on them are offered for sale throughout the city, and shortly after the Levesque murder, Fall River's new director of tourism said in a newspaper interview that the Borden murders were still the city's best selling point.

That rather pessimistic assessment may have been uncomfortably close to the truth. Fall River, which takes its name from a Narragansett Indian word, is a natural deepwater seaport on Mount Hope Bay. Its original prominence as a harbor, however, was eclipsed in the early part of this century by nearby New Bedford, which is still the epicenter of the deteriorating northeast fishing industry. Fall River's industrial epoch began in the 1870s and reached its acme before World War I, when the city boasted 140 operating mills and was the cotton-spinning center of the world. But the outstanding characteristics of that era were stubbornness, greed, and accelerated obsolescence. The price of prosperity for a small handful of mill owners was a ravaged landscape and choking pollution, along with exploitation and abject misery for the vast majority of workers. By the start of World War II, 80 percent of those mills were out of business because their machinery would no longer function competitively or they had moved south to escape the labor unions. In their wake, they left a plundered, depressed industrial ghost town. More than twenty thousand people—some 10 percent of the population—moved away during the nineteen fifties.

Sociologically, what was left of Fall River divided into three parts, the French Canadians living in the east section of the city known as the Flint, the Portuguese concentrated in the Globe along the waterfront and South End, and the Irish and founding Yankees occupying the area in the northwest between Main Street and the Highlands.

The civic buildings of the city tend toward monumental Gothic, punctuated here and there with the heavy Victorian whimsy of brick turrets and minarets, a style that reaches its bleak and threatening apotheosis in the overwhelming, yellow stone fortress that is Durfee High School. The favored residential motif in the Flint and Globe sections of town is the triple-decker tenement or the clusters of flat-roofed, two-story, red-brick cubes that comprise the city's public housing projects. At the time of the Levesque killing, the most infamous of those projects was on the escarpment above Battleship Cove, in the shadow of the Braga Bridge, known as Harbor Terrace. Most of Fall River's single-unit dwellings are contained in the reach toward the city's Highlands.

But the dominant architectural style is neither civic nor residential, but industrial. And in Fall River, industrial means immense, gray stone warehouses and factories seemingly modeled on English prisons and some as long as several city blocks, deliberately devoid of any concession to the aesthetic sensibilities of their human occupants. In the late 1970s, those stone buildings were the rotting heart of the city and many of them stood empty. The energy of Fall River had moved elsewhere. A lot of that energy had left town forever. Some of it had moved into the bars and fleshpots around Bedford Street.

Carl Drew worked on Bedford Street, starting with a string of armed robberies he committed in that area when he first came down from New Hampshire in his late teens and later when he returned as a pimp. Alan Silvia and Tom Joaquim worked there too.

And so did Doreen Levesque.

Four / A FINE EXAMPLE

Just a few days after his escape from the Fall River Police Station, Carl Drew was apprehended by New Hampshire police near the Canadian border. He got that far despite a historic winter hurricane that clogged highways in eastern Massachusetts with huge drifts and over three thousand abandoned vehicles, shutting down the city of Boston for five days. Drew told the police he had made it through the storm by stealing a succession of snowmobiles. He seemed proud of his story and showed no signs of regret or contrition for what had happened to his victim. He was sent to a house of correction to await trial for the beating.

The case dragged on, and before Drew was brought to court, the trick died. The victim was a drug addict, and there was no provable link between his injuries and his death. Moreover, because the DA's office had never gotten around to taking the victim's deposition, there was now no way the state could make its case against Drew for the beating. So instead of being charged with murder, as he fully expected, Carl Drew found himself suddenly free. Although he had spent several months in jail awaiting a trial that never happened, he couldn't believe his good luck.

He returned to Bedford Street and began recruiting more aggressively than ever. One of those recruits was a woman named Cookie Powers.

Cookie had been born Mildred Jukes in Corry, Pennsylvania, and was twenty-five. She had four children, ranging from age nine down to a year and a half.

She had come to Fall River just a few months earlier, and with the help of the Social Services Department had gotten an apartment which she shared with the man by whom she was expecting her fourth child. In June of 1979, eight months after the baby was born, the man was gone and all Cookie had to remember him by were the infant, a $1,200 stereo system, and a Plymouth Fury. One day Cookie was driving the Fury through town and saw a girl hitchhiking. It was hot. Cookie remembered the times, not long before, when she had done a lot of hitching herself, and she stopped to give her a lift.

The girl said she was headed to a place called the Penthouse, and when they got there, she invited Cookie inside for a drink. "I don't drink," she answered.

"Okay, I'll buy you a soda."

Cookie looked doubtfully toward the barroom. "I don't want to go into this kind of place," she said. "It's a dump."

The girl bounced out of the car. "C'mon," she said, laughing at Cookie's hesitancy.

Cookie shook her head, then reluctantly followed her. They had a soda, and the girl offered Cookie a couple of dollars for the ride. "I'm grateful," she told her. "You were really nice to pick me up."

Cookie refused the money, but was impressed by the gesture. She had few friends in Fall River, and the girl's enthusiasm and openness were refreshing.

After a few minutes, the girl said she had just come to the Penthouse to leave a message for a friend, and now was going to her grandmother's house on Bryant Street. "That's a long way," Cookie said. "I have a full tank. I'll drive you over."

The girl hesitated, then said, "You know, I'm a hooker—a prostitute."

It was not at all what Cookie expected to hear, but she was good at hiding her reactions. She looked at her and shrugged in an elaborate gesture of indifference. "So?"

The girl said, "Well, if you don't want to give me a ride, you don't have to, that's all."

"Why wouldn't I want to give you a ride? What you are makes no difference to me." The girl still looked doubtful, and Cookie said, "Hey, if I was the best Catholic in the world, would you hate me because I'm Catholic?"

The question sounded enough like a parable that they both considered it respectfully; Cookie began to think she had made a new friend. When they got to the house on Bryant Street, the girl invited her inside to meet her grandmother. Almost as an afterthought, the girl introduced herself as well. "Karen."

Cookie smiled and offered her hand. "Cookie. But my real name is Mildred." When Karen laughed with her, she added, "Isn't that awful?"

Karen laughed again, and her grandmother shook her head in sympathy, smiling.

A few nights later, Karen called Cookie and asked her if she felt like going out. "Not hooking, just out."

They went to a place in New Bedford called the International Club. They had barely walked in when a man came up to Cookie and said, "I want your car."

"It's not for sale," she told him.

The man reached into his pocket and took out a gun. "Give me the fucking keys."

"Oh." She gave him the keys. He got in the car and drove off.

Now both girls were hitchhiking, but Karen told Cookie not to worry, that she knew how to handle this kind of thing. They got a ride back to Fall River, and after Cookie checked in with the woman who was watching her children, they went over to the Penthouse. Karen said she knew someone who hung around there, and if Cookie was cool—if he liked her—Karen was sure he could help.

Outside the bar, sitting in his Mustang, was a big, muscular man in his middle twenties, taking in the street action and listening to his car stereo. His hair was shaggy, he had a cigarette behind one ear, and he wore a feathery blond goatee.

"Carl, this is a friend of mine," Karen said, presenting Cookie.

The man nodded. He had a nice smile: friendly but serious—and perhaps a little shy. He switched off the stereo and gestured toward the passenger-side door for the two girls to get into the car.

Karen described for Carl what had happened with the stolen car. He listened thoughtfully, then turned to Cookie. "I'll get it back," he said. He told her he belonged to a motorcycle club called the Sidewinders. "The cops won't be bothered with something like this. The club'll take care of it for you."

"Gee, great," Cookie said.

He looked her over, up and down, still smiling. There was nothing in the way he did it that was suggestive, just interested. Cookie was sitting in the back seat of the Mustang, and Karen was in front. The business of the stolen car apparently out of the way for the time being, Drew said, "Now, do you need a job?"

"No," she said, unsure why he had asked. "I have my kids."

Drew continued smiling, but he looked more serious than ever. "So how do you plan on paying me?"

She had not anticipated this, but in the instant she thought about it, there seemed to be nothing unreasonable in someone expecting to be paid for doing a big favor like recovering a stolen car. "Well," she said, "I get paid every two weeks, a hundred bucks or whatever, so just let me know how much, and I'll get it."

Drew took it in and seemed satisfied. "Okay. We can talk about it after."

The following week, he called her up and said they had recovered the car. "It's in New Bedford. It's in good shape, but they paid for it to be towed, and then there's their time. You owe them seventy-five dollars."

"Sure. Seventy-five dollars is no problem. That's fine." She had no idea who had recovered it, or why it had been towed, but when she met Drew a short time later, she got into his car and passed over the money without any questions.

Drew took the bills, counted them, and put them in his shirt pocket. "You owe me more than this," he said.

Cookie was glad to be getting her Fury back, and although she was surprised at what Drew had just told her, she was used to hearing bad news, and she prided herself in taking things in stride. Besides, she was anxious to avoid creating any offense. "Sure," she said, "what do I owe you?"

"Three months."

"Three months of what?"

"You're going to start working for me."

Cookie looked at him in puzzlement. "Doing what?" she asked.

"You're going to be out on the street—by seven o'clock tonight."

When Cookie realized what he meant, she was so amazed, she laughed. "I've never slept with anyone else than the fathers of my kids." He looked back at her from below his eyebrows, with no trace of a smile, and she stopped laughing. "Hey, I've never done anything like that, and I'm not about to start," she said desperately. "You've got me figured wrong."

Drew listened as carefully as he had listened before, but this time it was clear he had no intention of accommodating her. She talked for a minute or two more, and when she had run out of rational pleadings, he waited until he was sure she had stopped talking, then placed his hand firmly, almost paternally, on her arm. "You're going out tonight, or else, one by one, I'll take care of your kids."

Cookie looked at him with her mouth open, suddenly terrified and wondering if he were insane. "Hey, don't even say that."

"I'm going to get paid. I always get paid. I know where your kids are. No matter where you put them, one by one I'll find them."

That night, Cookie was out on the street, working for Carl Drew. When she showed some reluctance to do business with her first customer, Drew smashed her in the face. Later that same evening, after turning a couple of tricks, she was attacked by one of Drew's hookers, who hit her with a lead pipe wrapped in newspaper.

She had come into a dangerous world.

FIVE / **THE VIEW FROM THE TERRACE**

If the exodus of the textile industry and the concomitant rise in the flesh trade had elevated Bedford Street into a position of commercial dominance in Fall River, the cultural heart of that new order was in the Harbor Terrace public housing project, a waterfront appendix to the combat zone just above Bedford Street's northwestern end. The apartment complex had been familiar ground to all the detectives in the Major Crimes Division long before any of them ever heard of Doreen Levesque.

Since the beginning of the murder investigation, however, Silvia and Joaquim—and now Paul Carey—stopped by the housing project even more frequently than they had in the past, sometimes more than once in a night. Harbor Terrace was the natural place to pursue a specific lead or query: it was there, for example, that they were able to verify that Doreen had indeed been a prostitute and that she had worked the streets of Fall River. More generally, though, the Nighters and Carey visited the project because they hoped with persistence and familiarity to insinuate themselves deeper into the Bedford Street culture and eventually, either by gaining trust or simply by being there when defenses were momentarily lowered, to discover the names of those involved in the killing.

More often than not, their destination was the apartment of Maureen "Sonny Spikes" Sparda. Sonny was in her middle twenties, a few years older than the average Bedford Street prostitute, about the same age as pimps like Carl Drew and Carl Davis. She was different from the rest of the girls in other ways as well. She didn't look like what the detectives had come to expect of a hooker, either in her physical appearance or in the way she usually dressed. There was nothing soft or feminine about her—she was short, mannish, muscular, and just beginning to become chunky. Also unlike most of the other prostitutes, she had a strong personality, and although she drank a lot and used drugs, she usually managed to stay in control, not just of herself but of her environment. The detectives knew she had handcuffs snapped to the headboard of her bed, but even though she was apparently willing to play games of submission in that arena, she clearly was not the kind of person who allowed other people to push her around.

She was very, very tough. One of the most savage fights Silvia ever saw had ended with Sonny holding another girl's hair in her fist and repeatedly smashing her face into the cement sidewalk. She never gave the Nighters the impression that she was particularly bright, but Sonny had been around long enough to develop reliable instincts; she knew just how much space to keep between herself and the others who used her apartment as a social center, including the three detectives.

Even if Sonny had not been a central figure in the continuous street theater of Fall River's nightlife, she would have been of great interest to the MCD detectives for another, equally compelling reason. Although no direct references to Dr. DeVillers's suspicions about the ritual nature of the Levesque killing had yet appeared in the media, and the police had carefully refrained from discussing that aspect of the case with any outsiders, Silvia, Joaquim, and Carey were aware that the life of Bedford Street, and particularly of Harbor Terrace, included a deep, albeit primitive, strain of cultism. On the living-room wall of Sonny Sparda's apartment, the first thing they saw every time they walked in, painted in lurid reds and blues above the living-room couch, was an enormous, almost comically garish mural of Satan.

At the beginning, they suspected that the mural was there not because it necessarily expressed Sonny's religious convictions or even her tastes, but because she enjoyed the popularity and convenience of her apartment being the principal meeting place for the Bedford Street regulars and the picture was a kind of tribal banner. After the killing, Silvia in particular had made it a point to learn what he could about cult psychology, and the picture on the wall, like the pictures of the Devil tattooed on the skins of bikers and street people like Carl Drew, seemed more to be a sophomoric, counterculture political statement than a manifesto of some dark faith. Probably Sonny had donated the space on her wall in order to anchor her own position as a cornerstone in the Bedford Street culture.

That early assumption was seriously shaken when they learned that one of the uses of Sonny Sparda's apartment was as a gathering place for satanic meetings. The two Nighters were at a party there in early November, and Silvia heard of the meetings from a girl named Karen Marsden.

Karen got there late, long after the two detectives were settled in. Silvia had just returned from the kitchen with a fresh beer. Someone had taken his seat, and he was standing near the couch by the mural, looking around for another place to sit, when he saw her enter from the outside hallway; she was breathless from running, her cheeks were flushed, and her eyes were shining. It was a dramatic arrival, and although Silvia was talking with someone else—a neighborhood boy who sometimes baby-sat for Sonny's young daughter—he found himself repeatedly looking over at her as she moved about the room. He was impressed by the way she shook her hair and by her energy.

About a half hour later, when he finally got around to talking with her, the flush and breathlessness were gone—but the eyes had not changed. She was drinking a beer, but he was sure the unnatural brightness was from something else she had taken, not a result of the alcohol. He had to remind himself not to be surprised—most of the hookers were on something—but still, the realization was a downer, like the disappointment that follows the hope in seeing the flash of fool's gold.

"Sonny tells me you're a cop." She was smiling. Like the statement it was speculative, tentative.

"Yeah, well—" he said, shrugging and taking a pull on the beer. "Who are you?"

"Who or what?" It was partly teasing. She told him her name. Behind the shine, her eyes were nervous and intense, alternately studying him closely and darting away to other places in the room. Silvia saw them flit briefly to the portrait on the wall behind him, and he turned to face it as well.

"You an art lover?" he asked.

She looked at him sideways and made a wry face.

He tried to think of something to say about the painting, but before he could, Karen asked, "Do you know why the eyes follow you? It's because that's what the Devil does. He's everywhere. He never leaves you alone."

"That's so very true," Silvia agreed, trying to pick up on her style, at once earnest and mocking. "Really, I never have a minute's rest."

His remark did not get across exactly as he had intended. She looked at him defensively, apparently unsure whether he was laughing at what she had said or at her for saying it. "If it weren't for the Devil, you wouldn't have a job."

He resisted the impulse to say it back to her. "Sure," he agreed, grinning innocently. "That's what I meant."

At that moment, Silvia happened to glance across the room and saw that Sonny Sparda and Carl Drew were watching them from near the doorway. Sonny smiled abstractly and turned elsewhere. Drew did not; he looked back at the detective with an absolutely blank expression, neither friendly nor hostile, holding Silvia's eye. "You know this guy?" the detective asked Karen, still grinning, returning Drew's gaze.

"Everybody knows Carl Drew."

He could tell she had not turned to see where he was looking, and it occurred to him what the attention from Drew was about. "You're his lady," he said, letting go of the pimp's gaze and returning to Karen.

Her soft brown hair shimmered as she shook her head in denial, and he saw a flash, perhaps of anger, possibly of fear.

"Then he's after you," he pressed.

"Carl's after everyone. He's going to be the King of Bedford Street." She sounded edgy, apprehensive at the turn the conversation had taken, and Silvia worried for a moment that she was about to walk away. Instead, she looked up at the mural again, deliberately changing the subject. "You ought to come to one of the meetings. There's a lot of chanting. Some of the people speak in tongues. Sometimes the Devil comes right into the room."

He almost asked, "What meetings?" but he was smart enough to stop himself. In steering him away from a topic that was of only marginal interest to Silvia, Karen had suddenly led him to something of great potential significance. Until then, most of what Silvia had ever learned about Satanism came from episodes of "The Twilight Zone," movies like *The Exorcist*, or books like *Helter Skelter*. "I dunno," he said, putting on an ingenuous face that said he couldn't decide whether to be skeptical or believing.

Karen appeared to steel herself, then turned around at last and looked nervously across the room at Carl Drew, who by then had started a conversation with one of the girls who worked for him and appeared to have lost interest in what was happening on their side of the room. "Ask Sonny," Karen said to Silvia. "Tell her to let you know the next time they have one. Sometimes it's out in the state forest, but at this time of year it'll probably be right in the apartment. I'll be there. Carl will be there. It's the kind of thing you ought to see." She regarded him uncertainly, giving into the anxiety, now obviously poised for flight. "Especially," she said over her shoulder as she headed for the kitchen, "if you really are a cop."

SIX / **THE GIFT**

J anuary 26, 1980, was a cold, crisp Saturday in Fall River. The land was still in the grip of winter, but the days were getting slowly longer and the bite in the air held the slightest hint of softening toward springtime. It was the kind of day that lures hardy people out of doors to draw imagined warmth from the pale sunlight, to breathe natural air, to stretch briefly from the winter freeze.

It was a day to run the dogs.

Late that afternoon, in the big field behind Resco Printers & Lithographers, just off the lower end of Route 24 and Jefferson Street in Fall River, a man was training his two hunters. One of the dogs found something in the grass and busied himself with the distraction, not responding to his master's commands. Then the other one found the scent and loped over to join the first, his nose tracing the ground, the hair on his shoulders rising to a bristle. Their owner followed.

Lying in a small depression was the body of a woman. She was on her back. Her wrists were tied, and her arms were above her head as if defending against the blow that had destroyed her face and crushed her skull. Her flesh was black with decay and repeated freezing, thawing, freezing. The man pulled away his dogs and quickly walked back with them across the field, looking for a telephone.

Although it was a weekend, all the detectives in the Major Crimes Division were called in to work on the case, including the Nighters. Within an hour of the discovery, the landscape around the murder site was dotted with policemen, some in Fall River blue, some in state police gray, some in long, orange slickers, and others in civilian wear, taking photographs, making measurements, examining the body, collecting information, conferring with each other, clapping their hands in the cold. When Silvia and Joaquim left the discovery site, they returned to the police station and spent the evening going through the files on missing persons in the Fall River area.

In a relatively short time, based on size, coloring, and presumed age and time of death of the victim, they reduced the list to just three or four prospects. Of those, they decided the most likely candidate was a young Fall River girl named Barbara Raposa whose disappearance had been reported by her boyfriend three months earlier.

By that time, the body had been moved to the morgue at St. Anne's Hospital, and another few hours passed before MCD detectives were able to match specific articles of apparel on the body with descriptions of clothing from the missing persons report. It was after midnight before they confirmed that the victim was Barbara Raposa.

The missing persons report had been filed the previous November by Andre Maltais. The record showed that Maltais lived with his mother on Jencks Street in Fall River. At 5.05 A.M. Sunday, Paul Carey and another Fall River MCD detective knocked on the door. The mother let them in, and a moment later Andre Maltais appeared from the bedroom. Seeing the police, he asked, "Is this about Barbara?"

They said it was. He said he would get dressed and meet them at the Fall River Police Station.

Silvia and Joaquim considered Maltais a suspect even before they met him, simply because he was the last one to see the victim alive, and for Silvia, at least, those suspicions crossed over into near certainty the moment Maltais walked into the MCD offices at five-thirty Sunday morning. A little man intent on creating a big impression, he was half a head shorter than Silvia even with the cowboy boots, and he was wearing a Western shirt with darts sewn into the pockets and a wide leather belt with a big brass buckle that said TEXAS. He was also a lot older than Silvia, too old to be playing parts, and he seemed nervous and worn. In his hand was a Bible, which he carried before him like a shield. "So you found Barbara," he said.

The detectives took him into the captain's office, where he was offered a seat at a conference table. "We want to wrap this up," Silvia said. "We just want to get the details and close the case, Mr. Maltais."

"Sure, that makes sense." Maltais looked anxious to cooperate. He took off his sheepskin-lined denim jacket and sat down at a conference table next to the captain's desk. He pressed the Bible against his chest as though for added warmth, and Silvia noticed that he was trembling slightly, perhaps from the frigid outside air.

Carey read him his rights. Maltais said he understood them and waived the presence of an attorney. "I called the state police just before leaving the house," he explained. "They'll be down here at eight to take over the investigation."

Silvia looked up sharply; this guy was even crazier than he looked. "Is that right?"

Maltais nodded, trying to look sure of himself but wary of the edge in Silvia's response. "Eight o'clock," he repeated.

Then he began to talk. At first, it appeared that he was anxious to clarify his relationship with the state police, but his remarks quickly deteriorated into aimless, airy chatter, urgent in tone but almost empty of substance. After a couple of minutes of this, when he realized that the detectives were just watching him, he looked around nervously, then tried something different. "I used to be with Satan," he said.

"Yeah?" Silvia said, offering his most encouraging, no-judgment smile. He began to hope that this one was going to be easy.

"Now I'm with God," the little man continued, holding forth the Bible as evidence. "And God is with me."

Silvia watched him a moment longer, then sat down opposite him on the other side of the conference table. "Uh-huh."

Maltais looked back and smiled nervously. "Jesus Christ is my personal Lord and Savior. Once I worshiped Satan. Now I worship Jesus."

"You made the right choice, Andy," Silvia said, looking to his partner for affirmation. "At least, as far as we're concerned. Right, Tom?"

Joaquim was looking through the captain's desk for some paper to write on, and he nodded vigorously. "Absolutely. Way to go."

Silvia smiled back at Maltais, waited a moment longer, then said, "So?"

Maltais started talking again, this time about Barbara Raposa, his eyes all the while moving nervously about the room. Silvia busied himself writing something on a piece of paper, ostensibly making notes on what Maltais was saying, but actually preparing a small, hand-lettered sign on one side of a creased manila file folder. When Maltais was looking elsewhere, Silvia placed the sign on the desk where Joaquim was still searching for paper. A few minutes later, Maltais noticed it and pointed at it with his chin. "What's that?"

"What's what?" Silvia said, not turning to look.

Maltais eyed the sign uncertainly, glancing back and forth between it and the detective. He read aloud, "'Alan Silvia, Psychic Reader.'"

Silvia nodded absently, as though preoccupied with whatever he was reading in Maltais' face. "Umm," he acknowledged.

"Well?" Maltais asked again, after pondering the situation for a moment longer, grinning uncertainly. "What's it about, some kind of bullshit? I mean, or is it for real?"

Silvia turned and glanced distractedly at the sign behind him, as though seeing it for the first time. "That's something the state psychologist gave me." He looked back at Maltais in the same deep, thoughtful way.

"Oh," Maltais said. "Yeah."

Silvia reached for a blank pad of yellow foolscap. "You're into that stuff, aren't you, Andy?"

"What stuff?" Maltais obviously was interested in the bait, but he was approaching the subject obliquely, a step at a time, probably because he was afraid of looking stupid or of being played for a fool.

"Extrasensory perception, dream analysis, psychokinetics, that kind of thing. Mind travel. The invisible world."

"Well, uh, I know about it, sure—if that's what you mean," he said guardedly.

"Hey, don't be coy," Silvia said, offering the sly smile of a coconspirator. "You don't just know about it, you believe in it. And I know the reason why."

Maltais wasn't sure where this was heading, but he smiled back, tentatively, waiting for the rest. After a long moment, it became clear that Silvia was going to outwait him, and Maltais wasn't good at being patient. He finally asked, "So why?"

"Because you're like me," Silvia said, setting the hook. "You have the gift. You can tell in advance when things are going to happen. You know what people are thinking before they say anything. I could tell that right away, the first minute I saw you."

The would-be cowboy straightened in his chair. "Yeah?" He was clearly pleased to be likened to Silvia, and the invitation to verify the detective's judgment that they were, in a way, peers, especially when Andy knew it to be totally wrong, was irresistible.

Joaquim entered the room and sat down between them at the table. Silvia appeared not to notice. He leaned back and looked intently at Maltais, and after a moment his lids slowly lowered until they covered half his eyes, as though he were becoming drowsy. "I want you to relax, Andy. I think we can both use some of this stuff to help you remember."

"Sure," Maltais quickly agreed. He let his arms hang down limply beside the chair, and his expression quickly mimicked the slack, lethargic look on the detective's face. "I'm relaxed."

"Close your eyes," Silvia said.

Obediently, after only the slightest hesitation, he did as he was told. "Check," he said.

Silvia reopened his own eyes to confirm that Maltais had followed orders, then shot a quick, satisfied grin at Joaquim, who was shaking his head in amazement. Silvia closed his own eyes again. "This is good, Andy. This is very good. Can you feel it? Are you getting the same thing I'm getting?"

"Uh-h—" Maltais said, clearly fishing for a cue to his next response.

Silvia opened his eyes again, just in time to catch Maltais' lids flutter as he tried an exploratory peek. "Close 'em up," he warned. "Go with it."

Maltais' eyes shut tight, like a clam at the touch of the digger's rake.

"I can feel what you did, Andy," the detective continued, his voice slowing to a trancelike monotone. "I can feel it."

"Feel what?" Maltais said, obviously fascinated. "Did what?"

Silvia went on as though in a parody of a seance. "I can feel you getting out of the car, Andy. I can feel you walking around it, away from the highway."

Maltais was enthralled, but now he looked alarmed as well. His eyes opened again as he glanced quickly at Joaquim; he appeared to be less afraid of what Silvia knew than that it would be overheard by an outsider.

Joaquim reached across the corner of the conference table and gripped his partner's elbow. "Al—"

"I feel you walking through the bushes," Silvia went on, seemingly oblivious to the caution or even to his partner's presence. "I feel you fighting her, struggling with her body—"

Now Joaquim was shaking Silvia's elbow, and although his apparent intention was to stop what was happening, it had the effect of seeming to dramatize the scene as the other detective described it. But it worked. Silvia cut off in midsentence, then looked over at Joaquim as if surprised to see him.

"You're telling him too much," the younger detective explained quietly. "You're giving things away."

Silvia nodded, acknowledging that his partner was right, and he accepted the admonition in silence, stretching his shoulders and taking a deep breath to recover from the terrible strain of second sight.

Maltais watched Silvia intently, apparently unaware of the tears that were flowing down his own face, then slowly pushed his chair back from the table, hunched his shoulders, and let out his breath in a long, tremulous sigh of amazement. "Holy living shit," he said, almost in a whisper.

Silvia collected himself a moment longer, then snapped briskly back to the matter at hand. "About the murder of Barbara Raposa, Andy. What are you going to tell us?"

Maltais unconsciously brushed at the dampness on his cheeks and was silent, staring at the detective. He thought for a long time. Then he hugged the Bible tighter to his chest and leaned back in the wooden chair, stretching out his legs. "I think I'm going to wait for the Big Guy to show up before I say anything."

That wasn't the answer Silvia had expected.

"Big Guy?" he asked. He wondered for a moment if the suspect were referring again to God.

"Corporal Fitzgerald," Maltais explained.

Silvia's jaw dropped, and he looked up sharply at his partner. Joaquim had stopped rummaging in the desk and was now studying the witness, trying to place the name. Silvia said, "CPAC," pronouncing it as a single word, Seapack. Joaquim made a silent "Ah" in recognition. CPAC was the Crime Prevention and Control Unit of the Massachusetts State Police, attached to the office of the district attorney.

"How do you know Corporal Fitzgerald?" Silvia asked.

"Friends. I see him four, five times a week. I do a bit of undercover work for the state police, you know? He's been doing a lot to help me find Barbara, that kind of thing, and I try to help him out with a favor here and there, you know what I mean?"

"No, what do you mean?" Silvia asked.

"I work for him, see? He tells me, 'Andy, you got anything to say about this case, you say it to me, and not to the Fall River Police Department.'" Maltais smiled apologetically, a look that said he'd like to help, but that's how things are.

"You think you're going to wait for the state police to get here?" Silvia said, incredulous. "We're about to lock you up, to charge you with murder, and you tell me you're waiting for the state police?"

The news that he was about to be charged shocked Maltais, and his mouth opened and closed in surprise. But he recovered quickly. "Well, all I can say is Corporal Fitzgerald isn't going to like that. I mean, he's *really* not going to like that."

Silvia studied Maltais, weighing what he had heard, before he decided he was not about to be so quickly turned from his purpose.

"Listen, Andy," he said, in a voice that was measured, reasonable, even soothing, "if you talk to us now, if you get rid of this terrible burden, you're going to feel a whole lot better than you've felt at any time in the past three months."

Maltais nodded and stared back at him, the tears brimming again for an instant on his eyelids.

"It's too much for you to carry," Silvia continued sympathetically.

Maltais shivered, then pursed his lips in an attempt to control his emotions, nodding again. But he said nothing.

"So?" Silvia coaxed.

"Yeah," Maltais replied, staring now at the top of the table and still hugging the Bible.

Silvia smiled and made a gesture of encouragement with his hands, as though to draw out the pent-up truth. "Yeah?" he said. "Yeah, what?"

Maltais wouldn't look up. "I'm waiting," he answered, the picture of someone who has taken a position and decided to dig in.

Silvia sighed, then tried one last tactic, leaning forward angrily. "Listen, you're in the custody of the Fall River Police Department. The murder we're talking about took place here in Fall River, not in the goddamned statehouse, and if anyone—*any*one—comes in here to get you while you're in our custody before I'm goddamned good and ready to let you go, I personally will blow him away. Get it?"

"Sure," Maltais said, recoiling from Silvia's vehemence. "That makes sense to me." He finished lamely, "I didn't mean that the way it sounded."

"How did you mean it?"

"Well, it's just that Corporal Fitzgerald told me what he told me, and so that's the way I gotta do it, you know?" It was said very tentatively, but Silvia marveled at how quickly Maltais managed to turn off his emotions and switch into a new role, the character of the old sourdough, explaining the Way of the West to a new arrival.

Both detectives leaned back in their chairs, Joaquim studying the witness and Silvia examining the ceiling. After such a promising start, this wasn't turning out to be anywhere near as easy as it looked.

But it wasn't as though Maltais stopped talking. Once he had drawn the line, he rambled aimlessly on, inevitably answering some other question than the one that had been asked, sometimes excited, sometimes complacent, always irrelevant, crisscrossing the trail with one digression after another. By daybreak, the two detectives were as certain as ever that he knew more about the murder than he was telling, but it was clear that Andy Maltais was still a long, long way from admitting anything.

Shortly after six o'clock Paul Carey and the other detective took over the interview. Silvia got up to stretch his legs, signaling his partner to follow him out into the hallway. There, beyond Maltais' hearing, he asked, "Well?"

"This is the guy," Joaquim said.

Silvia was tense and disappointed. "We almost had a bingo."

"Yeah, well . . . " Joaquim didn't seem to be concerned. Both recognized that a fierce battle was taking place within Andre Maltais' soul, a contest between the instinct for self-preservation and the even stronger need to confess, to rid himself of a terrible guilt. "It doesn't have to be today," Joaquim said. "This one's not going anywhere. It's just a matter of when."

By nine o'clock, the witness was allowed to leave the station house. The state police still had not arrived. It was Sunday, and Andy Maltais, who now belonged to God, had to go to church. He promised to return early that afternoon to continue the interview, and he told the detectives that Paul Fitzgerald, the Big Guy, would be there when he came back.

In the hierarchy of law enforcement, state police are another level up from the locals: they can patrol traffic on any road in the Commonwealth, regardless of the town or city it runs through, and they act on similar higher authority, reporting directly to the district attorney, in the investigation of murder. The state police officer in charge of the Levesque homicide was a veteran detective corporal, Paul Fitzgerald, assigned to the Bristol County Crime Prevention and Control Unit.

Fitzgerald was the opposite number of Carey, Silvia, and Joaquim in every sense of the term. Tall, precise, methodical, intensely private, a family man, descended from policemen, at thirty-six he was a four-teen-year veteran of the state police and had been with CPAC since its inception in 1976. Like the Fall River Nighters, he was very good at what he did; the difference was in the way he went about it.

A big part of that difference lay in the respective roles of local and state police in any major case. The local police know the landscape, are familiar with the players, and follow the action at ground level. The state police are outsiders; the main function of the CPAC unit is to help make the case for the district attorney.

But the balance of the difference was Paul Fitzgerald himself and how he viewed his job. He visited Fall River frequently, interviewed witnesses, attended inquests and autopsies, worked closely with the local police, even followed up on some of their leads as well as his own. But he relied on his formidable intellect rather than on intimacy and on the natural power of the law rather than tricks or intimidation to get results. It would have been as out of character for Fitzgerald to insinuate himself into the netherworld of Fall River nightlife, for example, or to share intimately in the lives of witnesses and suspects, as it would have been for a square-rigged, four-masted ship of the line to shoot rapids or ride the surf. It was not his territory. It was not his style.

There were two CPAC locations in Bristol County: in the downtown New Bedford offices of the district attorney, Ronald Pina, and in the ramshackle house that served as the State Police Barracks in nearby North Dartmouth. Both Fitzgerald and his partner, Sergeant Dan Lowney, reported to District Attorney Pina, but because of space limitations in New Bedford they spent most of their office time in the North Dartmouth barracks.

In late October of 1979, a couple of weeks after the murder of Doreen Levesque, and three months before Barbara Raposa's body would be found, a trooper in North Dartmouth received a telephone call from a man who said he knew something about the Levesque killing. The caller was Andre O. Maltais, a distant acquaintance of the trooper's from the days when they had grown up in Dartmouth. Maltais said he was calling in the hope that the trooper could put him together with the detective in charge of the Levesque case.

The trooper receiving the call was younger than Maltais and knew him only slightly. Maltais had dropped out of school in the seventh grade, and now, in his early forties, he was a compulsive, unstable little man who worked at odd jobs around the Fall River and New Bedford area, mostly as a caretaker. The trooper also knew that a few years earlier Maltais had served time in the Barnstable County House of Correction on a sex conviction involving a couple of fifteen-year-old girls. He asked Maltais what he knew about the Levesque killing, but the caller put him off. He was evasive, given to long, rambling answers. The trooper gave Maltais Paul Fitzgerald's name as the officer in charge, promised to try to arrange a meeting, and said he'd get back to him.

Maltais was an obvious flake, but at that point the police still hadn't learned much about the murder, so when Fitzgerald got the message he decided instantly to talk with him. The trooper who knew Maltais tried several times over the following days to get back to him. He was hard to find. Eventually, he called in again and a meeting was arranged in the North Dartmouth Barracks for the week after Thanksgiving.

Late on the afternoon of the appointed day, just before dark, Andy Maltais showed up at the CPAC office on the second floor of the old wooden barracks. Paul Fitzgerald stood to greet him and offered him a chair beside his desk. The detective assessed Maltais as about five-feet-five, moderately built, and given to the nervous, ingratiating kind of cockiness which sometimes serves as a weak man's armor. Maltais' eyes darted about the office as he talked, and he talked nearly nonstop from the moment he entered the room—about his admiration for police work, about the state of his health, about the weather, about his shock and revulsion at the murder, about the many police officers he knew (all of them outstanding people), about what he'd had for Thanksgiving dinner, about why it had been so hard for the first trooper to get in touch with him and how sorry he was if that had caused any problems, about his faith in God, about what it's like to be born again—

Finally, Corporal Fitzgerald held up both his hands to stop the flow. "What do you know about the murder of Doreen Levesque?" he asked.

"Nothing," Maltais replied.

Fitzgerald looked at him without comment, waiting.

"I'm not the one. The ones who know about the murder are—two friends of mine. Two girls. I know that they know about it."

"How do they know?"

"I don't know."

"What do they know?"

"They haven't told me. I've heard them talking about it. They know."

Fitzgerald nodded. "Will they talk to the police—to me?"

More rapid eye movements, darting from thought to thought, beginning words without finishing them: "Well, see—," "It's, uh—," weighing the question, then clasping his hands together with conviction. "I think I can get them here. I'll ask them. Sure, I think they'll come. Yeah, I know they will. They'll be here."

Fitzgerald had enough experience in police work to know that it did not pay to prejudge people and that who people were was always less important than what they knew. Chances were, the president of a major corporation wasn't going to come in and tell the police about a street murder. Fitzgerald wasn't sure what to make of Andy Maltais, but when the little man scurried out of his office early the evening of that first meeting, the detective allowed himself to hope that Maltais would be able to convince the girls to come to the barracks and that they would have something to offer.

A week later, Maltais returned to Fitzgerald's office and told him he had the two girls. He wanted them to meet Fitzgerald, but was afraid to bring them directly there. "I don't want anyone to see my car in your parking lot. I gotta watch out for that kind of thing, if you know what I'm saying. I mean there are people who are going to wonder what's Andy and these girls doing, talking with the cops—"

Fitzgerald interrupted Maltais to ask if they were in his car. No, Maltais said, he had left them at the doughnut shop just down Route

6, the highway running in front of the barracks between North Dartmouth and New Bedford. He was sort of hoping the detective could bring them from the shop to the barracks in an unmarked car. Fitzgerald looked out the window at the rainswept highway. It was only about four o'clock, but already getting dark because of the weather. "Sure," he said. "Let's go."

Fitzgerald and Maltais walked quickly down the stairs and out the back of the barracks. Maltais got into his car, and the detective followed in his own. The entrance to the parking lot was on a side street, and Maltais took a right turn as he exited, away from Route 6, and drove to a dead end, out of sight of the station. Maltais parked, scampered around the front of Fitzgerald's car, and slid into the seat beside him.

A minute later, when they got to the doughnut shop, Maltais hopped out, sprinted inside, and reemerged almost immediately with two young women. He slid into the front seat as the girls got into the back.

Fitzgerald said "Hi," and the older of the two girls said "Hi" in return; the younger girl slammed the door behind her, studied the detective for a moment in the rearview mirror, then looked away. Fitzgerald had seen that routine before: the working girl's once-over, cool to the point of indifference, but counting the house. The detective turned the car back onto the highway, drove down the road until he was out of sight of the doughnut shop, then reversed direction and pulled into the barracks lot where he had started.

Upstairs in the CPAC office, Fitzgerald set up two more straight-backed wooden chairs next to his desk and Maltais offered introductions. The older girl, the one who had returned his greeting in the car, was Karen Marsden; also a hooker, Fitzgerald thought, but friendlier, not afraid to let him see she was nervous, even frightened. The younger one was Robin Murphy.

Fitzgerald's partner came into the room, and there were more introductions.

"Can we start with your ages?" Fitzgerald asked, looking at them in turn.

Karen, the nervous one, said twenty. Robin, the little brunette, said seventeen.

"Okay," Fitzgerald said, "Mr. Maltais tells us he doesn't know anything, but that he knows you know something. What do you know?"

Robin looked at Fitzgerald quizzically, smiled, and shrugged. She gave the impression she was uncertain why she was there, except as an accommodation to Andy Maltais.

Karen, on the other hand, was trembling. She looked back and forth in panic between the detective and her friend—Fitzgerald found himself wondering, just for a moment, whether he and Robin might be the two opposing sources of Karen's tension—and then she said, "Carl Drew killed Doreen Levesque."

Now here was something worth waiting for. Fitzgerald knew Carl Drew. He was a big, sullen young drifter who had come down from New Hampshire a year or two earlier, had been involved in several robbery and assault cases, and now worked as a Fall River pimp out of the bars on Bedford Street. The year before, Drew had escaped from custody and almost made it to the Canadian border before being rear-rested. Fitzgerald had been sent up to New Hampshire with Dan Lowney to bring him back.

"How do you know it was Carl Drew?"

Karen said, "I know it," and pursed her lips.

He looked at Robin, and she simply looked back, showing no reaction to what Karen had just told him.

"You've got to give me more information. Just saying you know doesn't tell me a thing. I've got to know *how* you know."

Karen shook her head slowly and looked at the floor. "I know it, that's all. He killed her."

Fitzgerald looked back over at Robin, but she now was studying her friend with the same curiosity as Lowney and Maltais, passive but engaged, apparently as unaware as they were of how Karen came to make this accusation. "What about you, Robin?" Fitzgerald asked.

If the question had been designed to catch Robin unawares, it failed at its purpose. She merely looked puzzled. She shrugged and shook her head.

"Do you know Carl Drew?" he asked.

"Yeah, I know him."

"Did he kill Doreen Levesque?

"Could be," she said. "I don't know."

"Do you know why Karen says he did?"

Robin shook her head again and deflected the question by looking back at her friend for the answer.

He next turned to Maltais, who raised his eyes silently to the ceiling in a pantomime of long-suffering disbelief at the ways of women. "Well, then," the detective said to them all, "we can't go much further with this until you're willing to trust us. If you're afraid of Carl Drew, we can protect you. But we can't protect anybody until they tell us something we can use."

Karen shook her head more vigorously when Fitzgerald spoke of trust, and when he got to the part about protection, she laughed. But she wouldn't say anything further about how she knew Carl Drew had murdered Doreen Levesque.

The detective backed away from the issue of how she knew and asked the two girls about other aspects of their life. Did they work for Drew? How long had they been prostitutes? Where did they live?

Karen told him she knew Drew because until a few months ago he had been her pimp; Robin said she knew him from the street.

Karen lived with her grandmother; she had a son, JJ, who lived with a foster family in Fall River.

Robin said she had been on the street at one time, but had given it up. She said she lived in Harbor Terrace.

But as often as Fitzgerald brought them back to the reason they were there in his office, neither of the two girls would tell him more. "Okay," he finally said. "Then that's about it."

Robin Murphy stood up first, then Karen Marsden. Andy Maltais had been perched on the edge of an adjacent desk, and as he let himself down to stand, he said to the two detectives, "Well, that's something, anyway, right?"

"No, it's not," Fitzgerald said. "By itself, a name doesn't mean a thing. Some guy could come in here and say Jimmy Carter did it."

Robin had started for the doorway, and Karen was right behind her. But before the older girl left the room, she turned back to Fitzgerald and Lowney, her voice trembling, and said, "If you find me dead, Carl Drew did it."

Robin Murphy was already at the top of the stairs, but Fitzgerald could tell she had heard what her friend had said to him. She slowed for a moment and then, without looking back, shook her head and skipped noisily down the wooden steps.

"Tell us how you know about Carl, so we can protect you," Fitzgerald said again to Karen Marsden.

Karen shook her head and started down the stairs, rushing to catch up with Robin.

Frustrated, Fitzgerald pulled on his parka and followed them out the back door and into the parking lot. The rain was still falling, and it was now night. He drove them back to where Andy Maltais had parked his car at the bottom of the dead-end street.

Despite her reticence about the Levesque case, over the next several weeks Karen Marsden telephoned Fitzgerald frequently about her fear of Carl Drew. Usually, the calls came into the barracks at night after Fitzgerald had already gone home. For a period of perhaps a month, they developed a routine where Karen would leave her name and a number which the desk officer would relay to the detective and Fitzgerald would call her back from his house. But all those conversations dead-ended in the same place as their first meeting. She never opened up. She was constantly saying how she feared for her life, but she was unwilling to tell him how she knew Drew had killed Doreen Levesque. By the end of the year, her calls had stopped.

The state trooper's relationship with Maltais, however, showed no signs of weakening. Through December, Andy kept in even closer touch with Fitzgerald than before. His calls were still unproductive, but at the beginning Fitzgerald suspected that he might hold a key, somehow, to the secret Karen was so stubbornly unwilling to share. And while Karen's calls during December became progressively more pressured, panicky, and even hysterical, Maltais would merely ramble endlessly on and on, and eventually the detective's hopes for him as a useful informant began to sink under the burden of endless digression. It was not uncommon in a conversation for him to start twelve different topics and go nowhere with any of them. Fitzgerald made an effort to control him, to keep him pointed in a direction, patiently bringing him back, again and again, to the question of how Karen knew what she knew, but with no tangible result.

One of the apparent digressions that began intruding with growing frequency during those calls from Maltais was his concern for his girlfriend. Her name was Barbara Raposa, and she had been missing, according to Andy, since sometime early in November—between Andy's first call to his friend at the barracks and his initial meeting with Fitzgerald. As far as the detective was concerned, Andy Maltais was that kind of person—you'd expect his girlfriend to be missing— and the topic of Barbara Raposa was just one more red herring that Andy kept dragging across the path as Fitzgerald pursued the killer of Doreen Levesque. It finally got to the point that if the name Barbara Raposa arose, Fitzgerald didn't want to hear about it.

Despite his early promise, by the end of December the facts suggested that voluble Andy Maltais didn't have a lot to offer on the Levesque case after all. But Fitzgerald was too good a cop to discount his instincts. There was still something there, perhaps not what Maltais had claimed when he first came to them, but something, and whenever he called, the detective continued to listen. Whether or not Fitzgerald needed Maltais, the compulsive little man clearly still needed him: his calls kept on coming even after Karen's stopped, almost every day through the dead of winter, with little or no information, just idle, undirected rambling, on and on and on.

The body of Barbara Raposa was delivered by police ambulance to St. Anne's Hospital in Fall River late Saturday afternoon, and it remained in the basement morgue overnight. The next morning, January 27, an attendant placed it on a portable steel table which he then rolled out into the hallway. Alan Silvia walked down the same corridor with two other Fall River detectives, just ahead of the table with the body. When they entered the examining room, Silvia saw that a couple of state police officers had arrived before them in the autopsy room, and they were talking with Dr. Ambrose Keeley, the state pathologist, who had driven down from the Boston suburb of Waltham.

As he expected, the observers from Bristol County CPAC were Paul Fitzgerald and Dan Lowney along with a state police photographer. Silvia nodded a greeting at the group, then singled out the tall state trooper. "How you doing, Big Guy?"

Fitzgerald nodded in response at Silvia and the other detectives, friendly but appearing slightly bemused by the greeting. Then the door from the corridor opened again, and the steel table with the body rolled in past them. The conversation stopped as Dr. Keeley unzipped the rubber bag.

Most of the encrusted snow from the day before had disappeared during the night, and the black granite flesh now glistened with the thaw. Otherwise, it remained in pretty much the same state as when it was discovered: the arms raised in languid, almost abandoned defense; the stained, weather-bleached clothing adhering stiffly to the body; grass and twigs entangled in the matted hair. Silvia forced himself to look again at where the face had been; then he turned away.

Dr. Keeley bent down to examine the face more closely and picked off some granular matter which he rolled thoughtfully between the thumb and forefinger of his gloved right hand. "Sand," he said, more to himself than to the detectives who were watching. But then he picked up a second, larger sample, which he examined more carefully. "Not sand," he said, this time looking at his audience as he spoke. "Cement. Small pieces of concrete."

The detectives nodded. Silvia made notes.

Dr. Keeley dropped the fragment into a steel tray on a stand at his side, then turned back to the body. "That's one thing. Let's see what else," he said, and began to carefully peel away the clothing.

Once the body had been unwrapped, the folds and texture of the fabric were still embossed in the blackened, unforgiving flesh. Dr. Keeley leaned over and examined two elliptical breaks in the skin, half hidden in the pattern left by the twisted brassiere. "This looks like a set of toothmarks," he said to the state police photographer, and another picture was taken.

The autopsy took over an hour. Under the strong lights, the thawing process accelerated. Despite the body's advanced decomposition, the law required the pathologist to follow standard investigative procedures, opening the abdomen and thoracic cavity, searching the cranium for further clues to the manner of death. Rivulets of water from the melting body fluids ran across the shiny metal surface of the table, and soon they commingled with darker, more viscous matter that began to ooze from within. Silvia's eyes burned from the stench, and he noticed that the others, like himself, had backed further away from the table as the autopsy progressed. The room lacked any method of renewing or cleansing the air, and Dr. Keeley asked Silvia to open one of the half windows at street level.

Although the Fall River detectives had matched the clothing on the corpse with the description of the clothing on Barbara Raposa's missing persons report, the state troopers remained privately uncommitted about the identity of the body. Fitzgerald and Lowney had interviewed Barbara Raposa's boyfriend the day before—not Andy Maltais, but a younger man named Dave Cowen—and learned that three months earlier, on the night she had disappeared, they had gone together to D'Angelo's on the corner of Plymouth Avenue and Pleasant Street to have a sandwich, after which she had decided to go uptown for a couple of hours to make some money on the street. Now, at the autopsy, Dr. Keeley opened the viscera. The others in the room drew back to avoid the overwhelming stench, but Fitzgerald and Lowney moved closer to the cadaver to follow the surgeon's progress.

"What time was it she had that sandwich?" Keeley asked. He drew his blade across a swollen section of the blue-gray stomach.

"About ten o'clock," Fitzgerald said.

All three men looked down into the body cavity as the medical examiner separated the viscera, still stiff from the three-month freeze, and sorted through its partially digested contents with the fingers of both hands. "And was it a crabmeat salad?" Keeley asked.

Fitzgerald nodded. His eyes were smarting.

Keeley nodded with amusement and satisfaction. "Then if you can tell me when she ate it, I'll give you a pretty good estimate of the time she died."

* * *

Near the end of the procedure, Silvia happened to look up at the window and see a boy of about twelve, watching them from outside. Perhaps on his way home from the nearby church, the boy was peering down into the autopsy room as the doctor sawed through the skull of the cadaver. Silvia wondered if the youngster knew what it was he was looking at: his expression was as detached and impassive as if he were watching television. "Hey, get out of there," he yelled sharply up at the open window.

At first, the boy's face didn't change; he stared back at him as though Silvia too were an abstraction, part of the same unreal tableau with the dissected cadaver as its centerpiece. But after another moment, before the detective spoke again, he apparently accepted the need to switch channels and with obvious reluctance turned and walked away.

By noon, the autopsy was over. Alan Silvia had been up since the middle of the previous day; he felt grimy and exhausted and was fighting nausea from the sweet, invasive stench of decay. He wanted to go home and change his clothes, to take a shower, to rest, to purge his mind and pores and lungs of all that had accumulated between his visit to the murder site the day before and this moment in the basement of St. Anne's. But he knew he could not; the treadmill of the murder investigation was already running at full speed beneath his feet. By then Andy Maltais was waiting back at the station house and Paul Fitzgerald was going directly there from the autopsy to continue the interrogation—on a Fall River case and on Fall River turf. Silvia had planted some important seeds with Maltais that morning, and if any of them should come to flower, he was determined to be in on the harvest.

But it was more than a sense of duty or of competition that gave him the energy to continue. It was the exhilaration of the chase—especially when, as Silvia was now certain, the most likely object of that pursuit was clearly in his sights.

As it turned out, nothing of any consequence occurred at the Sunday afternoon interview, and Maltais was again allowed to return to his mother's home. The state police felt they had a much better suspect in the victim's younger boyfriend, and they were not at all convinced Maltais had killed Barbara Raposa. For the next several days, Silvia, Joaquim, Carey, and the other MCD detectives interviewed other witnesses who knew either the young victim or her middle-aged lover, searched for evidence, for clues, followed rumors, gathered facts. They worked nearly around the clock.

EIGHT

IN THE GREEN WATER

On Wednesday, January 30, Alan Silvia received a call from a girl named Carol Fletcher, who told him that a friend of hers knew about the Raposa murder. Fletcher said the friend was distrustful of the police and nearly hysterical with fear and that she would never agree to going down to the station house to discuss what she knew. Perhaps, Fletcher suggested, they could bring the police to her instead.

Silvia agreed when he heard the friend was Karen Marsden.

Neither Silvia nor Joaquim knew anything of Karen's numerous conversations with Paul Fitzgerald from just after Thanksgiving to the New Year's weekend. Though both of the Fall River detectives had spent several months investigating the murder of Doreen Levesque, neither of them was aware that the state police considered Karen Marsden a key witness in that case. And they were unaware of any connection between either Karen Marsden or Robin Murphy and the principal suspect in the Raposa killing, Andy Maltais.

At six o'clock that evening, Alan Silvia knocked on the door of Carol Fletcher's apartment on County Street in Fall River. When he and Joaquim entered, Carol introduced them to her sister and another young woman, both of whom were visiting. All three were apparently in their early twenties. Silvia realized he had seen Carol before, perhaps along Bedford Street or at Harbor Terrace; she was rather plain, with stringy hair and the downtrodden demeanor that comes from living too close to the street. The other girls looked more kempt, and Silvia decided they were nearly pretty, but they had some of the same waifishness about them as well.

After the introduction, Silvia looked quickly around the room. He was relieved to see that Robin Murphy was not a part of this meeting, at least not yet. She had always been present whenever he had seen Karen in the past, and he suspected that was one reason she had seemed reluctant to talk openly with the police.

Carol quickly explained that neither her sister nor the friend knew anything about either murder. She told the two policemen that Karen Marsden was nearby; she repeated that she was sure Karen really wanted to talk with somebody but was afraid for her life and that this meeting had been planned without Karen's knowledge. "She may freak out when she sees you here."

The two policemen nodded, indicating that they were willing to take that chance, and Carol left to get her. She returned a few minutes later with her friend.

Karen Marsden was about five-feet-four or -five, and although her face was partially hidden by shoulder-length brunette hair, Silvia could tell she was wired the moment he saw her. She entered the room ahead of Carol, nervously brushed back the hair, and gave a shy, anxious, watery-eyed smile at Carol's sister and friend. Then she looked over at the two detectives with the same smile and, recognizing them, shivered and screamed in panic. "Oh, God, no!" she said, and turned back to leave.

Carol, who was behind her when they entered, now stood between Karen and the door. "Karen, they want to help you," she said, putting her arms around her. Whether to soothe her agitation or to keep her in the room, the gesture had the effect of blocking her exit. Still shivering, Karen began to sob, apparently abandoning her attempt to get away.

The two detectives remained seated and for the moment said nothing. Silvia was already aware that Karen, like many prostitutes, didn't think much of herself and was easily intimidated, and he wanted to avoid giving her any reason to view him as someone who used words or authority in the same way other people in her life used threats and muscle, to push her around and force their will on her. He also knew that under the influence of drugs, people were often inclined toward paranoia and the best way to get what he wanted was to play against her hysteria—calm, anchored, soothing.

"She's going to kill me if she finds out," Karen sobbed into Carol's shoulder.

One of the other girls explained to the detectives. "Robin."

Silvia already knew from his visits to Harbor Terrace that Karen was referring to Robin Murphy. Because they were anxious to avoid giving the appearance of an official interview, neither he nor Joaquim was taking notes, but he carefully filed Karen Marsden's exact words in his memory: "She's going to kill me."

For the next several minutes, Karen alternately raged and sulked. She sat on a couch, shivering and hugging herself and moaning, then looked up angrily to berate her friend for her betrayal, stomping both feet noisily on the floor like a child. "How could you do this? How could you *do* this to me?" Much of what she said was simply incoherent.

Finally, when there was a lull in the storm, Alan Silvia said very quietly, "If you're that scared, maybe we can help."

Despite the detective's even tone, the result was another violent, tearful eruption. "Help me nothing! Help them fill my veins with battery acid and leave me in the green water? Help them to kill JJ? What help?" More kicking her feet against the floor. *"What help?"*

Silvia made a calming motion with his hands, and after a moment the stomping ended.

"I'm a good person," she said, her voice between an exhausted moan and a whisper. "I believe in God."

Silvia nodded sympathetically and dropped his own voice even lower to answer, "Yeah, so do I."

"If you believe, then God will protect you," one of the other girls said. When Silvia looked up, she added, "Karen."

The detective grinned ironically—God's protection of the faithful evidently did not include policemen—and he kept on nodding. "Yeah," he said again, "that's right."

"Karen, honey," one of the girls said, "you've got to talk to these guys."

Karen looked up sharply, not threateningly, but frightened and feral. "What have you told them?"

"That you know about Doreen—about who killed her," the girl said.

"About Carl Drew," another added.

Karen screamed. She threw herself against the cushion of the couch, and when she screamed again the sound was muffled by the plush.

For the next two hours, Karen Marsden's three friends and the two detectives sat with her in the living room of the apartment on County Street, coaxing out an occasional small fact amidst a nearly steady stream of weeping, sobbing, screaming, the girls stroking Karen's soft hair and wiping with their cool fingers at the tears on her cheeks, the detectives speaking softly now and then to ask her questions which were seldom answered, interrupting her to clarify what she had said, pressing her for names, places, dates, proof—and getting very little of any. But despite the manner of the telling—the lack of details, the ambiguity, the incoherence, and the anguish—over the course of those two hours a picture began to emerge.

Karen spoke again and again of the Devil. This much the two detectives were able to clarify: when she said the Devil, she was referring to Carl Drew.

The Devil and Robin were going to harm Karen's child, JJ. But even though Silvia and Joaquim asked her more than once, she still had not said why or in what way that harm would be done.

"Tell them about the green water," one of the girls said, and when Silvia heard the request, he said, "The green water, yeah, and the battery acid."

Sobbing in fear, with Carol clarifying some of the incoherence and filling in some of the missing parts, Karen told them.

One afternoon about two months before, Robin Murphy had come by Karen's house in a car with Carol Fletcher, and all three girls drove over to the Freetown—Fall River State Forest, also called the Freetown Reservation, a large, undeveloped tract of campgrounds, woods, and state parkland that started at the outskirts of Fall River and sprawled on for several square miles to the northeast of the city. After following a long maze of dirt roads, they came to a secluded lane in the heart of the woods. "This is the place," Robin told them, and the car stopped.

Carol and Karen looked around. The woods were empty, but there was evidence from the ruts in the roadway and under the tall pines that other vehicles had been there in the recent past. "This is the place," Robin said again. All three girls got out of the car. Ahead of them was a dark, weathered structure, a table of stone or wood, among the trees. Robin said, "The altar."

It was here, she said, that Carl Drew had told Robin Murphy he was going to kill Karen Marsden and Carol Fletcher. He would offer their souls to Satan. He would inject battery acid into their veins. He would leave their bodies in the green water by the side of the road.

Silvia and Joaquim listened attentively through to the end. When it was obvious they were going to hear nothing more, either about Drew's alleged threat on their lives or about whatever Karen knew about the Raposa murder, Silvia decided to shift his tactics. "Okay," he said to all four girls, "get your coats on."

Karen took a deep breath as though she were about to scream

again, and Carol Fletcher, looking distressed as well, asked where they were going. Silvia said they were driving over to the Reservation to see if they could find the place the girls had just described.

Karen started to cry. "I won't go back there again." She stood up and began walking nervously around the room. "I won't do it."

"God will protect us," one of the other girls reminded her.

"And so will we," Silvia said. "You're not going down there with the Devil. You're going with the entire night shift of the Major Crimes Division of the Fall River Police Department."

Karen resisted for a few minutes longer, then finally agreed on the condition that they stop first at a nearby Catholic church, where she could speak with a priest. When Silvia and Joaquim said that was fine with them, she changed her mind about the church. "Let's just go."

Twenty minutes later, they turned into the dark, wintry, woodland roads of the Reservation. They drove around for nearly an hour, occasionally passing the long, concrete culverts that had been built as cisterns in defense of forest fires, their algae-filled waters now frozen in slick, dark slabs of green ice. But they never found the road where Robin Murphy had taken them two months earlier; they never saw the altar where Robin told them that Carl Drew, the Devil, had promised their souls to Satan.

And Karen Marsden never told any of them what she had done just before that terrifying visit to the Reservation, perhaps by only a few days: that she had gone to the North Dartmouth barracks of the state police CPAC unit with Robin Murphy and Andy Maltais and told Paul Fitzgerald that the murderer of Doreen Levesque was Carl Drew.

Silvia and Joaquim promised to return for another look in the daylight. The girls seemed both disappointed and relieved that they hadn't found what they were seeking.

NINE / **ANDY'S DREAM**

During the days following the discovery of Barbara Raposa's body, like a shipwrecked man who seizes at every piece of passing debris in the attempt to keep himself afloat, Andy Maltais redoubled the frequency of his contact with Paul Fitzgerald. On some days, he telephoned the detective in the morning, the afternoon, and again at night, talking with him about things he had seen in the paper, about people he had met who might have information valuable to the Raposa murder investigation, about new memories, and sometimes about random thoughts and feelings. Fitzgerald continued to listen carefully, and on a couple of occasions during the week of January 28 to February 1, he invited Maltais into the barracks at North Dartmouth to pursue a particular thought or to talk about any subject he wanted, for as long as he liked.

The talks always started off in the same direction, toward some substantial revelation about the Raposa killing, but Andy's excursions always seemed to wander hopelessly from their apparent goal, a long, incoherent tragicomedy that never quite reached a payoff or a punch line. Despite these false starts, Fitzgerald remained confident that Maltais was inching his way toward a result, and he was endlessly forbearing. And as the detective sensed that the goal was at last coming into view, he started meeting Maltais at the CPAC office in New Bedford instead of the barracks.

At that time, the Bristol County CPAC unit consisted of seven troopers, three of whom were in the North Dartmouth barracks; the rest, including the detective lieutenant in charge of the unit, were in nearby New Bedford. By diverting Maltais to the downtown office, Fitzgerald was able to invite other investigators, including District Attorney Pina and his assistant, Ray Veary, to sit in on these discussions and also ask questions. In each case, because they recognized the possibility that the suspect could either make a confession or trip himself up with an incriminating mistake, those meetings in New Bedford started with one of the officers reading Maltais his rights.

In all of this, they always took the greatest care that there was never any suggestion of judgment or even suspicion of guilt; they were simply following the law, and Fitzgerald was there to help the little man through a complex and sometimes bewildering passage—not exactly as Andy's peer, and certainly not as nemesis, but more as his shepherd—toward a goal which none of them could yet define but which they all sensed awaited them.

On February 5, ten days after the discovery of the body of Barbara Raposa, Maltais called Fitzgerald in North Dartmouth. The voice on the telephone was under control, perhaps more composed than in the past, but obviously excited. It said, "I know everything that happened. I had a dream last night."

It sounded like the call Fitzgerald had been expecting.

The state trooper knew of Maltais' interest in the occult, and he had heard a little bit from him about how, the previous week, one of the detectives down in Fall River had suggested that Maltais had psychic powers. A dream would be the perfect vehicle for dealing with information too painful or too dangerous to offer directly. "Come on over," Fitzgerald said.

"I don't have any gas in the car."

"We'll pick you up. We'll get you down here. I want to talk with you."

There was a pause on the other end, then Maltais let out a deep breath. "Okay," he said. "I'll be here."

Fitzgerald called Ray Veary and told him to alert his boss. "Andy's got the whole story, and he wants to tell us about it. He just called me and said he had a dream and knows everything that happened in the Raposa killing."

Fitzgerald then called the Fall River Police Department and told Detective Lieutenant Ted Kaegael about the call and the scheduled meeting. Did they want to be in on it? Kaegael said they did.

Fitzgerald said, "On the way, why don't you grab Andy? He's nearer to you than to me. We can all meet at the DA's office."

Lieutenant Kaegael sent two detectives to pick up Andy Maltais; they were Alan Silvia and Tom Joaquim. Kaegael and another detective, Tony Correia, headed down to New Bedford in a separate car.

When Andy Maltais arrived in the district attorney's office with Silvia and Joaquim, everyone else was already there. There was a recorder on the conference table, and Maltais saw two women who were introduced as stenographers. One was seated at a court reporter's console near the chair proffered to him by the district attorney. Fitzgerald stood up and said, "Hello, Andy," and Maltais, quick to seize on the public acknowledgment of their long association, smiled back and shook the Big Guy's hand.

"Andy, you have the right to remain silent," Fitzgerald said. Maltais laughed self-consciously and looked at the other detectives and attorneys who were seated around the conference table. "Anything you say can and will be used against you in a court of law," Fitzgerald continued. "You have the right to talk to a lawyer and have him present with you while we question you. And if you cannot afford to have a lawyer, one will be appointed to represent you before any questioning, if you so wish. You can decide at any time to exercise these rights, and not answer any questions or make any statements. Do you understand each of the rights I have explained to you?"

"Yeah," Andy said, still smiling. Then, straightening up, he said, "Yes, I do."

"Having these rights in mind, do you wish to talk to us now?"

"That's right. Yes, I do."

Fitzgerald made a gesture with his hand that said the stage was all his, then sat down with the others and waited. Maltais sat down as well.

Pina began the questioning.

"All right, Andy, try to remember as best you can. You had a dream last night."

Maltais nodded and looked around the room, composed but self-conscious.

"Okay, that was the date of February fifth, nineteen eighty," Pina continued, glancing briefly to the stenographer, then back to the witness. "What happened before you woke up? That dream was what?"

Maltais raised his hands above the table, palms down, as though to indicate a floating action. "In the dream I was up high."

"Up high—" the district attorney said, raising his own hands in encouragement.

Maltais nodded, his hands suspended before him, then peered down at the table as though viewing a landscape from above. "I could see this man standing on the ground. I was up high in the sky, like." He looked up sharply, searching the faces around the table for a reaction. Every person in the room was leaning forward, watching him intently. Alan Silvia, the Psychic Reader, was studying him closely as well, but unlike the others, he met the little man's inquiring look with the slightest trace of a smile. Maltais quickly amended his last statement: "I was not far off the ground."

Pina nodded encouragingly. "You were up in the sky, looking down."

"Somebody beating—" Maltais said, then stopped himself again. "I was in a tree—" Another stop. "He took rocks—" He looked back at Silvia, then lowered his hands nearer to the top of the table. "That high—but I was high and I had to move—I could see in my dream, the tree was in my way, I had to move—" Then back to Pina, "Was hitting with a rock. I took notice that he had a leather jacket on."

It was the same thing Fitzgerald had seen dozens of times before. Maltais's mind was racing like an engine in need of a tune-up, unable to drive the gears because all of the cylinders were firing at once. Exhausted before he had started, the little man sat back in the chair to collect himself. The difference this time, Fitzgerald knew, was that if Andy could adjust the timing, he clearly intended to take them to a place they all wanted to go.

Pina waited, then placed a piece of paper on the table in front of the witness. It was a Xerox copy of a clipping from the Fall River *Herald News* dated Monday, January 28, 1980, and it contained a picture of the field where Barbara Raposa's body had been found. Pina placed a pen on the table and asked him to mark the photograph with an X to indicate where he was located when this dream was taking place.

Maltais studied the paper. The photograph had been taken after the body was removed, and it provided no indication where in the field the victim had been located. Moreover, the investigators had taken great care at the site that none of that information was released to the press.

He picked up the pen and placed an X on the picture, slightly to the right of where the body had been discovered.

"Okay," Pina said. "And put an O where you thought in your dream you saw this man."

This time the witness pointed to the paper with the pen, precisely on the spot where the body had been found.

No one in the room moved a muscle.

"All right," Pina said. He studied the picture. "So you put an X there."

Maltais was like a tethered balloon, straining to the point of bursting with the story inside him, and he took the comment as an invitation to continue with his narrative. "I'm in the trees. Trees are not in the way—trunk of the tree—"

"Okay," the DA interrupted, smiling in sympathy at his eagerness; this had to be done a step at a time. "Now, have you ever been at the scene of the crime?"

"No."

"Never been there? Maybe as a boy or a child?"

"No."

"Okay," Pina said, apparently accepting the assurances, but now looking for another way to explain how Maltais could possibly know what he knew. "So this was just—"

"So," Maltais picked it up, nodding and trying to be helpful, "it just came into my mind."

The DA looked at him thoughtfully and nodded back. Maltais looked across for a reaction from Silvia; the Psychic Reader was craning his head to study the mark on the photograph, and his smile had given way to a frown of concentration.

"Do you see him?" the DA asked.

Maltais looked confused, then realized Pina was coming back to the man in the dream. "I could see him," he answered.

"Exactly what do you see?"

Maltais followed Pina's lead and returned to the present tense, his eyes closing slightly in a perhaps unconscious imitation of Alan Silvia ten days before as he too had described a vision of the murder scene. "He is a heavyset person."

"Short?" Pina asked. The DA was about six feet, and he held a hand at the level of his own chin, asking, in effect, if the man in the dream were the same height as Maltais. When there was no response, Pina began to raise his hand. "Tall?"

"In the neighborhood of—tall." As the DA's hand continued up, Maltais said, "Not in that neighborhood." The DA's hand had dropped back to the level of his eyebrow, somewhere in the area of five-feet-ten, and Maltais nodded. "And I could see his hand."

"What was in his hand? A knife? A gun?" The cause of death was another detail which had been deliberately withheld from the news media.

"Two hands—in the air—or something holding in between—" Maltais went on.

"Knife or a gun?" Pina asked again.

Maltais slowed down, trying very hard to be precise. "From what I could see, it looked like a rock."

The answer was close enough, at least for the moment; the actual murder instrument had never been identified in the press, and Pina was careful now not to question Maltais in a way that could later be construed as leading or entrapment. "What was he doing with that?"

"Leaning over. And he was hitting her more, coming down hard on her face." He mimed the action of striking, raising his hands over his head and bringing down his balled double fist repeatedly to the table, his expression a combination of wrath and remorse, his voice anguished. "I seen her body jump off the ground, and her feet. She was laying on her back, and he was back of her, hitting her, so her body would be lying out down of him. I seen her feet come up and he was, you know, like he was really mad at her—coming down with a rock on her face."

For the next several minutes, Pina concentrated on trying to get a detailed description of the man in the dream. But Maltais insisted that the face and other important aspects eluded him, as though the assailant had been aware that his crime was being observed from above and he had deliberately kept the witness from getting a good look.

"When did you find out it was Barbara?" Pina asked.

"When I looked around the tree, when she yells out, 'Stop,' and is looking for me, calling me."

"You heard her call you?"

Maltais hesitated, then plunged on. "I believe I heard her call, 'Andy, help me. Stop.'" He closed his eyes and concentrated, either on the recollection or on a present vision as the event repeated itself in his mind. "Can't stop, got to go to her. I tried, can't help her or him, can't stop him. She was hollering. She was not dead, but she couldn't get up and run, and this is what was bugging me. Something about her that won't let her get off the ground, you know? But I can see him, over and over, hitting her."

"Was he saying anything?"

"He was mad—couldn't understand what he was saying—very angry and violent—really mad at her for some reason or other, mad at her."

"Was he calling her names or anything?"

Maltais leaned back in the chair and held his face in his hands, rubbing his eyes with his fingertips. As he had done so many times before in his interviews with Paul Fitzgerald in North Dartmouth and with Silvia and Joaquim in Fall River, he answered a question other than the one that had just been asked. "Well, I think it might of been a love affair."

The room was absolutely silent. Paul Fitzgerald noiselessly lifted a page from his clipboard and wrote "Reason for murder."

"Myself—" Maltais started, then let his hands drop in his lap in despair, veering away from the word as though it had been a mistake. "She had a love affair with somebody—someone who liked her—and she double-crossed that person. So that led up to the killing." He closed his eyes, then opened them again, looking down at his hands. "And so on," he added, as though mocking himself or the futility of describing all he knew. "And so forth."

From across the table, Alan Silvia could see that the rims of Maltais' eyes had started to redden and there were the beginnings of tears.

Pina started to ask another question. "Could you think for a minute, Andy, if a man was—" But he interrupted himself and reached out to touch him on the shoulder. "Relax, just relax."

Maltais sat back in the chair and drew a deep breath. When he looked up, he avoided the faces around the table, raising his eyes to the ceiling as he slowly exhaled.

Pina gave him a moment more to compose himself, then started again. "Put yourself back there. Think about the man, what he is saying. You say he is angry—see if you can think of what he said. It would help us."

Maltais shut his eyes again and concentrated fiercely. "Somehow or other I can't get his face to move his mouth. I can see him, but not clearly."

"All right," Pina said, encouragingly. "And you know he's no little guy; he's a big guy?"

"I can see this, you know, that he's a big fellow—And the way the hands—what he had in his hands—it was easy for him to do. That's what I can see—myself—" He flinched at using that word again, rushing to get beyond it. "He was somebody that knew how to chop wood, you know?"

"And Barbara is saying, 'Andy, help me.' She says that once?"

Maltais wrestled with a concept, his eyes still shut and his head back. "I think this is—this is why I stepped in closer, you know? I was trying to get him, to make him stop. But I can't."

"Was he saying something at the time?" Pina urged gently.

"He was mumbling something. 'Andy isn't going to help you anymore.' I don't know—"

"Think if you can remember. Take your time."

Maltais opened his eyes and smiled apologetically, then closed them again and concentrated even harder. "I'm trying to think it, I'm trying." After a moment more, he shook his head and looked back at the DA. "Come and go, come and go, you know? This is one of those things." Self-consciously, he picked up the picture of the murder site that he had marked a few minutes before.

"The rock—" Pina said, trying a different tack. "Does it look like something that was around on the ground, or something special that he brought?"

Maltais studied the photograph in his hand. "The area was pretty clean there—" He stopped himself. Perhaps he was aware that he was slipping out of his role as psychic and into his other guise as police consultant.

Pina asked some more questions about the murder site and then, apparently sensing Maltais' eagerness to return to the role of seer, asked him why the man in the vision would want to kill Barbara Raposa.

Maltais closed his eyes again, but he evaded the question. "I don't know, I can't see this. I'm just floating away, that's all I'm doing, this floating away." His eyes popped open. "My mother woke me up. It didn't finish."

Pina persisted. "Was she going to fight in any way? Could you see that?"

Once more, Maltais obediently submerged himself in his vision. "I can see myself getting there into the picture. They were mumbling to one another. I knew she was alive. Can't hear his name. All I can see is him hitting her; that's all they're allowing me to see right now.

"Now I see him dropping her on the ground. She's hollering, and he's hollering back at her. He backs away—evidently to pick up an object—and he comes back. I'm getting closer and closer to him. He's mumbling, talking to her. He's very angry—a fellow of Portuguese descent. I can't hear what he's saying. I want to get closer. I feel myself trying to grab him, but I just can't."

"But she says, 'Andy, help me,'" Pina reminded him.

"She did holler that. 'Andy, forgive me.'"

"What was this they were talking about?" Pina asked again. "Something about Doreen Levesque?" It was the first time in the interview that Pina had mentioned the other murder, the one that had brought Maltais to the police in the first place, months before.

"I don't know," he answered cautiously, searching the insides of his eyelids for the answer. "I can tell you the way he's doing this—he knows what he's doing."

"So he could have heard about the other girl and planned it in the same way?"

"Somehow or other," Andy agreed.

"Why?"

"Either he didn't like prostitutes—something against them—" Andy thought for a moment longer, "Or he's doing it to find revenge on somebody, you know?"

He looked up at the DA to see how his suggestion was received. Pina nodded approvingly and waited for him to go on.

"I don't think there is no love affair because I can see she don't love him, you know?—this fellow, whoever she's with—don't love him, because she asks me for forgiveness, you know? I could see her crying."

Pina nodded again. "Does *he* love *her*?"

"This man? I don't know if he loves her." Maltais seemed surprised by the question, but then settled quickly on an answer. "I don't think he loves her. He's doing it through hate. He has something on her—keep her quiet, you know?"

"It would help if you could remember why he hated her," Pina said. "Sometimes it helps if there's a motive. Anything else you can think of?"

Maltais rubbed his forehead and his eyes with his hands. "No, not at this moment." He shook his head, apparently signaling that the vision was no longer accessible. "Gives me a headache to go in that far."

Pina was sympathetic. "I can imagine."

Still coming out of it, Maltais laid his hands palm down on the table, partly for the coolness and partly to frame the photograph. "I wanted to go to that scene because I could help."

The DA nodded; that was the next step. "You've never been to the scene at all?"

"Never been and—never been," Maltais said. "I wanted to go, you know, for obvious reasons, so there won't be no misbelief over something made up—cause I seen him. And maybe I might see what I see in my head, you know?" He blinked, swallowed, then added, "But I'm afraid to go, because I'm afraid to cry. I haven't been able to cry since this happened."

Several of the others around the table had already stood up, partly to relieve the tension of the past half hour, but also in anticipation of their departure for the murder site. If Maltais were going to incriminate himself further, that is where he was most likely to do it. But now, when he spoke of crying, there was an awkward silence.

"I don't want you to go if it bothers you," Pina said.

Maltais stood up as well, and everyone in the room was reminded again how small he was. "I want to go and get that person over with. Instead of sitting here, we can stop this other foolishness and, in fact, I might be able to come up with some pointer and go in there where she was found, how she was found, who found her, you know. Maybe I could see a car. This is all I can remember here; I'm only allowed to remember so much."

"Okay," Pina agreed. He looked around at the other police officers in the room, smiled, and turned back to Maltais. "We're all here to help."

And so they went.

There were too many of them for everyone to get into the elevator at the same time, so Maltais rode down with Pina and Veary, the state troopers, and the two stenographers; then the elevator went back up for the Fall River police. Once they got to the parking lot, however, they divided up the way they had arrived. Andy Maltais rode with Silvia and Joaquim; Fitzgerald was next, in his unmarked state police car; Lieutenants Kaegael and Correia followed in an unmarked Fall River unit; and District Attorney Pina, Veary, and the two stenographers rode in a state police cruiser driven by another CPAC detective named Brian McMahon. The convoy was almost a parade, and at its head rode Andy Maltais, the focus of more attention than he had ever had in his life.

But despite all the excitement, he was not so sure it was all the kind of attention that he really wanted. As he got into the cruiser, he said to Silvia, "I think they've got me now."

Silvia was startled by the comment, but he simply noted it and said nothing in reply. He knew that Maltais had a need for powerful alliances and that he still thought of Silvia as the Psychic Reader who knew his secret thoughts. It was unlikely Maltais would repeat the remark in front of anyone with lesser powers, such as the DA or the state police, but the way this was going, he would not have to.

A few minutes later, as the caravan came to a stop at Resco Printers in Fall River, Maltais looked around him at the other cars, at all the police officers and the two stenographers setting up the transcription equipment, and at the grassy slope of the murder site. "I know they've got me now."

Again Silvia didn't answer, but he wrote that comment in his casebook as well, after the first one. And this time, Tom Joaquim also heard the comment.

The day was bitter cold, and there was a wind. Trooper McMahon lifted the stenographic unit out of the trunk of the cruiser, but as soon as it was set up, the operator announced that it wasn't working. "It's frozen," she said.

The word was passed to Pina. "Okay," he said. "Then use short-hand." Shivering, the two women went back to the car and returned with ring-bound stenographic pads. One of the detectives said, "Next the ink will freeze." But at that point, Andy Maltais began to talk, and the two women followed him as he walked down into the field, each holding a glove in her mouth, each writing as fast as she was able on her small, yellow tablet.

"I'm getting vibes," Maltais said, spreading his hands toward the scene before them. "I was looking up at that tree on the other side."

Pina walked beside one of the two women and said to her in a voice that Maltais could not hear, "Points to exact tree." The stenographer nodded and wrote the remark, in parentheses, after the quote from Maltais.

Maltais stopped halfway to the tree, then continued. "I was looking from the other side of the tree, floating. It was very dark. I saw a car backing up in here." He indicated a grassy area near the tree, some distance from the parking lot. "Why did he go to this extreme, I don't know."

Following his lead, the entourage reached the tree. As the two stenographers and the group of policemen clustered beside and behind him, he pointed to the precise place on the ground where the body had been found, his words visible for an instant in the cold before being tattered by the wind. "He had to be over here, facing her with his back against the tree. He was in front of this limb. Head was near the tree. No, feet were near the tree, head was toward the other way. He was way to the right of her, over there."

At the back of the crowd, Alan Silvia shook his head impatiently in the bitter cold and muttered, "For Chrissake, make up your mind before we freeze to death."

One of the state troopers heard the remark and looked at the Fall River detective impassively with the subtlest of admonishments, at the same time making an obvious effort to stop his own shivering.

Maltais walked across the open area and took three or four steps up onto a stone outcropping. "He could of been standing on the rocks; he walked way to the right of her. He picked up something, something he could handle easy." He looked across the field and parking lot to the rear of the Resco plant. "There was shadow this way, no lights in back of the building. He backed up on the grass. He was standing here somewhere."

Pina asked, "What did you see him doing?" The wind carried his words away in ribbons of vapor.

"Saw him beating her," Maltais said from the top of the rocks, "her feet raising up in the air. He walked over from the grass"—he scrambled down and moved back toward the tree—"and placed her right here. He walked away nearby. Barbara said, 'Andy, forgive me!'" This time, the voice he gave her was a loud cry, almost a shout. "She was so immobilized, she could not get up and leave; she was lying down. I was trying to tell her to get up—in the dream. She kept saying, 'Forgive me, Andy!'" Again, the voice was a cry. "I could see him coming back into the picture and hitting her."

Maltais stopped for a moment, covering his eyes with his hands. "I see him walking away, out of the picture. He goes back and gets on the rock and beats her." He dropped his hands and opened his eyes again, looking at the DA. "From what I could see, she was gotten by surprise."

Pina nodded.

"She got surprised at the whole thing. He could of been going to have sexual relations with her. I could see her lying down. She was very upset."

Silvia smiled at the last comment and looked away so Maltais and the others wouldn't notice. "He's floating, all right," he said to one of the Fall River lieutenants, stomping his feet in the cold to keep the sound of his voice from the others.

Pina asked, "Did she know this man?"

"Yes, he was no stranger—someone she knew well." He turned again to look at the Resco printing plant. "I get bad vibes—this is so near the lovers' lane area—and I can't imagine it being so close to this building. A professional would never do this so close to this building."

Pina clapped his gloved hands together, more in apparent impatience at Maltais' asides than to restore his circulation. He looked at the printing plant and back at Maltais without comment. "Anything else you can remember?"

"He was cursing her, he had a mustache, a lot of hair on his head, and he couldn't speak English right." He was talking rapidly, perhaps because of the cold, perhaps to shift the focus back to areas where he knew the DA was interested. "I think he knows who I am. He might have seen me up there. He never looked up. He was scared for some reason or other." Almost furtively, Maltais checked his audience;

clearly he had recaptured their attention. "I know he's going to confront me sooner or later."

He sucked in his breath, trembling, and hugged himself. "It was cold out, like today. He had a leather coat on. After the first hit, she couldn't talk anymore. He was constantly hitting her with what he had in his hands. He kept hitting her. I get vibes—you see, it's a puzzle." He looked at the ground, pondering for a moment, and once more Alan Silvia saw the tears. "The Devil's got the best of her. I hope she goes to heaven."

The last time Silvia had heard about the Devil was from Karen Marsden, and Maltais' remark suddenly conjured an incongruous image in the detective's mind of Carl Drew on the night of the killing he'd just heard described, standing where the district attorney now stood, come to collect the soul of Barbara Raposa as it rose from her murdered body.

Pina asked some more questions—about what the man said, about what the victim was wearing. Maltais' answers were rambling, nonresponsive. Pina said, "Did you see any shoes?"

Andy put his head back for a moment with his eyes shut. "I don't see her with shoes." The eyes reopen. "He carries her and puts her down here. End of dream, when my mother woke me up. I didn't see him getting away; he was still hitting her when I left the dream."

Maltais may have imagined some reaction on the district attorney's face—disappointment, impatience, disbelief—because he suddenly added some more information. "He had an object, not too big, about one foot wide; it was a round rock. He could lift it and hit her and come back and hit her again. He was nervous. A car could have come by—it could have been a police car."

Pina asked where the killer's car was located in the dream.

Maltais had an inspiration. "Can we use Officer Fitzgerald's car in its place?" he asked.

Pina looked at Fitzgerald, and the trooper nodded in agreement and walked back across the field to his unmarked car. When he returned, parking the vehicle in the place on the matted grass that Maltais had indicated earlier, the little man called out new directions. "That's not quite it. Move over a little."

Fitzgerald pulled the cruiser forward a few feet, turned the wheel, and backed it up beyond where he had parked before. "You're getting warmer, that's it. Now open your trunk." Maltais turned back to the DA. "The car was not running. It had a big trunk."

Maltais walked over and stood behind the police car, looking down into the wheel well. "She was in the trunk. The car had two doors. She was in the trunk," he repeated.

Fitzgerald stood aside and Maltais leaned forward under the raised lid. "He picked her up. He was right-handed. He had a little trouble getting her out of the car. He tied up her hands in the car. She was high on drugs; he knew this. He was getting very panicky; he's very nervous. He walked over here"—Maltais simulated the actions of a man lifting a heavy object onto his shoulder, then moved with labored steps to the clearing under the tree, where he laid down his invisible burden—"and put her down. She said something to him. She was cold."

"What did he say?" Pina asked

Maltais thought for a moment before answering, apparently anxious to retrieve the memory with as much accuracy as possible. "He really didn't want to do anything wrong, but he didn't have any choice," he said carefully. "He was pleading with her. I can't grasp words. She was so immobilized, he walked away from her. I could see just enough; it was dark, she was drugged. She was saying, 'Andy, forgive me.'"

"Do you know what time it was?"

"For some reason or other, I think it was late night, in the morning hours, before three A.M." Maltais looked around again as though something new were being revealed to him. "Something happened here in the evening. She was living with this guy for quite a while. Something happened that night; they may have had an argument. There was a car. I see him taking her out of the trunk. Something draws his attention over there—" He pointed to a building beyond the printing company, to the plant of Swan Finishing. "They might have had an affair here before, in lovers' lane—an affair with a fight. Her shoes were rubber on the bottom; they would have left a print."

One of the secretaries blew on her exposed writing hand and winced with cold. Pina looked over at the Swan plant, then back to Maltais; it was certain that no footprints would have survived for the past three months. "Anything else you can remember?"

"I felt vibes when I got out of the car there," Maltais said, pointing to the lovers' lane behind Resco. "I had a feeling that a man and a woman sat there, making out. I don't know if it was Barbara."

The district attorney nodded, perhaps signaling, unintentionally, that the session was about to end. A couple of the officers at the edge of the group looked longingly back toward the shelter of their cars, and Fitzgerald clapped his gloved hands to restore the feeling in his frozen fingers.

Maltais must have known his time was running out. He took a deep breath and said, "The rock was square at the sides." Every eye turned back to him.

He walked over to a pile of concrete blocks. Every policeman there knew that it was a block of this type, and not a rock, that had been used to kill Barbara Raposa. To verify the findings of the autopsy, several chunks of concrete recovered from the murder site had been sent to the FBI laboratories in Washington, D.C., and scientists there had identified pieces of the victim's hair, samples of her blood—and pieces of her fingernails, from when she had defended herself against the blows—imbedded in the crushed, powdery aggregate. Maltais looked at the pile of blocks in the field.

"I sense a murder weapon here," he said.

He turned and looked back at the district attorney, at the collection of detectives, at the two stenographers whose frozen hands were poised above their pads, their discomfort forgotten, all listening attentively for the next words. Maltais turned again to the pile of blocks and added, almost with resignation, "It might have been a piece of concrete."

TEN / **PRIORITIES**

Back in 1972, when Alan Silvia was just out of the marines and a freshman at Bristol Community College, he was standing in front of a variety store near his father's house in Fall River when a car pulled to the curb and a pretty girl behind the wheel asked for directions to the Diman Regional High School.

He checked her out without being too obvious—she was fresh, bright-looking, and nicely dressed—then asked her, "Why do you want to go to the Diman? It's a trade school."

She laughed and told him there was a teachers' convention there.

"You're a teacher?" he asked. He could feel himself falling in love on the spot. He said he would show her how to get there. A year later they were married. Her name was Joanne.

For the first few years, they lived in his father's house in the South End of the city, but eventually they saved enough money for a down payment and bought a place of their own in the town of Dartmouth, fifteen miles to the southeast of Fall River. It was a beautiful house: way out in the country with plenty of room inside and out, complete with an in-ground pool. They had a daughter; at the time of the murders, she was two. To all appearances, they were a happy, prosperous family. But things were nowhere nearly as good as they looked on the surface.

Part of the reason they could afford the house was that Alan was finished with college and was putting in longer and longer hours on the job. But the more he earned, the less time he spent at home.

At work, Captain Reis had been waging a long guerrilla war with the chief of the Fall River Police, continually asking for more manpower in the Major Crimes Division and continually being refused. Reis's answer was to put the men on as much overtime as they could handle; it worked well for the detectives because their salaries often doubled and tripled, and it worked well for Reis because it demonstrated the extent of his need. Moreover, Silvia loved his job, even when it demanded as much as eighty and then one hundred or more hours a week. But over the course of time, it proved the adage about too much of a good thing. His work became an obsession, and part of the price was his home life.

When Silvia was just beginning his career as a detective, one of the veterans had warned him, "There are two things on this job that can ruin your life: the booze and the broads." It sounded so much like Mickey Spillane or *The Police Gazette* that Silvia had laughed at the time, but after a year or two the remark didn't sound quite as funny. It was commonplace for Silvia and the other detectives to make appointments with young women at bars or on the street at ten or eleven at night, or in their apartments at two in the morning, and although at first the ostensible purpose was usually in some way connected with police work—the women might have had some hearsay evidence about one of the suspects, or they could possibly be useful in the future—those meetings often, even predictably, led to other things. Silvia was convinced he was having the time of his life, and as long as he was working until five, six, or seven o'clock every morning, sleeping three hours, and then heading up to New Bedford for a nine-thirty meeting with the district attorney to coordinate strategies or review evidence, there was little time for introspection or thoughtful self-analysis.

Joanne had plenty of time, but very few of the facts. If she complained to Alan about the hours he kept, he would usually answer her with questions. "What do you want from me? How can I do my job if I stay home and watch television? How could we afford this furniture—or this house or this life—if I worked straight hours?"

But now and then Joanne got glimpses of what those long hours entailed, and she did not like it. One time, Alan was driving somewhere with Robin Murphy and he stopped at his house to make some telephone calls. Another time, he dropped by with Karen Marsden—not for any particular reason but that they were in the neighborhood, and he decided to show her where he lived. It was obvious to Joanne that the girls were prostitutes, and she could tell they were into drugs as well. Later, when Alan told her that both girls were lesbians and she didn't have anything to worry about, she looked at him as though he were insane. But even when Alan and Joanne both eventually realized their marriage had exhausted itself, he was too busy to consider a serious change.

Meanwhile, on the job, the detectives began looking at Captain Reis in much the same way as Joanne had looked at Silvia at home. Although the Nighters got along with Reis no better or worse than before, the captain's feud with the chief had expanded beyond problems of staffing and budgets and threatened to disrupt the entire division. The new focus of contention, like Captain Queeg's strawberries, was the departmental file on rapes.

As in most police departments, the Fall River files on rapes were intended to be confidential, and access was limited to the investigating officers. The rule of access was at odds, however, with another requirement related to the compilation of crime statistics for the FBI. The chief appointed a couple of civilians from Planning and Research to gather the appropriate statistical data from these files, and when Captain Reis heard about it, he decided to dig in. "I'm not going to let them break the law."

All the examiners had to do was read enough to confirm that there had really been a rape; they were civil servants doing a dull job. But Reis, as usual, stood by the rule book. He claimed the civilians were violating the privacy the law was designed to protect, and he suggested they were doing it at least in part for reasons of prurience. To Silvia and Joaquim, the continuing fiasco of the rape file was just one more instance of Reis using the book to define his police career and protect his bureaucratic turf.

Silvia was in the station house doing some paperwork one morning when the chief sent up a deputy chief to the Major Crimes Division. Silvia knew him slightly—the deputy chief owned a tenement on Pleasant Street, which he had bought cheap as an investment, and now he was Carl Drew's landlord. The deputy said hello to Silvia, then poked his head around the corner of the captain's office. "Good morning, John. The chief sent me up to get the key to the rape file."

"Fuck you!" Reis bellowed, charging out from behind his desk like a Bouncing Betty land mine. "He's not getting it. And you tell him next time not to send up a messenger boy!"

Silvia had been the target of the Reis treatment for such a long time, he took a certain amount of satisfaction at hearing it directed elsewhere. But he also knew that in this case Reis was on very thin ice; not even a captain can get away for long talking that way to a deputy chief.

"I wish you wouldn't feel that way, John," the deputy said, responding to the captain's outburst as though he were dealing with a naughty boy. "It just causes a lot of problems, and you know how the chief is."

"I don't give a fuck how he is or what problems it causes," Reis yelled back. "You tell him to come up here himself and get the god-damned key if he wants the fucking files."

Silvia looked warily at the deputy as he left the office. He had been framing a suitable remark—something like, "Gee, I wonder what the captain's really trying to say"—but this was clearly not one of those times when humor was a good idea.

A short time later, Reis took three weeks off. The problem, it turned out, was high blood pressure, although some of the detectives wondered whether that were the cause or just the result of an uncontrollable temper. Because of the murders, the subsequent rumors of Satanism, and the resulting unfavorable publicity for the city, the pressure on the Major Crimes Division was mounting, not just from the department but from the media, the city fathers, and the public. Reis's medical difficulties were a handicap even in normal times, and in this new, progressively more intense environment, spontaneous remission seemed unlikely. Silvia was in the office when the captain left, and he happened to be there again, standing in almost the same spot, the day he returned.

"Good morning, Cap, how are you?"

Reis arrived that morning, as he often did, with a folded newspaper under his arm—a perhaps unconscious imitation of a police captain on television which had led Silvia to refer to him as the K Mart version of Barney Miller. He didn't answer the question, but he greeted Silvia cheerfully enough and walked into his office. Just as he was settling himself down behind his desk, the telephone rang. Silvia was near it, so he answered on an extension in the outer office.

"Is your captain in?"

"Yes, he is," Silvia said, feeling the sudden rush that would rise when his instincts told him something big was about to happen. He put the call on hold and held up the receiver so Reis could see it through the sliding window of his office. "It's for you," he said. "The chief."

Reis hesitated just a fraction of a second, then reached out and picked up the extension on his desk.

There wasn't much conversation from Reis's end; he turned in his chair so he faced away from the window, and for most of the call he was listening instead of talking. Silvia continued about his business. After less than a minute, however, the detective happened to look toward the window just in time to see the captain rise up out of his chair as though he had been electrocuted. "Fuck you!" he shouted into the telephone, then threw it so hard across his office that it ripped the cord out of the wall.

"Whoops," Silvia said to himself, and turned back to his report. An instant later, the door to the office opened and the captain strode out, toward the hallway. The unread newspaper was again under his arm, and Silvia knew immediately that he was not headed down for a face-to-face chat with the chief but was leaving the building. As Reis passed by, he glanced over at the detective who had been the focus of so much concentrated and prolonged aggravation, and when their eyes met, an incongruous smile spread over the captain's livid face, a look of almost manic relief in the midst of his rout. He raised his free arm over his head in a combined gesture of salute and abandon and shouted, "See you later!"

Silvia stared after him. It was the last time he ever saw Captain Reis at the station house. A few days later, the division was notified that he had taken medical retirement.

ELEVEN / **MIDWINTER**

On the morning of Friday, February 8, 1980, Andre O. Maltais, now under arrest, was taken from Fall River to New Bedford and arraigned in the Second District Court of Bristol County for the murder of Barbara Raposa. The judge ordered him held without bail and transferred to the Barnstable County House of Correction on nearby Cape Cod, pending a psychiatric evaluation. His case was continued to the following Monday, February 11, at which time the court would hear testimony on the defendant's competency to stand trial.

Maltais had a hard time dealing with the failure of his performance at the murder site, and he felt wounded and betrayed. In particular, he was disappointed in losing the confidence of his friend on the state police, the Big Guy, and the apparent reversal of a relationship in which he and Paul Fitzgerald had become, in Maltais' wishful view, almost colleagues. Beyond vigorously defending his vision and denying his guilt, Maltais had nothing to say to Fitzgerald or any of the other officials who so recently had been his allies and were now his accusers. Parity had eluded Maltais all his life, and losing it again, when it had seemed so nearly within his grasp, seemed to weigh more heavily on him than the charge of murder.

He was not the only one who felt uneasy that Friday. For most of the morning, Alan Silvia had been involved with activities related to the Maltais arraignment, first in Fall River and then in New Bedford, and when he returned to Fall River and reported to the police station for his next shift late that afternoon, it was with an out-of-place, persistent sense that things were not entirely as they should be. Normally, there would be a certain amount of euphoria, or at least relief, in seeing a case settled as neatly as this one. That feeling which Silvia expected—and didn't have—was not just the satisfaction of a problem solved, or even that the side he served had moved way ahead; he knew from experience that it derived instead from the restoration of a natural balance, a return of symmetry where there had been disorder. It was one of the reasons he had become a policeman. But the feeling eluded him. What he felt was apprehension.

Silvia knew that his unease was not directly related to the murder of Barbara Raposa, whom he had never known, or to what had happened to Andy Maltais, who was just where he ought to be. It was true that there were still plenty of loose ends—he found himself wondering how Maltais really had become involved in the Levesque case, if he *had* any connection with Carl Drew—but the little man had passed out of his jurisdiction and those questions were now beyond the province of the Fall River police.

Whatever the cause of Silvia's apprehension, he realized that its focus was on Karen Marsden.

Both Silvia and Joaquim had done everything they could to keep lines open to Karen since their meeting at Carol Fletcher's apartment several nights earlier and their trip to the Freetown Reservation. They and other detectives in the Major Crimes Division had met with Karen three or four times, they had spoken to her on several occasions by telephone, and had even made a couple of daytime excursions, with and without her, through the Reservation to search for more evidence of the cult activities she had so fearfully described. Over and over they reached out to make it clear they took her seriously. But Karen remained elusive. Barricaded by her fears, insulated by drugs, she was obviously begging for help but, for more reasons than Silvia understood, unable to accept that help when it was offered.

Late one gray afternoon, he and Karen were driving alone through the rutted, slush-filled roads of the state forest. They had not spoken in several minutes, but Silvia's eyes were everywhere, searching among the bare, twisted trees, the rocky outcroppings and bleak ledges for some sign of the evil she and the others had described. In the course of scanning the passing landscape, he glanced at her sitting beside him. Karen's earlier frantic anxiety had slipped away from her and she was looking dully ahead, lost in reverie, as though she had absorbed the hopeless remorse of the forest itself. Although they still had found nothing, Silvia felt for an eerie moment as though he were now looking at what they had come for. "Shake it off, Karen, for Chrissake," he said, surprised at his own impatience. "You can at least make an effort."

She looked at him guiltily, then turned back to the window and resumed her search of the passing woods. She did not acknowledge the remark, but for a moment it had brought her back.

On February 8, the day Andy Maltais was arraigned, Karen telephoned Alan Silvia at the station around dusk, returning a call he had made to her the evening before. Her voice was tremulous, nearly inaudible, but Silvia recognized it immediately and with relief.

The night before, he and Tom Joaquim had discussed Karen's situation with Captain Andrade, Reis's replacement, and he told her now on the telephone that he had a proposition to discuss with her. At first there was no answer. Silvia wondered if she had heard, and said, "You there?"

"Fine," she said, edgy but resigned. "Whatever."

They agreed to meet. Karen would wait on a street corner a few blocks from the station. "Don't forget it's cold," she said plaintively.

Three minutes later, Silvia and Joaquim drove up to a corner on Bedford Street in an unmarked police car. The weak winter sun had set a few minutes earlier, but there was still a smoggy afterglow that sponged the color out of the streetscape and gave the few pedestrians the complexion of cadavers. At first, the detectives could not tell in the gloom if anyone were in the doorway where Karen had said she would be waiting, but when Silvia peered more closely into the shadows he saw a vaporous contrail of breath, and he pulled to the curb. Karen stepped quickly across the sidewalk and got into the rear seat. She huddled, hugging herself and shivering, her back to the door and her head down, as Silvia turned the car back into the traffic. "This sucks," she said, her voice shaking. "I must be out of my mind."

The two detectives didn't answer. Silvia took a turn at the next intersection and headed away from the congestion and bright lights of Bedford Street, crossing on a series of side streets into an area of single- and two-family homes. It was now deep twilight, and when he pulled again to the curb, he could barely see Karen's face in the rearview mirror. "Safe," he said, and turned off the engine.

When he turned around to talk to her, there were tears in her eyes.

"Karen, we can take care of you," Silvia said quietly.

She shook her head, still hugging herself and shaking. She leaned further back into the shadows and sobbed.

"After we talked the other night, I called Captain Andrade at home," Silvia said. "I asked him to meet me at the police station, and he did."

"He's one of the good guys," Tom Joaquim said.

Both detectives liked Reis's replacement as a person and respected his competence and dedication as a policeman.

Karen took a deep breath, trying to gain control over her tears. The two detectives waited until the sobbing stopped; her eyes watched back, glistening in the dark. At last she said, barely in a whisper, "It doesn't matter."

"I told him you had talked with us, that you are in fear for your life," Silvia said.

She looked at him as though trying to comprehend what he was saying, her eyes still shining, then turned them vacantly away. She mouthed the words, "It doesn't matter," her voice so low that neither of them could hear it.

"He knows this whole scenario, what's building up here," Silvia continued. "I suggested we place you in protective custody."

Karen answered as though she were in a dream, "It's almost over," and slowly shook her head.

"We want to put you in a safe place," Silvia persisted.

Karen continued looking out the window without answering. Joaquim asked, "Do you understand what we're saying?"

Suddenly she started to weep again, this time in loud spasmodic sobs that bent her forward until her face was nearly touching her knees. Both detectives put a hand across the back of the seat and stroked a shoulder in consolation.

"*I* understand," she said. "You're the ones who don't understand."

"Because you don't tell us," Silvia said. "But even if you don't tell us, we can still give you help, and that's what we're offering."

She raised her head again, gulping for air. Now, her voice was loud. "I did tell you. I told you the Devil is going to kill me. I told you a hundred times."

Neither detective picked up the challenge. Their hope was to get her to accept the protective custody so they could get her off the street and off the drugs, and then when her brain was clear and her nerves were untangled, they could work with her for as long as it might take to tell how she knew all that she said she did—about the Raposa murder, about the Levesque killing, and about Carl Drew.

"I want to see a priest," she said, plaintive again.

"Fine," Silvia answered.

Now it was Joaquim's turn. "See a priest," he said, "but let us protect you, Karen."

"God will protect me." She pursed her lips as though to suppress more tears and looked out the window into the deepening darkness.

"If you help yourself," Joaquim agreed.

Karen shook her head emphatically in denial, and the crystal gleamed again on her eyelids. "God will protect me, no strings."

Both detectives had heard this several times before, not only on the first night they had spoken with her nine days earlier, but in most of the meetings and conversations since. "Then how come you're scared?" Silvia asked quietly. "How come you cry?"

Karen's body shook, this time a combination of tears and laughter. "I think it must be the stuff I take—uppers, downers, Valium, greens, reds—that's what it does. I dunno, they say it isn't good for you, and maybe that's why."

Silvia waited for the laughing/crying to taper off, then said, "Maybe. But I think it's also because you're afraid of the Devil. And dying. And hell."

She wrapped her arms around herself again, and then her face puckered once more in uncontrollable fear and sorrow. "I want to see a priest!" she repeated, sobbing wretchedly.

"We can take you to a place where the Devil can't reach you," Silvia offered again.

She shook her head in the same childish, stubborn-passive way as before, the tears rolling down her cheeks. "No you can't. You can't."

"Why not?" Joaquim asked.

"Because I won't go," she said simply.

"Why not?" Joaquim insisted.

"Because I won't," she insisted back. She hugged herself, grieving and thoughtful, then, still sobbing, said, "Because the life I've got is the life I've got. I have a little boy, JJ. I have a grandmother and a mother and a father. I have friends. You can't put everyone I know in protective custody. You can't put Bedford Street in protective custody."

Silvia looked at her without answering, and finally nodded wearily. He had heard that logic before, but he still didn't know how to deal with it. Besides, with Karen, the offer of protection was the only card he had to play, and he refused to give up without a fight. "Let me tell you what we can do," he went on.

They sat in the car on the side street for another half hour, until it was so dark they could no longer see each other except in silhouette and the muscles in the detectives' necks were strained from craning. Silvia and Joaquim offered protective custody in every possible combination they could think of, from Karen moving into another apartment with JJ and her grandmother, to being alone in a motel in a nearby town, to moving out of the state. And each idea, in turn, was rejected, sometimes with a shake of the head, sometimes with words, sometimes with pursed lips and silent tears.

"Well," Silvia said, throwing up his hands and accepting defeat at last, if only for the time being. "At least, we've given you something to think about, right? Maybe you'll change your mind."

He turned back to face the steering wheel. The motor was still running. He shifted into drive.

"Wait a minute, where are we going now?" Karen asked, sounding alarmed.

Silvia tried to see her in the mirror, but it was too dark. "Wherever you want," he said. "If you want to talk some more, we'll talk. We can stay here, we can go to the police station, we can drop you somewhere, just tell us. Are you headed back down to Bedford?"

Karen nodded, yes. "But—"

Silvia waited. "We're all yours. Say the word. Anywhere."

Suddenly, Karen erupted again in a deluge of tears. "Oh, my God, I don't know, I just don't know. I'm a good person, I know I am, and I'm about to die."

Silvia left the car in drive, but kept his foot on the brake. He didn't turn around, and he didn't answer. Joaquim too was silent. She sobbed noisily in the dark. Finally, Silvia again said quietly, "Do you want us to take you somewhere safe?"

The sobbing continued for another full minute, and the detectives waited. When Karen collected herself this time, it was to ask, in the tiniest possible voice, "Can you take me to St. Mary's? Can you take me to a priest?"

And so they did.

The last time they saw Karen, she was standing on the sidewalk in front of the rectory. She gazed up at the gray Gothic symmetry of the cathedral which rose softly into the darkness behind her, then turned back for one last look into the police car, her hair caught in the glow of the street lamp, successful for the moment in holding back the tears but cold, wired, trembling, and vulnerable. Silvia asked her from the police car, "Would you call me?" Listening to his own voice, he sounded like a child. "Please, call me?"

She was about to reply, but behind the door a light had been switched on, and they could see through a window that a priest was coming to answer the bell. The two detectives watched her for a moment longer, then the door opened. By now, Silvia's unease had ripened into premonition, a nearly tangible sense that they were about to lose her. But as strongly as he felt it, he also realized there was nothing in the world they could do unless they had Karen's help. With a deliberate effort of will he looked away. A moment later he turned the car out into the traffic.

Hours later, at three in the morning, Silvia and Joaquim were sitting at a table in the back corner of a tiny after-hours bar diagonally across from Charlie's on Pleasant Street, each drinking a beer and waiting for an order of chouriço and chips from the kitchen. They had not been there more than a couple of minutes when a girl in her early twenties walked in, stood near the corner of the bar, and began looking deliberately around the room, not in the usual languid way that asked to be noticed, but apparently with some other purpose. Silvia recognized her as a hooker he had arrested on his way into work two or three weeks before, and he was curious to see what she was after. A moment later, when she spotted the two detectives at the far table, she smiled and walked toward them. Silvia smiled back, but guardedly.

She looked pretty good. Her straight blond hair was precision cut, and she was wearing a black leather skirt and a black lambskin bolero over a red mesh tank top. She stood in front of the two detectives, her eyes on Silvia, and threw out her hip, half provocatively and half self-mocking. "My, but don't we work long hours."

"You seem to be holding up," Silvia said, "considering the time of night."

"I get to lie down a lot," she said, and the two detectives laughed.

Tom Joaquim hooked his foot into the rungs of a chair at the empty table beside them and pulled it toward the girl. She turned to include him in the smile as well, then glanced back at Silvia to make sure it was all right if she accepted the offer. He nodded, and she sat down, crossing her legs and looking at him teasingly. "You're not going to arrest me again, are you?"

"Why should I do that?" Silvia said. "Once is usually enough—for most people, anyway. It's obvious you've learned your lesson."

"I'm completely rehabilitated," she said. She turned again to Joaquim with the same coy look. "I helped your friend make quota the other day."

Joaquim nodded. Every afternoon for nearly a month, Silvia had checked into their shift with a different girl, usually making his arrest within a block or two of the station house. He joked that it was a way of warming up for the night's work. It was also his way of making a point about a situation which most of the daytimers were willing to ignore: when the pimps and hookers stood on the sidewalk in front of

Pier 14 and peered down the block at Police Headquarters, the police seldom looked back. In that part of the city, the business of prostitution had taken over.

In fact, it was the pimps, hookers, and tricks who patrolled the streets and the outnumbered police who watched them from in hiding. Lots of nights, Silvia, Joaquim, and Carey—or Silvia and one or two of the other vice detectives—would sit in an unmarked car up the hill from Charlie's or the Pier, keeping track of the white Lincolns with the Rhode Island plates, watching the pimps move from bar to bar as their girls worked the sidewalks. In particular, they would see a lot of Carl Drew; his two principal hangouts were Charlie's and the Pier, and on some nights they would watch him move back and forth between the two bars as many as a dozen times. It was a little promenade, an important part of the night's ritual, a way of marking territory in the same way the town fathers sometimes are required by law to stroll the municipal bounds in certain Massachusetts villages or like dogs who lift their legs at ordained intervals, pissing the corners in the timeless ritual of possession. Drew and the other pimps would check with their girls, collecting from them the money they had taken in during the latest interval at that end of the street. Sometimes they would even look up the hill toward the unmarked car. If they knew they were being watched, they didn't care.

It was clear to Silvia that the reason the girl had come into the bar was because she had seen him and his partner enter a minute earlier, and she wanted to get next to them. The detectives were used to it; the women they met in their work were attracted to them because they were detectives, because they were young and good-looking— and almost inevitably because they could give something the women wanted. Not protection, not even approval. Just tacit allowance, tolerance, a willingness to look the other way—the natural seepage that follows the erosion of boundaries. Permission.

The bartender arrived with the platters of chouriço and chips, along with another couple of beers. A few minutes later, Silvia saw one of the truckers from the dress-transportation company across the street, leaning against the bar and taking in the activity around the small corner table. Like the two detectives, the drivers started and ended their workdays in the middle of the night. Silvia had seen this one in here before and had even talked with him a few times, but could not now recall his name. The driver grinned and raised his head in salute. "Hey," he called across the small room, "what size dress is your girlfriend?"

"What size?" Silvia asked back, trying to look incredulous. "What the fuck do you care what size dress my girlfriend wears?"

By now the girl had moved the chair around so she was sitting beside Silvia; in fact, she was leaning against him, her arm over the back of his chair and her hand resting on his shoulder, telling a long, pointless story about two friends of hers who had gone to Miami, her breast against the detective's arm as she spoke. She laughed at Silvia's reply to the driver, and before the man at the bar could say anything else, she turned her head and called over to him, "I'm an eight."

Silvia pushed away the plate of food and turned in his chair so the girl was no longer touching him. He knew the reason for the question was that drivers used to steal dresses from the deliveries they took to New York from the local mills, and the guy at the bar was trying to do the same thing with stolen property that the girl beside him was doing with sex. Still grinning, and in a voice that only she could hear, he told her, "Get lost."

Startled, she searched his face to see whether he had said it as just one more bit of banter or if he meant it. Despite the grin, there was not the slightest trace of humor in his eyes. She said, "Oops," looking apologetic, but when the detective's expression still did not change, she stood up and said, "Well, gotta go."

The driver saw what was happening, and he turned quietly back to the bar. The girl walked around him and back onto the street.

Silvia and Joaquim drank the rest of their beers in silence. When they were finished, Joaquim stretched out with fatigue and said, "I think I'm going to pack it in."

Although the night shift had officially ended more than two hours before, at one in the morning, Silvia was surprised to hear his partner decide to leave so early. "You okay?" he asked.

Joaquim nodded and shrugged. After another moment's thought, he said, "It's that stuff about battery acid and the green water. I can't get it out of my mind."

"It stays with you," Silvia agreed. He looked at his glass. "It's a good story."

Joaquim leaned forward earnestly, relieved to unburden himself. "I mean, I know Karen's a hooker, I know she's flaky and does a lot of dope. But my God, battery acid—it's something right out of a horror movie."

"That's probably where it came from," Silvia said. "'Night of the Living Diehards.'" He grinned. "As threats go, it's a lot better than a wallpaper steamer."

"I was thinking something else," Joaquim went on. "Here we have this murder investigation and a witness who seems to know what happened. The reason she isn't telling us is because some guy strong enough to gut a patrol car has said he's going to fill her veins with battery acid and throw her in the green water. Somewhere along the way, I remember hearing that using threats against a witness in a murder investigation is a serious crime—like, theoretically, punishable by life in prison."

Silvia leaned back, shaking his head. "Yeah, but that isn't what we've got. We don't know if Karen is really a witness, because she won't tell us what she saw or if she saw anything at all. And even if she is a witness, Drew hasn't used any threats on her. He may have made the threats to someone else—and for that matter, maybe he didn't. But who's *using* the threats? Who's gone to the trouble of driving everybody out to the altar in the woods? Who keeps insisting Carl Drew is Satan himself? Who describes in loving detail what will happen if anyone talks? Not some monster pimp or backwoods devil from New Hampshire, but a kid of only seventeen, a little sweetie from right here in Fall River. In fact, Karen Marsden is supposed to be Robin's best friend—and Robin is using these stories to scare her to death."

TWELVE / **AN UPSETTING EXPERIENCE**

T he next day, February 9, was a Saturday—exactly two weeks after the discovery of Barbara Raposa's frozen body in the field behind Resco Printers. At a few minutes before one o'clock in the afternoon, a telephone call came into the Fall River Major Crimes Division for Paul Carey. When Carey hung up, he told another detective, Joe Phelan, that the caller was Robin Murphy and that it looked like a new break in the Raposa case. The two detectives immediately left the police station and headed over to Harbor Terrace, above Battleship Cove, where they were to meet Robin in the apartment of Maureen "Sonny Spikes" Sparda.

Carey, along with Detectives Silvia and Joaquim, had spent a lot of time cultivating Robin, Sonny, and the others in their circle over the past several months in connection with both the Raposa disappearance and the Levesque murder. Despite the arrest of Andy Maltais, the police still believed the two cases were connected. Robin had never given any indication to the Fall River police that she was directly involved in either of them, seldom offering information and usually deferring to others when asked direct questions. But nevertheless, she stood out.

Carey and the other detectives realized early on that Robin was a lot more intelligent than the rest of the girls and women on the street. And even her occasional shows of deference to the others could not disguise a strong, commanding personality. On the way to the apartment, Carey told Phelan that this time Robin sounded stressed and almost hysterical on the telephone—that she had something to tell them about the Raposa murder that she said was "driving her crazy."

Phelan and Carey realized almost as soon as they arrived at Harbor Terrace, however, that Robin wasn't going to be an ideal witness. She was sprawled on the sofa under the garish, crudely painted mural of

Satan that occupied the longest wall in Sonny's living room. When the Fall River detectives had visited there before, the picture had always seemed childishly theatrical, a crude attempt at stage design that was contradicted by the drabness of the setting—the bleak prospect of the rest of the housing development from the window and the Salvation Army—style furnishings in the room itself. But if the mural had missed its effect previously, today it perfectly complement-ed the tableau. Robin's hair and clothes were unkempt, her speech rushed and semicoherent, and she looked badly in need of sleep. She smelled of alcohol, and they suspected she was also on drugs. "I've got to get this off my mind," she said, sitting up abruptly and clutching the top of her head when the detectives walked into the apartment. "I can't stand it."

Sonny Sparda, the tough, butch den mother and mentor for the prostitutes, pimps, runaways, and hangers-on at Harbor Terrace, watched Robin's performance warily as the two detectives took out their notebooks. In her middle twenties, she was seven or eight years older than Robin. Sergeant Carey had heard that the two women had previously been lovers and perhaps still were. Sonny's attitude was pro-tective, clearly apprehensive about the consequences for her younger friend of what was about to be told. But by her intense concentration, and because she had lent her apartment for this use, she also appeared to be encouraging Robin in whatever she was about to reveal.

"I was there when Andy killed Barbara," Robin said, and she start-ed to cry.

"You were where?" Carey asked.

It took a moment for Robin to collect herself enough to answer. She held her hands over the lower half of her face, speaking through a cage of fingers. "In the car," she sobbed. "Andy's. In the back seat."

Carey looked quickly over at Phelan. This was exactly the kind of result Carey had hoped for, but because what they were hearing was so serious and the potential consequences so grave for Robin, he was worried that any evidence she gave in her present condition might be disallowed when the case finally got to court. "When was this?" he asked cautiously.

"Three months ago," she coughed out between sobs, still speaking through her hands as though she were trying to hold back the words. "Early November."

Joe Phelan sat down on the edge of a wooden chair and began writing in earnest. Detective Carey led her through the basic details— where the killing had taken place, how it had happened, the degree to which Robin had been involved, why she hadn't come forward until now. At some points in the interview, Robin wailed hysterically, at others she shouted in rage, and sometimes her voice dropped to a fearful whisper. But despite the emotions, the alcohol, and the possible drugs, her answers were coherent, consistent, even measured. She had witnessed the crime. She had fought with the victim before the killing, but had not been a participant in the murder. She had remained silent until now for fear of her life.

Carey listened carefully, and when he was sure that he and Phelan had a complete outline of what she knew, he closed his notebook. "You're going to have to tell this all again," he said to her. "More than once."

Robin hiccuped in acknowledgment; behind the grief, the fear, the horror in her tearful eyes, Carey thought he still saw a certain watchfulness.

"We have a problem." He was aware as he said it that Robin's inner defenses were going on alert. "You've been drinking."

She visibly relaxed, laughing into her hand and glancing at Sonny Sparda in relief. "I'm scared to death," she said. "This isn't easy for me. What do you expect?"

Carey nodded, smiling in sympathetic encouragement, and looked at his wristwatch. He asked her if she could come down to the police station at five o'clock, sober, see Detective Phelan in the Major Crimes Division, and do it all again. She brushed some long strands of black hair back from her face, composing herself, and glanced quickly, speculatively, at Phelan. Then she nodded and said she would.

Later that evening, Detective Roger St. Pierre, the Identification Officer with the MCD, wrote his report of that meeting.

At 5:00 PM this date, Robin Murphy came into our office, at which time she made the following statements to Detective Phelan and myself.

Robin Murphy stated that on November 7, 1979, between the hours of 11:00 PM and 1:00 AM, while in the Mahogany Cafe located on Pleasant and Flint Streets, she called Andy (Andre Maltais) at his home and asked him for a ride to her mother's home located at 169 Walnut Street in Fall River. During the telephone conversation, Andy told her he had just received a call from Barbara (Barbara Raposa) asking him to come and pick her up at Sambo's diner on Pleasant Street. A short time later, Andy picked up Robin at the corner of Flint and Pleasant Streets and proceeded to Sambo's.

Enroute to Sambo's, Andy made the statement, "I'm going to kill that Barbara for going out with that Cowen."

Robin stated that when she and Andy reached Sambo's, she jumped into the back seat upon the request of Andy, allowing Barbara to get into the front seat.

An argument began with Robin as to what Robin was doing in the car with Andy; it continued until they reached the intersection of Jefferson Street and Brayton Avenue, at which time Barbara turned and punched Robin in the face.

In return, Robin grabbed Barbara by the hair and neck, pulling her into the back seat. They continued to fight while Andy proceeded south on Jefferson Street. At one time during the fight, Robin remembers biting Barbara somewhere on the breast.

The auto suddenly made an abrupt left turn, causing both Barbara and Robin to be thrown against the right hand rear door. A short distance after the turn, the auto came to a stop. Andy got out of the car and opened the rear door and pulled Barbara off of Robin, [and restrained] Barbara outside the vehicle.

Robin stated that she heard Barbara and Andy talking outside, but she could not hear what they were saying. Barbara began to calm down.

Andy released Barbara and went to the rear of the car. He opened the trunk and removed a brown paper bag. Robin described the bag as containing Andy's gadgets, such as a rubber penis, etc.

Barbara and Andy [walked] a short distance from the car. Barbara removed her coat and placed it on the ground. She also removed her jeans. Barbara then lay on the ground in the area where she had put her coat, and Andy lay on top of her. We asked Robin if Barbara's blouse or bra had been removed, and Robin said, "No," because it was cold out that night.

She stated that Andy then turned Barbara over on her stomach and [Robin] saw him insert the rubber penis in the anal area. He continued to have intercourse with her. At this time, Robin noticed Barbara's elbows up and away from her body. She said it was as though she had her hands tied.

A short time later, Robin said she heard what sounded like an argument between Andy and Barbara. She saw Andy beating Barbara with his fists. Robin turned her head away. Upon hearing a scream, she turned back. Andy [was] sitting on top of Barbara with his two hands raised, holding a rock over Barbara. She then saw Andy come down with the rock in . . . the approximate area where Barbara's head would have been.

Andy then got up and put the gadget back in the bag. He looked down at Barbara and said, "Let's see you crawl home from here." Andy then placed the bag back in the trunk, got back into the auto and drove off.

He asked Robin where she wanted to go and Robin told him to please take her to her mother's house. She was so scared, she could not recall any conversation.

On November 8, 1979, in the morning hours, Robin received a call from Andy. Andy [asked], "What happened to Barbara?"

Robin answered, "I don't know."

Robin stated that on several occasions Andy had dated different girls and had hurt them. Each time, he would call Robin the following morning, asking her how (whatever girl he had dated the night before) was. On each occasion, Robin would answer the same. "I don't know."

Detective Phelan informed me that the statements just given by Robin were the same statements Robin had given to Sgt. Carey and [him] earlier that morning.

At approximately 6:15 PM this date, Robin directed Det. Phelan and myself to the area of the crime scene. When we arrived at the intersection of Jefferson Street and Brayton Avenue, Robin stated that this is where the fight began between her and Barbara. She told us to continue south on Jefferson Street, [and] to turn left off Jefferson before the overpass to Dave's Beach. This was the entrance to Resco Printing.

We paused at the entrance to try to determine where the abrupt left turn might have been made. She also indicated that she thought she was on a dirt road shortly before the abrupt left turn.

An area that matched [her] description was found at the northeast corner of the Resco Printing building. Also in this area is a large tree located in the center of a lawn between the building and a wooded area. We drove onto the lawn and made a turn around the large tree.

Robin said, "This lawn is what I thought was a dirt road." She said, "Pull the car ahead a little more." She [then] said, "Hold it. Oh my God, this is the place."

Robin at this time was pointing to the area where Barbara Raposa was found on January 26, 1980. Robin then got out of the car, walked a few steps, pointed and said, "That's the place. I remember the stones."

She then asked to be taken home because she had become emotionally upset. Enroute, Robin explained that the reason she did not come forth sooner about this information was due to the fact that she was petrified of Andy from that day until his arrest.

On that same Saturday, the police received another telephone call and another visit to the station. This caller was a gentle, elderly woman who said that her granddaughter, who lived with her, had left home the previous afternoon and had not returned. It was unlike the girl to stay out all night; the granddaughter had a small child of her own and was a good mother. The police helped her fill out a report on a missing person.

At three that afternoon, Captain Andrade called the Nighters at home—Silvia first and then Joaquim—to tell them about that report.

"The lady's missing granddaughter," he said, "is Karen Marsden."

Alan Silvia had just gotten out of bed for the telephone, and he shivered when he heard the news. "This isn't just a missing person," he said.

"That's right," Andrade agreed. "She's probably dead."

THIRTEEN / **SKIN PICS**

K aren's grandmother called the station again at nine o'clock
the next morning, Sunday, February 10. She wanted to
hear if the police had learned anything about Karen's disappearance. She spoke with a policewoman in Major Crimes, and on
being told there were no developments, she offered some further
information.

She said that the last time she saw Karen was about three o'clock
Friday afternoon. The next day, between nine and ten on Saturday
morning, just after she had called the police to report her granddaughter missing, she had received a telephone call from a friend of Karen's
saying that she and Karen were supposed to have met at around ten
o'clock the previous night, but that Karen had never shown up.
Karen's grandmother told the friend that Karen had been out all night.
The caller seemed to be very upset on hearing this and had hung up.

"This is one of Karen's friends?"

"One of them, yes."

The officer asked if she knew the caller's name.

"Robin Murphy."

The policewoman wrote it down for her report.

"Karen is reliable," her grandmother went on. "She comes home
every night, at least by one o'clock."

The policewoman was sympathetic. She told her the department
was looking for Karen and that if she heard anything else, or if her
granddaughter returned home, to let them know right away. Karen's
grandmother said she would. There was a moment's hesitation.

"Karen doesn't say too much," she offered, tentatively. She was
struggling with whether to go further. "But—now and then, I have
overheard her talking with people on the telephone, friends of hers."
Another pause.

101

The officer encouraged her to go on. "Anything you can remember might help—appointments, plans she may have made to visit someone, names—"

"There is a name—Carl Drew. He's supposed to be asking the girls on the street if they have been talking to the police about the Doreen Levesque murder."

The policewoman started writing in earnest. "Carl Drew," she said. "And Doreen Levesque."

"That's right." She thought for a moment, perhaps gathering her courage to take a further risk for her granddaughter and herself, then added, "Karen has a friend named Carol Fletcher, and I heard Karen mention that Carl Drew was supposed to have given Carol a beating this week."

"He did beat her, or he was going to beat her?"

"Did or going to," she said. "I don't know." She hesitated. "I worry about Karen. I don't think she seems to be hanging around very nice people."

"No," the officer agreed.

"The reason Karen doesn't say too much at home—well, maybe the reason—is that she's afraid some one of these people might hurt me."

"Might hurt you?"

"She hasn't said so, but with what I've overheard, that's what I've been starting to think—that she doesn't want me to know too much about these people, and then they won't have any reason to think about me."

As soon as the call was finished, the policewoman typed a report to Andrade and sent it up to the Major Crimes Division.

Meanwhile, Alan Silvia and Paul Carey began a systematic canvass of everyone they knew who had been connected with Karen Marsden. The Fall River Police Department now listed her as a missing person, but the decision had been made unofficially to treat her disappearance as a probable homicide. And although the police had still made no public connections between the disappearance and the two known murders, all three cases were quickly merging into a single investigation.

At two-thirty Sunday afternoon, Carey and Silvia drove over to Woodman Street in Fall River and spoke with a young man named Dave Cowen. They had first run into Cowen during the Levesque investigation, and they knew him to have been one of Karen's friends. Cowen said he hadn't seen or heard from her since last Wednesday, when he had run into her by chance in the middle of the afternoon. He recalled that Karen had told him she was going to get a job. Cowen said he had asked her where she would be working, but she wouldn't say. He added, "She also said she was afraid of Carl Drew."

"Did she tell you why?" Carey asked.

He shook his head. "Just that she was afraid of him."

Cowen promised to call the station the following day, once he had checked with some of Karen's other friends.

The next stop was Robin Murphy. Just after sunset, Carey and Silvia knocked on the door of her apartment on Walnut Street.

Barely twenty-four hours had passed since Robin's revelation that she had been a witness to the killing of Barbara Raposa, but she appeared to have made a good recovery from the strain of the previous day. Her straight black hair fell limply across her face, giving her a wan, bedraggled look, and she was still tense, but she was far more composed, and there was no evidence of alcohol or drugs. She did not seem particularly happy to see them, although her mood was more somber than hostile. She stood uncertainly with her hand on the doorknob as they walked past her into the apartment.

"This isn't about Barbara or Andy," Silvia said, and she seemed to relax a little.

Carey asked her when she had last seen Karen Marsden.

She looked at them thoughtfully, as though trying to understand the purpose of the question, then said, "Two nights ago." She perched on the arm of an overstuffed chair, without offering them seats. "Friday."

"You know she's missing?"

She shrugged. "I heard she didn't come home, if that's missing."

Alan Silvia asked, "What about Friday night?"

She looked at him blankly. "What about Friday night?"

Silvia set his jaw and cocked his head, letting her know he was not willing to play the game.

"What about it?" she repeated.

Carey said, "C'mon—"

"The last time I saw her, we were hitchhiking together on South Main—"

"From?" Silvia interrupted.

"From Forest Street—the people who take care of her kid, JJ—the Nolins. We were there for a while, talked with them, then headed downtown."

"Where downtown?"

Robin squinted at a spot above Silvia's head, trying to get it exact. "Well, we were up around St. Anne's—about in front of the church— and this guy stops and gives us a ride. I was headed for Sonny's, and he says he's going to the Hub, so I only went part of the way and got out near the Government Center."

The Hub was a pool hall on Pleasant Street, at the corner of Sixth. In a reversal of the usual pattern, it was on the second floor of a building whose downstairs was empty, and the corner where it stood was a popular area for prostitution. There was a small bar nearby called Pigeon's Cafe. Both the Hub and Pigeon's were near an access ramp of the depressed interstate highway, which made the block convenient for tricks who drove in from out of town and were reluctant to cruise further up, nearer the congested center of the city.

Carey said, "So Karen was going on up to the Hub too, with the guy in the car?"

Robin nodded.

"Was he a trick?" Silvia asked.

She shrugged and shook her head, "Just a guy—far's I know."

"And you—?"

"Walked over to Harbor Terrace. To Sonny's. I only stayed there a little while. Karen and I were supposed to meet later, downtown, but she didn't show up. I haven't seen her since."

"Heard from her?" Silvia asked.

"Haven't heard from her or seen her since." Robin looked at Silvia steadily, and then at Carey. There was nothing challenging or defiant in her manner, but she had a sternness to her, an intensity that belied her relaxed posture. Her black hair, as usual, was parted in the middle and, perhaps because of that, her eyes were almost fierce. She looked back at Silvia. "I think she's dead."

"Why do you say that?" Carey asked.

"Because this isn't Karen. She doesn't do this kind of thing. She'd call—at least her grandmother. She wouldn't be away from JJ this long. It's been two days."

"A minute ago you weren't even sure she's missing, and now you're telling us she's dead?" Silvia asked.

She looked blankly back at him as though she did not understand what he was saying.

The next stop was Sonny Sparda's apartment. Sonny greeted Carey and Silvia at the door as though she had been expecting them. "You're here about Karen," she said, and when Silvia looked at her quizzically, she added, "Robin told me you were coming."

"Well, there you go," said Silvia, dropping wearily onto his usual place on the couch. Carey remained standing; he walked casually around the living room, checking on whether they were the only ones there. "So," Silvia asked Sonny, "what do you think?"

Sonny leaned across the back of a chair and weighed her answer. "I don't know what's happened to her, but I think Robin had something to do with it."

Silvia nodded. Carey sat down on a lounge chair beside the sofa.

"Robin likes to hurt people," Sonny said. "She scares me."

"She's a sadist?" Silvia asked.

Sonny did not respond. Silvia wondered for a moment if it was because she did not know the meaning of sadist, but then he recalled that Sonny had handcuffs attached to the headboard of her bed, and he decided it was simply that the question did not require an answer. She sat down on the arm of the chair, facing them. "When Robin called to say you were coming, she told me not to talk to you."

"No shit," Silvia said, half ironically and half in anger.

"She told me Joe Savitch had Karen and that he was going to kill her. She said you guys work for Savitch, and you're going to kill me."

Joe Savitch was a local troublemaker who had put a lot of effort into developing his own legend as a barroom brawler and street thug. He had accumulated a long file of charges for assault and battery and related offenses. But the lurid image of Joe Savitch as a crime lord who could hold hostages and buy the police was absurd, the kind of story kids would make up to sound street smart and to scare each other.

At first, Silvia laughed, then he stood up. "Give us a break," he said. He looked at Carey, who was grinning, then sat down again. "Hey," he said to him, "this really pisses me off. Ten minutes ago, you'd think butter wouldn't melt in Robin Murphy's mouth."

"I keep trying to tell you, Alan, some girls just don't go for brainy guys. You gotta work on a different image. Does she know you were a marine?"

Both men stood up. On the way to the door, Carey asked, "When was the last time you saw Karen, Sonny?"

"Thursday."

He wrote "Thursday, 2/7/80" in his notebook and told her they would probably drop in again the next day.

Both detectives were angry and ready to go back and confront Robin with what Sonny had just told them. Once they were back in the patrol car, however, they turned southeast to check out the early Sunday night action along Bedford Street. Robin could wait. It was time to talk with Carl Drew.

At about seven-thirty, as they approached the corner of Ninth, Carey rolled down the passenger-side window for a closer look at a figure standing in front of Charlie's Cafe. Silvia saw him at the same time and pulled the police car up to the curb. They got out.

The man in front of Charlie's was in his middle twenties, about six feet tall, with the muscular shoulders and arms of a bouncer. His dark hair was close-cropped and brushed back, and he wore a goatee. He had on a motorcycle jacket, and beneath it the collar of his shirt was open, showing gold chains around his neck. As the police approached, he nodded and eyed them indifferently for a moment, then turned his attention back to the passing traffic on the street.

Detective Silvia said, "Carl, we'd like you to come with us down to the station."

Carl Drew dropped his cigarette to the sidewalk and stepped on it. The request didn't appear to surprise or shock him, and when he answered, his tone was calm and mildly curious. "Am I under arrest?"

"No, it's about the disappearance of Karen Marsden."

"I'll be glad to help any way I can." Drew looked pleased. He crossed the sidewalk and got into the back seat.

Silvia drove the two blocks and parked in back of the police station, then took Drew upstairs to the second-floor offices of the Major Crimes Division. Carey read the Miranda warning. Drew had heard it several times before, but he listened courteously and made the appropriate acknowledgments when they were requested. Silvia next asked him when he had last seen Karen Marsden.

"Last Friday night."

Carey was seated at a typewriter beside an office desk, and he began filling in a legal form as Silvia continued the questions.

"Where?" Silvia asked.

"She was with Carol Fletcher and Robin Murphy in Carol Fletcher's car. Karen was sitting in the back seat."

Silvia repeated the question, "Where?" adding, "And what time was it?"

Drew thought for a moment. "It was seven, seven-thirty P.M., I guess. I was standing in front of the Pier, having a joint."

Silvia made sure his expression gave away nothing, but the comment about the joint raised a small red flag. He, Carey, and Joaquim had been a lot of places where marijuana had been smoked openly, and from early on they had made a practice of looking the other way. They knew the kids who were selling drugs all over the neighborhood, even right down the street from where the detectives were drinking with the women and their pimps, and the Nighters sometimes even lent out money so some of the guests at these parties could run out and make a buy. Their rationale was that they were not looking for drugs: they were investigating a homicide. Silvia would say, "When you're picking watermelons, you don't stop for blueberries."

But it was a flaw in the way they felt they were forced to work, and it left them potentially vulnerable. Now they were in the police station, not in somebody's apartment at Harbor Terrace, and they were taking Carl Drew's official statement. Drew's open reference to smoking a joint might have been a subtle piece of bait, a scrap of information which had the potential for compromising the police if they included it, but which could compromise them far more seriously if they chose to leave it out.

The other thing that crossed Silvia's mind, but only for a moment, was that by making himself so deliberately vulnerable with respect to the joint—admitting to something irrelevant, but for which there were potential consequences under the law—Drew was positioning himself as an open and cooperative witness. It was a technique he had seen before. After all, if Drew were the kind of person who would admit to smoking dope even when no one asked him, who could doubt whatever else he said?

"And they drove by, while you happened to be standing there?" Silvia asked.

Drew nodded, serious, helpful. "I haven't seen her since."

Carey saw a buck knife in a scabbard on Drew's belt, and he asked if he could look at it. Drew unsnapped the holster and passed it over.

Silvia had been looking Drew over since they had walked into the MCD office, and now he pointed to a tattoo that was visible behind the gold chains at the open neck of his shirt. "What's that?"

Drew didn't look down. "Satan," he said, "that's a tattoo of Satan."

"Uh-huh," Silvia said.

"You probably already heard," Drew continued matter-of-factly, "I worship Satan. There's no law against worshiping Satan. I worship him like you worship God."

"No kidding," Silvia said. Beside him, Carey looked up and then resumed his typing.

"No kidding," Drew said, his face darkening. But it passed, and when he spoke again, his tone was patient, explaining. "If you believe in God, you have to believe in the Devil. Any religion that teaches one teaches the other."

"How about if we take a photograph of your chest?" Silvia asked, indicating the ID camera which another officer passed Carey through the sliding glass door from the next office. "Would that be okay?"

Drew didn't hesitate. "Sure. I'll do anything." He took off his jacket, and as he started to unbutton his shirt, he asked, "Has someone said I had something to do with Karen being missing?"

Silvia widened his eyes, as though surprised by the suggestion. "No."

Drew laid the shirt on top of the jacket, across the back of a metal chair. "I'll do anything," he repeated. "I have nothing to hide. I didn't do anything wrong."

Before the photographs were taken, Carey rolled the paper out of the typewriter and passed it to Drew. The sheet was entitled Consent Search Authorization. "We'd also like a sample of your hair, if that's all right with you."

"Sure it's all right," he said. Drew reached up and, with one pull, yanked several strands of hair from the front of his scalp and held them out to the detectives.

Carey got a plastic evidence bag from the desk and held it open so Drew could place the hairs inside. While Drew signed the form, Carey sealed the bag, set it aside on the desk, then photographed the tattoo of Satan on Drew's chest. The camera clicked and whirred.

"Here's another one over here." Silvia pointed to a smaller tattoo on Drew's left forearm. "What does this one say?"

"It says, 'Satan Avengers.'" Drew was not looking at that one either.

"And that's the Devil again, is it?"

"That's right. It's an old, old tattoo."

"We'd like a picture of that one too," Carey said. Drew obediently held out his arm while the detective took another photograph.

Drew was reaching for his shirt when Silvia asked, "How about you take off your pants, Carl?"

He looked at the detective as though unsure what he had heard. Silvia looked back without any expression, waiting for him to do as asked.

"Come on," Drew said.

"Come on," Silvia answered in the same tone. "Are you cooperating or not?"

Drew weighed the request a moment longer, then undid his belt and dropped his jeans. He was still wearing his motorcycle boots, and he made no attempt to step out of the trousers.

Silvia was looking for identifying marks, and he was astonished at the enormous red welts on Drew's knees. They looked like friction burns, gray in the center and red on the edges, almost as though infected. "What's that from?"

"Fucking."

"Fucking?"

"Yeah, on a rug. A mat."

Carey took a photograph of the sores. There were not the usual sort of identifying marks, and they could hardly be expected to last. But if the district attorney ever made a case against Carl Drew, this was the kind of thing that the right prosecutor could use to advantage with a jury.

Drew pulled up the trousers. As he rebuttoned his shirt and put his jacket back on, the two detectives asked him some more questions about Karen Marsden. Getting no new information, they returned the knife and told him he was free to go. They had no basis for holding him.

"We'll be talking to you soon again," Silvia said.

"Any time," Drew said. "Any way I can be of help."

Silvia turned his back.

The next day, a state police cruiser from the Bristol Country CPAC unit picked up Robin Murphy at her apartment and drove her to the Groveland Motel, near the State Police Barracks in North Dartmouth. In due course, the DA's office advised the Fall River Police Department that Robin was now in protective custody.

When the district attorney prepares a case for the grand jury, an important part of that process is a culling of the herd of participants, separating the sheep, who will become targets, from the goats, who will help lead them to conviction. Robin's new status was a clear sign to the detectives of the Major Crimes Division that she was a goat, being groomed as a potential witness for the prosecution.

FOURTEEN / MISSING

Alan Silvia was certain that Carl Drew was another bingo.

Both detectives felt frustrated and angry at having to let him go. They could take some comfort from their recent experience with Andy Maltais, but they also recognized that there were important differences. Before they tied Maltais to the Raposa case, they had found a body. There was a body in the Levesque murder, but so far there was no direct link to Drew, and in order for the police to prove that Carl Drew had killed Karen Marsden, it was first necessary to demonstrate that Karen was dead.

Besides, despite the ferocity of the Raposa homicide, it was obvious from the first meeting that Maltais was a pathetic, self-delusive poseur. Carl Drew was a poseur as well, but of a much more dangerous variety—and he was far more successful than Maltais in being what he pretended to be.

Although Andy and Carl were so clearly opposite in character and appearance, one of the first rules of good police work is to look beyond the obvious, and Silvia was careful not to dismiss out of hand the many ways in which the two suspects were also alike. They both knew Karen, who may well have become a third victim. They both knew Robin Murphy, Sonny Sparda, and the supporting cast at Harbor Terrace and on Bedford Street. They knew each other. And, at least up to the point where Andy found Jesus Christ, they had both worshiped the Devil.

Once Drew left the station on Sunday night, February 10, Silvia wrote a quick report of their interview, then he and Carey headed back to the street.

They drove over to County Street and at 9:00 P.M. stopped in front of the apartment where Silvia and Joaquim had met with Karen Marsden just a week and a half earlier.

110

This time, they didn't stay as long. Carol Fletcher told them that the last time she had seen Karen was forty-eight hours ago—about eight-thirty Friday night—in the Hub Pool Room at Sixth and Pleasant. This agreed with what Carey and Silvia had heard a few hours earlier from Robin: the Hub was Karen's destination when Robin got out of the pickup truck that had stopped when they were hitchhiking, near Government Center.

Carol could not recall that Karen had said much. "It was just sort of like, 'Hi.' She hung around outside for a while, maybe a few minutes, then she got picked up by a trick and took off."

"Did you know the trick?" Carey asked.

She hesitated. "I didn't know him, but he looked, kinda, like—I don't know, I thought it was a guy I might have seen before."

"Where?" Carey asked.

Carol frowned, straining at the memory, then said lamely, "Around."

Detective Silvia asked, "What was the car?"

"One of those muscle cars. I think a Duster."

"A Plymouth Duster," he confirmed.

"A light-green Plymouth Duster."

"Describe the guy," Carey asked.

She thought back. "Middle-aged. A Portuguese-looking guy. Round face. Hair down to about here," indicating shoulder-length.

"What color?" Carey asked.

"White," she said.

"I mean his hair," Carey said.

"Brown," she said. "And brown eyes."

"Would you be able to recognize a photo?" Carey asked.

"Yeah, I think so."

Silvia studied her for a moment. "What were you saying earlier? About him looking like someone you'd seen around?"

She hesitated again, then said, "He looked like a trick that beat up on me a few days ago."

"Was he driving the same car?" Carey asked.

"I don't remember, but I think so." She thought harder. "Yeah, I think it was—a light-green Duster."

Silvia wrote down what she had told them. When he was finished, he asked, "Anything else?"

"I thought it was kind of funny he didn't make a deal about the price."

"You heard them talk price?" Silvia asked. "How much?"

"Karen told him thirty-five. He didn't say a word, just motioned for her to get in, and she did."

Silvia wrote that down as well, then asked again, "Anything else?"

Carol made a mouth, halfway between a smile and a grimace. "Yeah, I saw Carl Drew that same night."

"With Karen?" Silvia asked, hopefully.

"No, later, up at Pier 14. He called me over to tell me that anybody who mentions his name to the police is going to pay."

An hour after they left Carol Fletcher's apartment, Detectives Silvia and Carey spotted Robin Murphy near the entrance to a bar on Bedford Street.

"There's the DA's protected witness," Silvia said to Carey, "out on the town." He pulled up to the curb and gestured for her to get in the back seat, then turned and faced her irately. "What's this crap you're giving Sonny Sparda?"

"I don't know," Robin said, trying to decide between puzzlement and indignation. "What crap am I giving Sonny? What are you talking about?"

Paul Carey cut across between them, the peacemaker, patient and reasonable against Silvia's vehemence and Robin's umbrage. "Sonny said you told her not to talk with us."

Robin said, "Oh," and slumped back against the seat, smiling very slightly.

"How come?" Carey asked, still friendly and forbearing.

Robin shrugged, looking out the window as though something of interest had diverted her attention to the sidewalk. She glanced back at Carey, then quickly away again. "I don't know." She sounded almost meek.

"If you don't know that, then you probably don't know why you told her we were working for Joe Savitch and that we'd kill her," Silvia said.

Silvia could see her mind was working, and when she looked back this time, she fixed him straight in the eye and held it. "I *do* know why I said that. Andy told me to. He said it might scare Sonny, to keep her quiet. He said he didn't want her talking to you about Karen's disappearance."

Silvia studied Robin for a moment longer, then nodded, appearing to accept her answer. He indicated that she could get out of the car.

When she shut the door behind her, Silvia pulled out into the traffic. As Carey wrote down his notes on the conversation, he said to

Silvia, "By the time Karen disappeared, Andy was already in jail. Under the circumstances, why would Andy care one way or the other what anybody said about Karen Marsden?"

Silvia nodded in agreement. "Besides, how could Andy tell Robin anything? The court ordered him to Barnstable two days ago."

Carey leaned back thoughtfully as the car continued down Bedford Street. "Well, that wouldn't be a problem for Andy. He could have projected his spirit. He could have come to her in a dream."

The next night, Monday the eleventh, Carey and Silvia went back to Harbor Terrace to continue their interview with Sonny Sparda. This time there was another visitor there ahead of them. Sonny introduced him as David Roche; Carey guessed him to be in his early twenties. Carey asked Sonny if she had seen either Robin or Karen the previous Friday.

Sonny looked at him with mistrust and reproach. "I told you already: the last time I saw Karen was Thursday; I didn't see her Friday. You asked me that last night. Don't you make notes?"

Both Carey and Silvia smiled. Carey said, "What about Robin?"

Sonny glanced over at the man whom she had just introduced, then back at Carey. "Yeah, she was here Friday night." Looking at her visitor again, she said, "What time would you say?"

Roche thought. "I don't know. Maybe ten."

"You were here, Dave?" Silvia asked.

"Yeah, for a while," Roche replied, trying to be noncommittal.

Carey asked Sonny, "Did Robin say anything about Karen?"

"Robin was going down to Bristol," Sonny said, looking again to Roche for affirmation. "Bristol, right?"

"Bristol," the young man agreed.

Bristol was a Rhode Island town on a peninsula in Narragansett Bay, across from Fall River.

Sonny continued, "Robin said she'd just been with Karen. She said she had already told Karen she was going to Bristol, so I shouldn't expect Karen to come by here looking for her."

Silvia wanted to be sure he had heard Sonny correctly. "Robin was going to meet Karen here, and then Robin told you she had canceled the date?"

"That's what she told us," Sonny answered. "She said Karen wasn't coming because Robin told her the date was off."

"Okay," Silvia said, glancing at Carey.

"Maybe they were going to meet later, somewhere else," Carey suggested.

Sonny shrugged, a gesture that said she had no way of knowing. "Robin was only here for a few minutes. At first I thought she was sick; she was all out of breath and sweating. When I asked her, she said it was from running."

"Why was she running?" Carey asked.

The same shrug. "Didn't say—just that she been running."

Carey asked David Roche if he had seen the same things that Sonny had just described, and he said he had. Carey asked him to repeat the events anyway, and he did, adding nothing new.

"Where do you live, Dave?" Carey asked.

Roche looked startled. "What do you mean?"

"Your address." Carey had his notebook open and was waiting to write it down.

"I'd rather not give it," Roche said.

Carey considered for a moment. Harbor Terrace—and most particularly this apartment—was the division's principal source of information into two known murders and a possible third. He wanted to protect their relationship with that source. He looked at Roche a moment longer, closed his book, and said, "Okay."

The value of Harbor Terrace to all three investigations was even more obvious when the detectives compared their access there and the quality of the information they developed with what was available to them elsewhere. They got more cooperation from their Harbor Terrace contacts than they received, at least in the beginning, from any other sources, including Karen Marsden's mother.

Nancy Marsden lived in Bay Village in Fall River. After trying unsuccessfully to reach her on several previous occasions, Joe Phelan and Alan Silvia went to her apartment and knocked on the door at 12:30 A.M. on Thursday, February 14. Silvia could hear sounds from inside, but their knocking went unanswered. They tried for another couple of minutes, and then Silvia called the office from the car radio and asked Paul Carey to try reaching Mrs. Marsden by telephone from the police station. No luck there either.

They drove around for a time, got some coffee at a diner, and after nearly a half hour had elapsed they tried calling again, from an outdoor pay phone. After several rings, Silvia heard a woman's voice at the other end of the line.

"Mrs. Marsden, this is Detective Alan Silvia with the Fall River Police Department. I'm calling about your missing daughter, Karen."

"What about her?" Mrs. Marsden asked.

"We'd like to meet with you for a few minutes to ask you some questions that might help us find her."

There was a moment of silence. "Do you know what time it is?"

"We've tried reaching you; we've called, and we've gone to the house—we were by there earlier tonight."

"Any questions you want to ask, I can answer on the telephone," she said.

But when Silvia did start to question her from the pay phone, she soon became impatient with that approach as well. She told him that Karen didn't live with her, that she couldn't remember exactly when she saw her last, but that it was certainly before Karen's grandmother had reported her missing. In fact, Mrs. Marsden had only just learned of her daughter's disappearance. When she reminded Silvia again of the hour, he said he would drive by in another day or so in the hope of talking with her personally. She repeated that there was nothing to talk about that couldn't be done by telephone.

The next day was Friday, February 15. At four-fifty that afternoon, her memory apparently refreshed by a night's sleep and a day of reflection, Nancy Marsden called the Fall River Police Department to report that she recalled hearing, three weeks before, that there had been a contract out on her daughter's life.

Tom Joaquim took the call. She told him that one afternoon three weeks ago, she had gone to her mother's house, where her daughter, Karen, lived as well, and while there she had met a friend of Karen's named Cookie. Mrs. Marsden didn't know her by any other name, but Joaquim recognized Cookie as the nickname of a woman named Millie Powers.

Cookie had been very nervous and in tears. Sobbing, she had told her friend's mother that there was a contract out on her and Karen and that they had no place to go. The contract had been placed by Carl Drew. Mrs. Marsden told Joaquim that she knew Drew, although not well—she had met him a couple of times—but that she hadn't taken Cookie seriously.

Joaquim asked whether Mrs. Marsden had been in touch with Cookie again. She said no, that they had walked together to a bus stop in Bay Village and that Cookie had taken a bus downtown. Mrs. Marsden didn't know where Cookie lived, and she didn't think she had any relatives in the area.

When Joaquim put down the phone, he leaned back and let out a long breath. Twenty-four hours before, when they had appealed to her motherhood, Nancy Marsden gave them little more than the time of day. He wondered how she could tell him these things now—of an ignored death threat, of a possible next victim—without the slightest hint of responsibility or remorse.

Karen's mother was not the only call on the case forwarded to the MCD that afternoon; she wasn't even the only Nancy. Detective Ron Saucier took a call from a girl who identified herself as Nancy Numan. She lived at 16 Harbor Terrace. "Robin did kill this girl," Ms. Numan said, referring to Karen. "Check an abandoned building or well for the body. I am telling you the truth."

Saucier told her someone would be getting in touch with her. Thirty minutes later, Tom Joaquim and an MCD daytime detective were back at Harbor Terrace.

Ms. Numan told them she had known Robin Murphy for the past five years, since Robin was twelve. She also said she felt very sure that Andy Maltais had been responsible for several unreported deaths in the Fall River area over the past several months.

Joaquim repeated what he and Alan Silvia—and Paul Fitzgerald—had so often told Karen Marsden. By itself, *what* people know doesn't mean much. They must also be able to tell the police *how* they happen to know it.

Nancy Numan understood. She explained that she had seen these things in a vision.

"Ah, a vision," Joaquim said, suppressing the temptation to add, "Of course." He wished Alan Silvia were there to hear this.

She then repeated what she had told Saucier on the telephone. She had seen that Karen Marsden was dead and that her body was in an old abandoned building or a well. She said she didn't have a specific location, but the site was somewhere in the Freetown Reservation. She added that some unknown male had helped Robin with this latest murder.

"Robin will admit their guilt," she told the two detectives.

"You think so?" Joaquim asked her.

"I do. She just needs help—a program of psychiatric help."

Joaquim thanked her for the information.

Later that night he typed his report, for reference "in the event Ms. Numan calls again." He found himself wondering if Silvia's stratagem as the Psychic Reader had launched a purely local phenomenon—or if it might be the beginning of a whole new trend in criminal discovery.

FIFTEEN /**SPEAK OF THE DEVIL**

The following evening, Alan Silvia and Paul Carey drove back to Sonny Sparda's apartment. There had been a fine, steady drizzle blowing in from the bay all afternoon, and after dark, now that the temperature had dropped, the trees had turned to rock-candy light shows. The street that went down to the cove below Harbor Terrace glistened dangerously with a quarter-inch veneer of black ice. Silvia approached their usual parking space gingerly, but even with studs in all four tires, the car skidded the last two feet and the wheel rims scraped noisily against the curb.

"One small step for man," Carey said. "One giant crash for mankind."

Silvia laughed. "I pity the poor kid who buys this car when the City finally dumps it. I can just see him pissing down to Horseneck Beach some night, trying to outrun the state cops, when the two right wheels fall off."

"We'll be old by then." Carey picked up a brown paper bag with the six-pack they had bought around the corner, opened the door to the sidewalk on the passenger side, and put his foot out, testing the traction. He stood up slowly, turning to hold onto the car with his free hand, and as he did he stopped to look down the hill at the icy trees, gleaming like crystal whirligigs in the lights from Battleship Cove.

Silvia got out the driver's side. The sand trucks had been by recently, and the footing was better in the street. He locked the door and walked carefully around the back of the cruiser. Enough grit adhered to his soles that he had no trouble keeping his footing as he crossed the glazed sidewalk. Carey, clutching the six-pack, skated after him into the brick-and-cement entryway of number five.

Sonny had been expecting them. Her second-floor corner apartment commanded a good view of the street, and she opened the door before they knocked. She watched Carey give the usual quick glance toward the other rooms in the back. "No one else is here, just me and Darnella. Anybody with any brains doesn't go out in this kind of weather."

Darnella was Sonny's child, a few months younger than Silvia's own daughter. She was just teething, and the detectives had seen her on past visits, crawling around the floor and biting furniture legs, plastic toys, clothing, shoes, and whatever else she could get her mouth on. Apparently, Darnella had already gone to bed. It was late.

Carey said, "We came up by Charlie's and the Pier, and it's hopping. There's a lot of people down there with no brains."

"That's no surprise."

Silvia glanced as he usually did toward the mural; the fiery eyes followed them now—an obvious gimmick, but still a bit spooky—as Sonny led her visitors toward the back of the apartment. In the kitchen, she offered two chairs at the breakfast table, draped with an oversized floral-printed plastic cloth.

Carey tore open the bag he had been carrying and pried up one end of the cardboard carton, setting out three king Buds. He passed one to Sonny. "An apple for the teacher."

Silvia snapped back the aluminum tab and held up his can in the manner of a toast.

Sonny took a sip of her own beer, leaning against the kitchen sink and looking down at them uncertainly. "I'm not really sure how much I'm going to be able to tell you that you haven't heard already. It isn't like I ever made a study of it or anything. You may know more than I do."

"Yeah, that's right," Silvia said. "I took Satanism 101 at Northeastern. For the final, everyone got to kiss a toad and bite the head off a chicken."

In fact, since the time several months earlier when Karen Marsden had first told him about the meetings, Silvia had learned a lot more about Devil worship than he let on.

Just a few days earlier, moreover, Andy Maltais, late of Satan but now of Jesus Christ, had told them of having served as a personal conduit, at one time or another, for both the voice of Satan and the voice of God. Andy had shown Silvia the passage in the New Testament where Saint Paul described speaking in tongues as one of the gifts of the Holy Spirit—along with wisdom, knowledge, faith, healing, the working of miracles, prophecy, and the ability to understand tongues when they are spoken by others—and he said that the same powers, or their corollaries, were equally available to those who served the Devil.

Silvia had subsequently made a point of finding out more for himself. There were other passages in the Bible that appeared to support what Carl Drew had said to him and Carey about the relationship between God and Satan. Saint Paul referred to the Devil as "the God of this world," and Matthew described the temptation in the wilderness, where the Devil offered Jesus "all the kingdoms of the world and the glory of them." The Devil slithered through the Old Testament as well, in support of Drew's thesis: in Genesis, the serpent told Eve in the garden, "When you eat of the fruit of the tree, your eyes will be opened, and you will be like God, knowing good and evil."

Eventually, Silvia had gone beyond the Bible, to the local library. He learned that in later centuries, the Manichaeans and the other Gnostic sects carried this dualism several steps further, seeing the world as essentially evil and mortal life as a sentence in prison. But just because the Gnostics did not like it here did not mean they were Satanists, and neither were most of the heretics who followed them. He also read that most of the people who had been accused of Satanism over the centuries were guilty of something substantially different, usually related to pantheism, paganism, or witchcraft. He was certain, however, that there was no such confusion in the satanic cult activity of Fall River.

He learned that the lurid metaphysics of modern-day Satanism are nowhere near as old as the Devil, but in large measure are the legacy of an anomaly in the Romantic tradition which started with such figures as Swinburne, who invoked "Good Satan" in warning Rossetti against the "criminal lunacy of theolatry," and Crowley, who was said to have baptized a toad as Jesus Christ and then crucified it in order to fix his position as the "wickedest man on earth." That anomaly peaked in the end-of-the-century reaction to Victorian restraints on a wide range of natural expression, particularly in the area of sex. The Black Mass, which had been practiced in one form or another as a travesty of Catholicism since the Dark Ages, did not introduce the body of a naked woman into the service until relatively modern times.

Silvia also knew the likelihood that Carl Drew had ever heard of Swinburne, Crowley, Gnosticism, or even the gifts of the Spirit was somewhere around zero. He suspected that Drew and probably others were simply using the fear of the Devil as von Clausewitz had used a definition of warfare: as an extension of politics by other means. Whether or not they really believed in it themselves, either as a philosophy or a religion, it was undeniably an effective method of controlling the people around them.

By the same token, common sense told them Sonny Sparda was

unlikely to know anything more about the ancestry of modern Devil worship than Carl Drew did; the most Silvia or Carey expected of her was what she would be able to tell them from her own experience.

Sonny didn't appear to understand that at first, and she seemed uncomfortable. "Well, what I mean is, that's pretty much the kind of thing I know about it, you know? Stories. Meetings I've been to, here and in the forest."

Silvia said, "Stories are exactly what we want to hear. Whatever you can tell us from what you've personally seen or done."

"And names," Carey added. "Every name you can remember."

"A lot of the names I don't know," she said, looking doubtful again. "Sometimes there's all the same people and I know every one of them, and sometimes it includes a lot of people who just come once or twice, for the kick. If I don't know a person already, from someplace else, then even if I've seen him three or four times at the services, I wouldn't be able to tell you his name."

Silvia made a small gesture of dismissal with his hand. "Why don't you start off by telling us what these services are for? What happens at them?"

She thought for a moment. "What they're for is to worship Satan. Just like in a church. We pray to Satan. We chant. We try to conjure him."

"Conjure?" Silvia asked.

"Plenty of times we get him right into the room—either in a form where we feel his presence, or he takes possession of one of us. You can tell when Satan is there. Some people even let him speak through them, in his own language. It isn't human speech; there's no way anybody on earth could fake it."

During the course of the next half hour, as Sonny Sparda and the two detectives sat at the kitchen table drinking beer, she told them what she knew about Satanism in Fall River, circa 1980. She described the ritual sacrifice of animals at ceremonies in the reservation. Sometimes warm gore from goats or stray cats slaughtered at the site was dropped onto the heads of participants, some willing and some not, who were bound to a tree or at a makeshift altar in place of the crucified Jesus. She also said that even before the Levesque killing there had been rumors of human sacrifice, but she knew of no such murders.

She explained the mural of Satan that had been painted on the wall of her living room. It was no different from the portraits of Jesus Christ that adorned the living rooms of other houses throughout Fall River or the country or the world. Christians had faith in the power of

God and the promise of life beyond death—a better life than the misery of earth. Satanists believed the real light came from Lucifer, that Satan was the true Savior, and that physical pleasure in the here and now was a lot better than false promises of spiritual delight in some nebulous afterworld. "When we have meetings here in the apartment, we sit in front of the picture and try to conjure him into the room. That's what we're going to do tonight."

"Conjure," Silvia repeated again. This time it was not a question.

The meeting was scheduled to begin in another half hour, and although they had been invited to stay for the service, they knew their conversation with Sonny was almost at an end. "What do you think is going to happen?" he asked.

Sonny finished her second beer. "Tonight? Probably not much. There could be twenty people or more—but with this weather it could be a lot less. We'll sit in a circle. There will be some praying and chanting. If you let yourselves get into it, you'll be able to feel Satan in the room. He'll be here."

Carey said, "If he's coming anyway, couldn't you get him to melt a little of this ice?"

Silvia started to smile, but at that moment he felt something brush against his left ankle under the kitchen table. At first he thought it might have been the other detective's shoe, but as he pulled back to withdraw his legs from under the plastic tablecloth, he realized with a rush of panic that it was something far different. It was warm and moist, and now it grasped him around his leg, and there was a sharp pain as whatever it was bit suddenly into his ankle. Silvia yelled out in terror, kicked back his chair at the same time he pushed violently against the table, and tried frantically to get his feet out where he could see what had attacked him. "Ah-h-h!" he said, attempting to stand. "Holy shit!"

Sonny was startled at first, then she suddenly started to laugh.

Silvia saw it at the same time. Teething Darnella was under the kitchen table. After a moment Silvia started to laugh as well. Off and on, he kept laughing for the next several minutes, until the first guests arrived. He was shaking, and it was hard to stop.

By the time the pizza was eaten and everybody had settled into the ritual circle, there were only a dozen other people in Sonny's living room. But the service was a disappointment for more reasons than the low turnout. Sonny had told the detectives that at a meeting a month earlier, after the chanting had gone on for more than an hour, the presence of Satan had been so palpable in the room that the person leading the service had turned purple. If that was the litmus test for this evening, the Devil was nowhere in the vicinity of Fall River. The person in the middle of the circle was a prostitute from Providence, and although she led the group in the chant of "Hail, Satan, Hail, Satan," until the effort raised the veins in her neck, it never had a corresponding effect on her complexion; she retained her midwinter nighthawk's pallor throughout.

Another part of the disappointment was that the ceremony did not involve any people other than those who were known to the police already. Carl Drew was there, Nancy Numan from around the corner, David Roche, and other Bedford Street regulars. Robin Murphy, whose new status as a protected witness had apparently changed little more than her address, was there as well. Although Carey thought he heard Drew lapse once or twice into incoherence—something that might have passed for speaking in tongues—eventually the chanting died away and the ritual came to a faltering, indecisive conclusion.

When the ceremony was over, the party atmosphere, never entirely in abeyance, returned. Participants drifted into other rooms. At one point, Silvia heard a deep, unfamiliar voice from a bedroom saying, "Satan will have his toll." It was the kind of thing Carl Drew said frequently, and he thought at first it was Drew speaking. But then he realized Drew was sitting in the kitchen. Silvia walked by the bedroom door and looked in, just as the phrase was being repeated.

The speaker was Robin Murphy. The only other person in the room was one of the prostitutes who worked for Drew, and she was watching Robin with obvious astonishment and fear. The voice coming from Robin's mouth had nothing to do with a petite seventeen-year-old girl. It was not young. It sounded exactly like a man. Silvia felt the hair rising on the back of his neck.

SIXTEEN / WATCHERS IN THE WOODS

In the first week following the report of Karen Marsden's disappearance, Alan Silvia and Tom Joaquim each worked at least ninety hours on the case, seeking out everyone they knew who had a connection with the missing girl or who might hold a clue to her whereabouts. Indeed, with two known murders and a suspected third, all the detectives in the Major Crimes Division were carrying a heavy added burden. But it was especially hard on the Nighters, who now included Paul Carey. Because a lot of the follow-up to their after-dark activities could only take place in the daytime, the process of discovery crossed back and forth between two worlds.

On the afternoon of February 16, Tom Joaquim and a daytime detective were in the State Forest, assigned to check out possible leads in connection with all three cases, but particularly the disappearance of Karen Marsden. They were working with a K-9 officer and a dog that had been trained to sniff out dead bodies. During the course of their search, they came upon the rusted skeleton of a burned-out automobile. They looked in and around the car, saw nothing suspicious, and made note of the location. But as Tom Joaquim was about to leave the area of the burning, he saw something in the woods that made him stop.

He called over the other two officers. "What do you make of this?" he asked.

What he had seen was several rocks, laid out as though they had been stacked by hand or heavy equipment; they formed two large steps, or perhaps shelves, at successive heights. All three policemen studied the formation without speaking and finally agreed that it looked like an altar.

They moved to another area which they had been assigned to

search, and on the way back to Fall River they reported the location of the burned car to the Freetown Police Department. Joaquim also mentioned the car, as well as the altar, in his report to Captain Andrade.

That evening started out like any other Saturday night. Silvia checked into the MCD second-floor offices and went straight to the file. He had been in and out of the police station several times during the afternoon, but this was his first chance to catch up on any relevant case reports from the day shift. He exchanged some information with Paul Carey, then they both got into an unmarked car and cruised slowly down Bedford Street, stopping at bars along the way or wherever they saw people they recognized on the sidewalk.

Traffic was heavy. Because it was Saturday night, a lot of other cars were cruising the streets as well, some with boys in pairs or groups, some with men by themselves, checking out the activity, searching faces, making choices—in much the same way as the two policemen, if with different motives.

At a few minutes before eight-thirty, Silvia turned the car onto Robeson, leaving the turmoil and congestion of Bedford Street behind them, and drove a dozen blocks north.

At the corner of Robeson and Stanley, Silvia pulled over to the curb. Carol Fletcher, the last known person to have seen Karen Marsden, came out of a doorway and got into the back seat.

Silvia turned long enough to say hello, then watched her in the rearview mirror as Paul Carey asked her where she wanted to go.

"The Reservation," she said.

Silvia pulled onto the nearly empty street, continuing north.

"There's this place in the forest, near the power lines," Carol told them. "I know she's there because Robin once took me to the same spot. It's the only place she could be."

Carey nodded. "We'll go anywhere."

Silvia, however, said nothing. Now and then he glanced at Carol in the mirror, but when she made occasional comments as they continued through the outskirts of the city and into the countryside near the beginning of the state forest, his eyes would return to the road and he made no reply. Finally, when he felt reasonably sure that this treatment was beginning to make her feel uncomfortable, he said to her, "Carol, we've got a problem."

She looked at him apprehensively in the glass, then turned to Carey for help, but now Carey was watching her in silence too. Clearly, whatever problem she had with Silvia, she had with Carey as well. She bit her lip and waited for one of them to go on, the expression on her face wavering between apprehension and solid fear.

"You're not telling us everything you know," Silvia said.

They both watched her closely for a reaction. Carol had been sitting with her forearms on the back of the driver's seat, but now she slumped to the rear, sucking in her breath sharply and covering her face with her hands.

Carey said, "If you did tell us, we could help you."

Silvia pressed harder. "You say you're a friend of Karen's . . ."

Before Silvia could go further, she interrupted with a sob, then began to weep loudly. "If they know I said anything—anything"—she gulped for air—"they'll kill me."

Silvia pulled the car to the side of the road and put the selector on park, leaving the motor running. The road was nearly deserted. "Carol," he said, turning to face her, "you've got to tell us."

Carey said to her, "Life doesn't give that many second chances."

She sobbed some more, still not speaking. Silvia had the impression she was weighing their words, balancing them against her fear. He said, "If Karen had told us everything she knew just a week ago, we wouldn't be here now. And she wouldn't be wherever she is either."

Carol struggled for control, sitting up in the seat and wiping the tears from her face with the sleeve of her coat. "Oh, God—" More sobs. "I don't know where to begin—"

"Friday night," Silvia said decisively.

She sniffled some more, then brought a handkerchief from her pocket and blew her nose loudly. "Oh, God help me," she moaned. "What a mess."

"You were in the pool hall on Sixth, with Karen—" Carey coaxed.

"No, we weren't," she said. Her voice squeaked with the strain, as though it were barely escaping from a body that was fighting to keep her secret within. She folded the handkerchief carefully and used the dry side to wipe at her eyes. "We were sitting outside in my car."

"You and Karen," Silvia affirmed.

Carol nodded, her eyes darting back and forth between them, still welling with tears; she winced and held up a hand to shield them against the headlights of an oncoming car. "Robin told her to get down there and make some money."

"You heard her say this, or Karen told you?" Silvia asked.

"Karen told me," she sobbed. Carol leaned back in the seat, drawing and exhaling three deep breaths before going on. "And she talked about Carl Drew. She was worried—she was very, very worried."

"About Drew," Silvia said, and Carol nodded.

"Carl told the both of us, anybody that talks to the cops will pay," she said. "Karen was scared to death. It was one of those things— almost like, because Carl said we'd pay, it made her go to the cops. She went to the state cops in North Dartmouth. She talked to you guys. It was, you know, like she was so scared to open her mouth, she couldn't keep it shut."

"Yeah, we know all right," Silvia said angrily. "And look where it got her, not telling the whole story. She was sitting right where you are, crying the same as you, telling us her life was over. And because that's *all* she told us, there was not a goddamned thing we could do for her."

Carol winced at Silvia's vehemence and averted her face without taking her eyes from him, looking at him sideways as though she half expected to be hit. Silvia shook his head in disgust and turned to face forward again, looking out into the darkness.

Carey waited while Carol unfolded the handkerchief and blew her nose again, then asked, "So, what's the story on this guy in the Duster?"

"There was a guy," Carol said quickly. "There really was, and what I told you was the truth: he pulled up beside us, she told him thirty-five dollars, and she got out and took off with him."

Silvia said, "And—"

She held his eye for a moment, then looked down at the floor. "And, fifteen minutes later, he comes back, lets her off, and Karen gets back in my car."

"So this Duster stuff is bullshit," Silvia said. Every detective in the Major Crimes Division, and every uniformed patrolman in Fall River, had spent something on this false lead, combing the area around Bedford Street and Bay Village for the car in question, looking for the middle-aged Portuguese driver with shoulder-length brown hair and brown eyes.

"There was a Duster, there was a guy," she said, defensive and tearful, adding lamely, "It's just that he brought her back."

"Hey, Carol," Paul Carey said, patting her shoulder, "good for you. C'mon, what were we just saying about second chances? See?"

Silvia could not help remembering that he had almost this same conversation with Karen Marsden, sitting in this same car at night, hearing the fearfulness, seeing the tears, just a week before. And it didn't stop with Karen; his thoughts suddenly shifted further back, to the ice-blackened body in the autopsy room of St. Anne's and to the other mutilated corpse under the Diman School bleachers last October. He looked again at Carol Fletcher and nodded in agreement with Carey. "He's right. You're going good. It's never too late to tell the truth."

Carol folded the handkerchief in her lap and leaned back again, looking out the window into the darkness. She sniffled, apparently still trying to compose herself.

Carey gave her another moment, then said, "So Karen is back, sitting with you in your car, out in front of the Hub."

Carol squinted down the highway; the lights of another vehicle were coming into view, and she listlessly held up a hand again to shield her eyes. "Yeah, there we were," she said.

No one spoke as the light inside the police car intensified, but when the pickup truck passed them and it was dark again, she said, "I drove around the block. When we got back more or less where we started, I spotted a couple of guys sitting in a car in the parking lot across from the pool room."

Carey started to ask, "What kind of—" but she held up her hand to forestall the question. "I think a Mercury. Dark green, with a black top. I don't know, maybe it was a Montego. The driver was blinking the lights off and on to get Karen's attention."

"Why do you say Karen's?" Silvia asked.

"Because that's who they were looking at. They weren't that far away. They weren't looking at me."

"The guys," Carey said.

Carol put her face in her hands, her elbows on her knees, thinking. "Both white. About six-one, six-two."

"Both of them?" Carey asked.

She looked up at him sharply, as though worried she had said something wrong. "Why not?"

"So what happened?" Silvia interrupted.

"Karen gets out and starts to cross the street. She gets to the middle, and these two guys get out and start around to the front of their car. They meet on the sidewalk."

"On the far side of Sixth," Silvia said.

She stopped to place the event in her memory. "On the curb, on the far side of Sixth. Maybe one of them even stepped down from the sidewalk into the street to meet her. Both guys take her by the arm, one on each side, and walk her to the car. They put her between them in the front seat, pull out of the parking lot, and head down Pleasant."

"Which way?" Silvia asked.

"Down," she repeated. "Toward Eighth, Ninth, Tenth."

"East," Carey said.

"And that's it? That was the last time you saw her?" Silvia asked.

She nodded, looking at the floor. "That's the last time. Driving off with these two guys."

Silvia turned on the overhead light and opened up his notebook. So far, except for the type of car and number and nationality of the tricks, this story didn't sound that much different from the one that had started the wild goose chase after the Duster. Carey asked, "Who were these guys? Did you know them?"

She hesitated. "I'm not sure. I've seen them before."

Silvia shut his book and flipped off the inside light, then pulled the car out onto the highway.

The place Carol wanted them to take her was deep in the state forest, but before they had gone very far off the highway, Silvia realized the driving conditions were worse than either he or Carey had anticipated. There had been a slight thaw during the day, but the temperature had dropped sharply after sunset; the car slewed dangerously on the iced-over flat stretches, and in the unpaved, wooded areas the roads were too deeply rutted for them to pass. They agreed to return to the police station and come back to the Reservation Sunday, during daylight.

Once they were upstairs in the Major Crimes Division, Silvia took Carol Fletcher into an empty office. When and where, he asked her, had she previously seen the two men who had driven off with Karen Marsden?

"A few months ago," she said, "with Carl Drew. They were all going into Sonny's place up at the Terrace."

"And before that?"

"All told, I've seen them maybe four times: twice in the pool hall, once at the Pier—and going into Sonny's."

"What are their names?" He knew the question was a reach, considering that an hour earlier Carol was unsure whether she knew them at all.

"One of them is Jim," she said. "Carl called him Jim."

"What's the other one?" he asked.

"I don't know. I don't think I ever heard it."

He asked her to describe the one called Jim.

"Well, about six-one or -two. Like blond hair—sort of blond—"

"Dirty blond?" Silvia offered.

"Yeah. Medium length." She thought a moment longer. "Built husky."

"Like Carl Drew?"

She hesitated again, then said tentatively, "Yeah, like Carl."

"Complexion?" Silvia asked.

"Complexion? Light complexion. He has a little acne; maybe not now, but he did once and it left a mark—you know."

She described the second man as being about the same build and height, with dark-brown hair.

Carol said that Carl Drew knew everything about the disappearance of Karen, but when Silvia pressed her for details, she was as vague and evasive as Karen herself had been, volunteering almost nothing. Silvia had to extract the information from her a fragment at a time. "He told me to stay away from Karen and Robin because something bad is going to happen."

"What bad? Didn't he give you any idea?"

"He gave me an idea, but he never said it right out. Just stuff like 'Satan's toll must be paid,' and 'Satan is everywhere, Satan sees everything you do. Satan, Satan, Satan.'"

Silvia half seated himself on the end of a battered wooden desk and smiled at her. "Well, I was hoping he might have told you something we could use—like where he left the body."

Carol looked thoughtful, as though trying to recall a forgotten detail. Then she said, "A graveyard in Assonet."

Silvia looked at her in astonishment.

"A graveyard in Assonet," she repeated. "I asked him."

Silvia stood up. "Exactly what did you ask him, and exactly what did he say?"

"I saw him the other night, on the street. I asked him where he thought Karen's body might be found. And that's what he said."

"What did you mean, 'Might be'?"

"Might be found. I meant, if she was dead, where did he think they might find her body."

"So Drew could have been guessing. Maybe he thought you were asking him for a guess, and he gave one."

"Maybe," she said, shaking her head dubiously, "but it didn't sound that way to me."

Silvia stood up. "Then why the hell were we driving around in the woods all night? What were we looking for in the state forest if she's in a cemetery in Assonet?"

Carol flinched, watching him out of the side of her eye, fearful of his anger. "I don't know," she said meekly. "I thought we were looking for the place she died."

Sergeant Carey came into the room. Silvia made sure he was listening, then turned back to Carol and asked the most obvious question of all.

"Who killed Karen Marsden?"

Without a moment's hesitation, she said, "Carl Drew did it. I've seen the two guys with him before. He said he was going to do it, and he did. Other people are involved too—Robin is involved. It was Robin who sent her to the pool room."

Silvia and Carey thanked Carol. Carey drove her back up to the corner where they had picked her up earlier in the evening.

While Silvia was typing his report to Captain Andrade, Joaquim came into the office and stood behind him, looking over his shoulder. "A dark-green Mercury," he read aloud.

Silvia looked up. "Yeah, you can forget the light-green Duster."

"Okay," Joaquim said, "I'll start looking."

On Sunday morning, Andrade called in Silvia and assigned him to join the dog officer for another look at several specific locations in the state forest. As soon as Silvia arrived in the Reservation, the officer told him about the burned car and the altar.

"What kind of a car?" Silvia asked quickly.

The officer hesitated—after a fire, it was sometimes hard to tell.

"Could it have been a Montego?"

"That kind of car," he agreed, apparently not certain of the exact make.

"What color?"

"Well, it was burned—"

"Dark green?"

His face lit up. "That was it—dark green."

Silvia felt the small rush that can come when things begin to look like they are falling into place. He tried not to sound excited. "Where is it?"

"It's been towed."

Silvia immediately called into the station on the car radio; Captain Andrade told him to contact the Freetown police, find where the car had been taken, and check it out.

Two other Fall River policemen and a Reservation officer overheard the conversation on the police band and joined them. All of them went to the location where the burned vehicle had been found, and after that they looked over the altarlike formation of stones. Two of the new arrivals had been with Tom Joaquim the day before, and when they showed Silvia what they had found, they kept looking back and forth between him and the pile of rocks, anxious for his reaction. It was obvious they were uncertain whether their discovery was merely an odd collection of glacial erratics or a deliberate construction of man with all the significance and mystery of a satanic Stonehenge. Silvia didn't know either, and he said nothing. But it was not hard for him to imagine this same place at night, with twenty or thirty people chanting "Hail, Satan" by candlelight and the body of a sacrificial victim lying across the upper slab—perhaps even the body of Karen Marsden.

The five policeman and the dog spread out through the surrounding woods for a thorough search.

One of the new arrivals from Fall River, the only other MCD detective in the group, found some shreds of red-and-white cloth. They appeared to be from a woman's blouse.

More officers arrived from the Freetown Police Department to comb the area, but nothing new was found. One of the Freetown police gave Silvia a copy of the Incident Report on the burned car; the vehicle was a 1973 Chevrolet Monte Carlo, and it was, indeed, dark green. The car came from Fall River and had been stolen on the morning of February 6, two days before Karen disappeared. The two Fall River detectives and the dog officer followed the Freetown police out of the park and over to John's Auto Body in East Freetown.

They searched the burned hulk inside and out as thoroughly as they were able, but found nothing that could be construed as evidence. Silvia and the other detective decided to open the trunk, which turned out to be unlocked. The lid rose easily, despite the strained, kinking sounds from the charred springs. They looked inside. There was some residue in the tire well, and both detectives bent over to examine it more closely.

"That could be bone," Silvia said.

The other detective agreed. "It just could."

Silvia called Andrade.

SEVENTEEN / ASHES

Andrade was on the scene within a few minutes of Silvia's call, along with a couple of Fall River identification officers. One ID man collected samples from inside the car, and the other began taking interior and exterior pictures of the burned vehicle, including close-ups of the residue in the trunk. All of the officers at the garage examined it as closely as they were able without touching it.

At almost the same time, an unmarked Massachusetts State Police car pulled noisily into the parking area. Silvia recognized the driver as a member of the CPAC unit assigned to the office of District Attorney Ron Pina. An assistant DA followed the trooper over to the charred automobile, along with Bristol County Medical Examiner Paul DeVillers. The ID man stopped taking pictures, and the other officers moved aside so the new arrivals could peer into the open trunk.

Two more cruisers arrived: Chief Norman Allison and one of his detectives from the Freetown police pulled up in the first; the other, from Fall River, was driven by Paul Carey.

All together, there were six Fall River policemen at the scene, five more from Freetown, and three law-enforcement officials from the state. They all hovered around Dr. DeVillers.

After a few minutes, DeVillers knelt down at the rear of the car and leaned into the trunk, studying the residue as closely as possible before it was moved. Then the ashes were carefully collected in plastic bags; the bags, in turn, were sealed with evidence tape and placed in the trunk of the unmarked state police car.

Andrade asked the medical examiner when he would have a report.

"Tomorrow," DeVillers promised.

*   *   *

Early Sunday afternoon, on orders from Captain Andrade, Tom Joaquim picked up Carol Fletcher and brought her back to the Fall River Police Station. Her hair was a mess, as though she had not done anything with it since getting out of the shower. She said she was glad to be there, that she wanted to do everything she could to help. But she was nervous, and her expression was anything but happy.

At about five o'clock, Joaquim showed her several reels of color slides. From the hundreds of police portraits on them, Carol selected two individuals, positively identifying one of them as the passenger in the dark-green car that had driven off with Karen Marsden. Carol was not as sure about the other; she said he looked like the man who had been at the wheel.

When Andrade returned to the police station, he made arrangements for an office to be set up where Carol could stay overnight. "We need your permission," he told her. "It's for your own protection."

She was slow to answer, but, when she did, she accepted Andrade's offer.

The next morning, Dr. DeVillers called Andrade and told him the residue taken from the trunk was not bone and was not of human or animal origin. Andrade then checked with his own department's ID officers; no other evidence had been found linking the burned car to the disappearance of Karen Marsden.

As the day wore on, Carol Fletcher expressed a growing dissatisfaction at sitting around the MCD offices and acted progressively more lethargic and bored. At about four o'clock, she told Paul Carey she wanted to leave.

When Carey dropped her off at a friend's apartment, he told her that if she needed help or had any more information about Karen, to call. But even as she agreed, he had a depressing sense that she was only saying what she thought was expected of her and that she had been doing the same thing since Joaquim brought her in the day before—pretending to participate, pretending to be helping, and all the while releasing wild geese, one by one.

EIGHTEEN / **GIRL TALK**

The local name for the northern wind that determines much of New England's wintertime weather is the Montreal Express, and for three days, despite crackling blue skies, it had sluiced bitter arctic temperatures across the whole northeastern stretch of the country between the Great Lakes and the Atlantic Ocean. By late afternoon of February 20, however, the Montreal Express was temporarily derailed. Just before sunset, a warmer weather pattern intruded from the southwest, pushing a front of pink-topped, gray-bellied rain clouds across the streaked-slate waters of Mount Hope Bay, and by nightfall, when the tropical squall had passed, the temperature had risen twenty-five degrees.

At about ten-thirty that night, Joaquim and Phelan were cruising downtown Fall River when they spotted Judy Jennings, a sixteen-year-old girl who occasionally hung out at Harbor Terrace. Joaquim pulled over to the curb, and Phelan rolled down his window.

Judy seemed to know what she was going to be asked. Yes, she had seen Karen Marsden a week and a half ago. She wasn't sure if it was on Friday, the night she disappeared, or the night before. Karen had been walking north, up South Main, at about seven o'clock. And yes, she was sure it was Karen. "I know Karen very well."

"Did you have a chance to talk with her?" Phelan asked.

"She said she was looking for a place she could hide. She was afraid someone was after her."

"Did you tell her a place?"

Judy shrugged. Her quilted coat was too big for her, and the whole garment rose and fell with her shoulders. "I told her I was on the run myself, that there wasn't anything I could do for her."

"Well, sure, if you're on the run too—" Joaquim said, doubting her story instantly but careful to suppress any irony in his tone. "I

134

don't suppose you remember which way she went?"

"North is all I know," Judy said, shrugging her coat again. "She just kept on walking."

"And she didn't say who was after her."

"Nope, that was it—what I said."

The two detectives thanked her and were about to drive on.

"I saw her last night, and she looked awful." It was said almost as an afterthought.

Joaquim put his foot on the brakes, and Phelan stopped rolling up the window. "You saw *who* last night?"

"Karen."

"Karen Marsden," Joaquim repeated.

"She asked me to light her cigarette, and she was really shaking, you know?"

"You're sure it was Karen Marsden?" Joaquim asked.

"Hey, I know Karen, okay? Her hair looked different—lighter than usual. But it was her."

"Where did you see her?" Phelan asked.

"South Main Street, walking in that direction," she said, this time pointing south.

"Hold on, Judy—" Joaquim said.

"What was she wearing?" Phelan asked.

She put her hand to her eyes, attempting to recall. "One of those fleece-lined jackets, like blue jeans—denim. And blue-jean pants. It was Karen, all right."

The detectives looked at her, then glanced at each other. Phelan asked Judy to let them know if she saw Karen again.

"Sure," she said. "I'll ask around. I'll try to find out where she's living."

As Joaquim pulled away from the sidewalk, he ran his fingers through his hair and shook his head. In the rearview mirror he watched for a moment as Judy continued down the street, her legs moving under the quilted coat like the clappers of a large muted bell. "Why the hell would she lie like that?"

Phelan shrugged as though to say, "Who knows?" and rolled the window the rest of the way up.

The next evening, when Paul Carey stopped in at Sonny Sparda's apartment, Robin Murphy was sitting in the front room. She stared at him without speaking for a moment, perhaps imitating the image of Satan on the wall behind her. Then she appeared to relax. He asked her how life was treating her down at the Groveland Motel, and they passed a few minutes in casual conversation. Carey mentioned, just as casually, that someone claimed to have seen Karen Marsden just a couple of nights before, on South Main Street.

Robin went back to the stare, saying nothing.

"A kid named Judy Jennings," Carey added, as an afterthought.

Robin looked away. She didn't seem interested.

Officially, Robin Murphy was a protected witness, under the aegis of the district attorney's office and the Massachusetts State Police, but she was free to come and go pretty much as she pleased. In conditions of extreme threat, witness protection can mean around-the-clock armed guards and even holding the subject in isolation in jail. In Robin's case, however, the objective was more modest. Andy Maltais was already in custody, so the purpose of the protection program was partly to stop trouble from finding her in some other form, such as Carl Drew, and to keep Robin from finding trouble on her own initiative.

Robin was not registered at the North Dartmouth motel in her own name, but she had frequent visitors from among her Fall River street friends. She was to stay in the vicinity, and it was expected that she would keep the police informed of her whereabouts, but otherwise she moved about at will. She visited Harbor Terrace. She visited her mother. She visited the Pier, Charlie's, the Hub.

Meanwhile, every detective in the Major Crimes Division was working overtime on the two murders or on the disappearance of Robin's friend, Karen Marsden. The earlier clear distinctions that had set apart the Nighters became blurred and eventually irrelevant as their hours increased. Silvia, Joaquim, and Carey found themselves sharing daytime assignments with the other MCD detectives, and frequently they all worked together at night as well.

Robin was kept up to the minute on developments in all three cases, not so much by the police as through her network of street connections. Many of the visitors who dropped in at the Groveland Motel came there just to report on what they had heard and often to recite their recent interviews with the Fall River police. And whenever Robin went downtown, gathering information seemed to be her principal agenda. She badgered Sonny, in particular, for every detail and nuance of the many visits by the police.

Clearly, Robin wanted to keep in touch with the excitement, even the titillation, of being at the center of the action. But this was also a way of trying to maintain some control of the situation. She knew

Sonny was not likely to be intimidated and that she could generally be relied on to tell the truth. Robin appeared to weigh Sonny's version of events against what she had been told by others, using her answers as bench marks in determining the loyalty of the other friends and the candor of the police.

On February 22, the second Friday since Karen's disappearance, Tom Joaquim and Paul Carey returned once more to Sonny's apartment at about 8:00 P.M. They found that Sonny already had four other guests: a neighbor named Carol Dias; a sometime baby-sitter for Sonny named Robert Bohun, age sixteen; another teenager, a girl whom they had also seen once or twice before; and, again, Robin Murphy.

Carey and Joaquim nodded at each of them, and Joaquim said, "Hey, Robin, taking a vacation from your vacation?"

She gave them a blank, unamused look, then turned back to finish whatever she had been saying to the young girl. In her role as a protected witness, Robin was not handling her new notoriety, as modest as it was, with much gravity. It was evident to both Carey and Joaquim that she was high. The two detectives found seats and soon were in conversation with the others.

For the first few minutes, the party continued in the living room. But the pitch of the conversation, especially from Robin, soon reached a level where Carey had difficulty hearing what Sonny was saying to him, so they moved to a bedroom just around the corner. Carey had barely sat down again when there was an outburst from the living room.

"What are you telling the cops?" Robin screamed. "You shut your fucking mouth or I'll break your jaw."

He quickly got up and went back into the living room. The young girl, who had obviously been the object of the explosion, looked pale and unsteady, but she continued sitting next to Tom Joaquim and trying her best to ignore Robin, who was glowering blackly across at them.

Joaquim, as anxious as Carey to preserve the fragile balance of their relationships in this place, stood up as though to say the incident was closed and walked to the other side of the room to talk with Dias and Bohun. Although Robin was now silent, she continued to fix the young girl with a poisonous, basilisk stare.

Carey watched from the doorway, then walked in and took the seat that Joaquim had just left. Robin, obviously still in a rage, stood up and stormed out of the room.

Carey asked the young girl what had happened, but she made a show of turning away. The detective asked her name.

She was trembling, and after considering for a moment she said, "Theresa Deschenes."

"What's the matter with Robin?" Carey asked, but the girl ignored the question.

He tapped her on the shoulder to get her attention. When she looked around, he said, "Where do you live, Terry?"

"Fall River," she said, turning away again.

Carey leaned forward, still friendly, and asked quietly, "Where in Fall River? What address?"

She held her head down and didn't answer.

Carey tapped her on the shoulder again, this time with his ballpoint pen. "What's your address, Terry?"

Reluctantly, she told him the street and number. Carey wrote it down.

"And how old are you?" he asked in the same gentle voice.

"Seventeen," she said.

He tried talking with her further, but got nowhere. She seemed intimidated by Robin's outburst and determined not to repeat whatever it was that created the offense—or the appearance of offense—even though Robin was no longer present. After a few minutes, Carey gave up and walked back down the hall to the bedroom.

There on the bed were Robin and Sonny. Robin had her arms around Sonny and was kissing her face, at first brushing her lips against her cheek, then nuzzling her more forcibly with wet, smacking sounds, groaning in a travesty of ardor. Carey stood in the doorway and waited.

Robin suddenly jumped from the bed and advanced threateningly toward him. "Why don't you get out of here? Can't you see I want to get a piece of ass?"

Behind Robin, still sitting on the edge of the bed, Sonny shook her head vigorously at the detective, silently imploring him to stay. Perhaps reading a reaction on Carey's face, Robin swung around sharply toward Sonny; Carey was unsure whether the move was fast enough to catch Sonny's signal. Then Robin swung angrily back at him with a wicked, wired grin. "Hey, if you guys are still looking for Karen, this time why don't you try Bessie's Beach?"

Carey didn't answer. He walked back into the living room and gestured to Tom Joaquim, and they left.

At eleven o'clock that night, Carey called Sonny's apartment. He apologized for leaving when they did, but he said he had been afraid things would just get worse if they had stayed. Sonny agreed.

"Did we miss anything?" Carey asked.

There was a pause on the other end of the line. "Yes. You did."

"Something you can tell me?"

Sonny took a deep breath. "I told Robin I thought she killed Karen."

"Uh-huh," Carey said. There was more silence, and he asked, "Any reaction?"

"Robin told me, 'I killed her, but it will take the cops two years to figure it out.'"

Carey waited in silence for her to continue.

Sonny said, "I asked her if I was next."

"And—"

"Robin just laughed and said, 'We'll see.'"

Carey let out his breath slowly, audibly, into the phone.

Sonny went on. "Robin told me, 'If I do kill you, Sonny, I'll use a gun. If I kill Carol, I'll beat her to death.'"

Carol Dias had started living with Sonny and helped take care of her daughter, Darnella. "What's that about? Why would Robin say something like that?"

Sonny said, "Robin loves me. She'd kill Carol if she thought she could move in with me."

Late the next afternoon, Carey went to see Theresa Deschenes. He found her alone at her sister's apartment. Without Robin Murphy around, Terry was much more relaxed, starting off the conversation by telling Carey she was five months pregnant.

"You know why I'm here," Carey said.

"Sure—on police business. About Karen Marsden."

"To start, let me ask you about your relationship with Robin Murphy."

Terry frowned, and then smiled. "I think a lot of her."

"Okay," Carey said. He wrote nothing down, but watched her encouragingly.

She leaned toward him. "Look, I'll tell you anything you want to know, but there are two 'if's.'"

Carey spread his hands in a gesture of invitation.

"If it will be kept secret," she said.

He nodded in agreement. "From her, you mean."

"And if you'll help Robin."

Carey hesitated. "That depends. Help her in what way?"

"Whatever way you can. Robin is a very sick person. She needs any help she can get—desperately."

"Sometimes people who need help the most are the ones who want it least." When Terry said nothing in response, he added, "I don't know what, and I can't make any promises, but I'll do what I can do."

Terry watched him, unsure whether she had the commitment she had asked for.

The detective said, "I want you to start by telling me what you talked about on the way back to Dartmouth last night, when you took Robin home."

Terry began to weep. At first her expression didn't change; the tears appeared in her eyes and rolled slowly down her cheeks, without the accompaniment of sobbing. "Do you understand how I really feel about Robin?" she asked softly.

Almost as gently, Carey said, "Yes, I do."

Terry clasped her hands in her lap and stared at them for several seconds before continuing. "In the car, on the way back to the motel, Robin told me she had killed Karen Marsden."

Carey leaned back in his chair. He realized that his own hands were clasped as well, gripping his pen and notebook. He unfolded them, smoothed the blank page, and said, "In so many words?"

She nodded.

"Do you know why?"

"She said Karen was always on her case, that she wouldn't leave her alone. Karen kept accusing Robin of cheating on her, and it got to the point where Robin couldn't take it anymore."

"Did she say where Karen is?"

Terry shook her head. "I didn't ask—I didn't want to know. I already knew too much, more than I could stand. I dropped her off at the Groveland Motel, and then I turned around and drove home."

For one hour after Detective Sergeant Paul Carey left Terry Deschenes, he sat in his parked car in the dark on Central Street, across from the Harbor Terrace apartments, hugging himself against the cold but resisting the temptation to turn on the motor for a moment's heat. At a few minutes after eight, another vehicle pulled to the curb on the opposite side of the street and Carey watched as Robin Murphy got out and walked up to number five.

Once he was sure that she had entered Sonny's apartment, Carey got out and walked across the street to the other car. He showed his badge and asked the occupants to identify themselves.

The driver, a nineteen-year-old boy, was from Fall River. So were his two passengers—another male, age twenty-three, and Judy Jennings.

Carey took a close look at the girl. "Judy Jennings. Did you tell two detectives the other night that you saw Karen Marsden at about seven P.M. on February nineteenth on South Main Street?"

Judy nodded nervously. "I think it was her," she said.

"How long have you known Karen, Judy?"

"About a month," she said.

"And how long have you known Robin Murphy?"

She hesitated and looked chagrined at the question. "Longer. A long time. I used to live in the apartment below her on Walnut."

"What are you doing with Robin tonight?"

Judy glanced anxiously toward the Harbor Terrace apartments, then quickly at her two companions before looking back at Carey. "My date picked me up, and Robin was in the car, that's all. I didn't expect to see her. I didn't know she was there until I got in."

Carey was watching her carefully and listening to her answers without showing any reaction of his own. "Did Robin ask you if you had seen Karen Marsden on South Main Street last Tuesday?"

"No."

"Didn't mention it, didn't ask you anything about it?"

Judy looked worried. "No," she said again.

Carey looked at her for a moment longer, then walked back across the street, got into his car, and headed toward the police station.

At 1:30 A.M. that same night, Tom Joaquim turned his unmarked car into a parking lot just a few blocks from the Groveland Motel. Robin had been interrogated for several hours that evening at the Fall River Police Station, and things had been set up so that Terry Deschenes would accompany Robin at the long session, then drive her back to her motel. Joaquim waited a few minutes, his engine idling to keep the heater warm, before Terry pulled into the lot and parked in the space to his left. She got out, walked around the two cars, and slid onto the front seat next to the detective.

"How'd it go?"

"I don't know—you'll have to tell me," Terry said in the dark, her voice shaking with anxiety and cold.

"Did you get a chance to ask about Karen again?"

Terry nodded. "She says Karen's dead. She kept saying it. I asked her how she knew, and she said, 'I'm not stupid.'"

"But nothing specific this time," Joaquim said.

"She was very nervous—I guess from being with you guys at the police station. When someone mentioned the Reservation, I noticed her eyes got big, and she started gritting her teeth."

Joaquim was not interested in Terry's interpretation of how Robin had reacted at the police station because he already knew everything that had taken place there. He tried to avoid sounding impatient. "What happened on the way home?"

"Well, that's the thing," Terry said. "Robin kept insisting that Karen was dead, but she never said it was because she had killed her. I brought it up two or three times, but she just wouldn't say it. I did what I could." She sounded hurt by the possibility that she had disappointed him.

"You're terrific," Joaquim said quickly. "You are. You're terrific."

Early the following evening, Judy Jennings called Carey at the police station. "You left a message." She sounded abrupt and nervous.

"We were just checking in with you, Judy." Carey's tone was easy and paternal. "We were interested in knowing if you have any more information that might be helpful to us in the Karen Marsden case."

"No," Judy said quickly.

"Nothing at all, Judy? Can't think of anything?"

"No," she replied again. Then she said, "It's bad enough I told you I thought I saw Karen."

"Bad enough?" Carey's voice was all innocent curiosity. "Why's that?"

"I don't want to get involved anymore. I just don't want to be involved at all."

The next check-in was at Harbor Terrace. Silvia and Carey drove to Sonny Sparda's apartment building on the corner. Upstairs, her door was opened by Robert Bohun, Darnella's sometime baby-sitter. He told them Sonny was out.

"Well, that's okay," Carey said. "You're good company. We'll talk with you instead."

As he usually did, Carey looked casually around to determine whether there were others in the apartment, then he and Silvia sat down in the living room. "Well, Robert, how's the world treating you?"

Bohun offered a slight, shy smile. "Not so bad."

Carey loosened his tie. "Did we just miss her? How long has she been gone?"

"A couple of hours—a few hours, I guess."

Carey nodded affably. "You spend a lot of time over here."

"Yeah," the boy said. He thought about it. "Not all that much. I baby-sit."

"When did you get here today?" he asked.

"Uh—well, this afternoon. Say, three o'clock?"

"Sure, what the hell, say three o'clock," Carey agreed. "So you were here when Robin Murphy was here."

Bohun nodded, then looked over at Silvia. Silvia smiled back.

"I've been wanting to ask you," Carey said, "what do you think happened to Karen Marsden?"

"I don't know," Bohun answered.

"Do you think something bad has happened to her?"

"Well—I don't know," he said again.

"What do Robin and Sonny think?" Carey asked.

Bohun hesitated, looking uncomfortable, and glanced again at Silvia, who was still smiling affably. He said, "Sonny asked Robin this afternoon."

"Asked her what?"

Bohun squirmed in the chair. "Where Karen is."

Carey said nothing. Both detectives were now watching him as though they expected him to tell the rest.

"That's it. Robin didn't answer," Bohun said defensively.

"She didn't say a thing?" Carey said, looking surprised.

"Not about Karen, no. Sonny asked her several times, and she just wouldn't answer."

"Hmm," Carey said. "Did Robin say anything about anything?"

"Yes, about Doreen Levesque," the boy answered.

"What about her?"

"That she was right there, up at the Diman High School, when Doreen Levesque was killed—and that she saw the whole thing."

Carey let Silvia off on Bedford Street, then went back to the station. At ten forty-five, he and Joaquim stopped in at the apartment of Richard Guinen and Robin Murphy's mother, Maureen, on Walnut Street.

By now they had spoken with Guinen and Robin's mother on several occasions. The detectives asked if, since their last conversation, either of them had heard anything new about Karen Marsden. They were told they had not.

"Can you think of anything you may recall that you didn't tell us before?" Carey asked. "Things that Robin may have told you?"

Guinen, looking uneasy, was the first to speak. "The night after Karen was reported missing, Robin told us that Andy was the one who killed the girl they found under the bleachers at the Diman last fall."

"Doreen Levesque," Carey said.

Mrs. Murphy nodded in agreement. "She said Andy picked up Doreen at Pigeon's Cafe and then killed her."

Mrs. Murphy looked at Guinen. Apparently, they both considered the story complete.

"What's the rest of it?" Carey asked. "That couldn't have been the end of the conversation."

"Well, yes, it was," Guinen said, looking slightly embarrassed. "She was extremely upset, and we didn't want to make things any worse by asking her questions."

"So you didn't ask her anything? Not then and not later?" Joaquim asked, trying to keep the astonishment out of his voice.

Mrs. Murphy's expression was anguished. "We sent Robin to a doctor once, to get her psychiatric help, but—"

"What doctor?" Carey interrupted.

She shook her head. "An associate of Doctor Sousa on Hanover

144

Street in Fall River—I don't remember his name. He gave Robin a personality test, and afterward he said he thought she lied on it."

"Why? What reason would she have for lying on a test?" Carey asked.

"Because Robin may have thought if she told the truth, the results would show she shouldn't be allowed to live in a normal environment."

Later that evening, Carey met with Phelan, Silvia, and Joaquim in the second-floor offices of the Major Crimes Division. The room was poorly lighted, colorless, and gritty, and the gathering had the look and feel of a council of war. The detectives were weary and on edge, worn down by sorties and excursions, anxious for open battle. Carey straddled a chair.

"What we've got so far on Karen Marsden amounts to little more than gossip. There isn't a shred of evidence that a crime has been committed," he said.

"She's dead," Silvia answered quietly, and the other detectives nodded.

"She's dead," Carey agreed.

He went on to explain that the division still had almost no funds budgeted for additional help and that there was a tremendous amount of overtime involved in what they were planning. It was not an appeal to greed; they were already making more money than they had ever earned before. What he was acknowledging was that the case had become an obsession, not just for Silvia and Joaquim but for them all. He was also aware of the personal price they were paying at home.

There was no doubt in any of their minds that the two known murders and the disappearance were tied together, and that collectively they were about to become the biggest case they were likely to see in their police careers. It had all the elements that appealed to the media—sex, violent slaughter, Satanism, mystery. And this handful of detectives had it within their grasp to unravel the knot. They knew the city. They had spent months cultivating the players. If they gave it everything they had from this moment on, the case could produce the biggest payoff of their lives. Recognition. Gratitude. Even national publicity. In a city that had been on a century-long slide to depression and decay, it was the kind of satisfaction that street cops seldom even dream about, and nothing would be able to take it away—not the fucking state police, not the goddamned city council, not the showboat DA.

When Carey finished talking, it was as though he had drawn the sword from the stone. Despite Silvia's fatigue, and despite his long experience with bureaucracy both within the department and in competition with CPAC, he could feel the blood of resolution, of hope, running through his veins. And he could see the same reaction in the others.

They all knew that the key to all three cases was Robin Murphy. From that night on, for as long as she was in state police custody at the Groveland Motel, an airtight program of surveillance by the Major Crimes Division of the Fall River police would keep track of her around the clock.

TWENTY /DEEPER

After supper one night, Paul Carey and Joe Phelan drove the fifteen minutes from Fall River to New Bedford and knocked at Cookie Powers's door. They were following up on their conversation with Nancy Marsden, who said that some weeks earlier Carl Drew had placed a contract on Cookie's and Karen's lives.

Cookie told them she had not seen Karen for a month and maybe longer. "I remember the last time I saw her. We were running scared."

"What about Drew?" Phelan asked. "When did you last see him?"

"Around Christmas," she said. "I was working the streets for him, then I left. That's why I was frightened. Carl has this thing, like they say about the Mafia—nobody leaves the mob. He'll kill anybody who screws him, anyone he thinks isn't, you know, loyal."

Phelan asked Cookie if she could recall either from her own experience or from any conversations with Karen instances of Drew threatening people or hurting them.

"Karen told me about this group; Carl runs it, or at least he's one of the people in charge. They meet in the Reservation and have rituals and kill people, offering their souls to the Devil. Karen told me, once they took a baseball bat and stuck it up—you know—up this guy's ass. She said there's a sacrifice tree in the reservation, where they hang their victim and pour blood on him before he dies."

"Where's the tree?" Carey asked.

"I don't know. She just told me about it." Cookie thought a moment. "I heard Carl say once—back in November—that he was going to take someone for a long ride."

"Who?" Phelan asked.

Again, she said, "I don't know. He didn't say any more than that. These are just things I remember."

Phelan asked Cookie if she had known Doreen Levesque.

"Yeah, as 'the girl from New Bedford.' She was working for Carl, and Carl was mad at her because she was keeping some money. He said, 'Satan will take his toll'—things like that."

"Doesn't he talk that way all the time?" Phelan asked.

"Just when he's shooting up," she said.

"What else did Karen say about him?"

She thought for a moment. "You know, Karen didn't tell me too much about Carl—she didn't get too specific—because she was afraid for me. This is dangerous stuff to know."

"Try to think of things you learned directly from Carl," Carey said. "Can you think of anything?"

Cookie pondered for a moment. "Well, I know he has a house in Florida. It's not his—I mean, he rents it. Wait a minute." She got up from her chair and left the living room, returning a moment later from the rear of the apartment with some papers. "For a little while, he lived with a guy on Seabury Street, in Fall River. In December, Carl made some calls to Florida, and I have one of the phone bills."

Phelan scanned the sheets and wrote down two numbers in area code 305. He saw telephone calls listed to New Bedford and Warwick, Rhode Island, and he wrote them down as well.

Cookie added, "Whenever Carl wanted, this guy let him use his place for tricks."

"What about the group?" Carey asked. Based on Carey's own reports as well as those of Silvia and Joaquim, along with what had been found in the Reservation, the police and the newspapers had come to regard the satanic activity around Fall River as an organized cult. "Did Karen tell you more about them?"

"She said they kill every thirty days or so—on the full moon. She said it's always a ritual, that they offer up the victim as a sacrifice to Satan." She stopped and slowly shook her head. "God, just listen to me."

Back in Fall River later that evening, Carey and Phelan picked up Alan Silvia at the police station and all three detectives drove over to Seabury Street. It was hardly worth the trip. The man Cookie had named told them almost nothing; he said he really didn't know Carl Drew very well at all.

Perhaps that was the truth. At the very least it was prudent. But if friendship with Carl Drew was now a social liability when dealing with the police, the rumors and suspicions that attached to his name were visible assets in the marketplace of Bedford Street. Far from driving him underground, Carl Drew's notoriety preceded him like an advertising campaign. He was still in the bars at night, still cool, still very much in business, reportedly with more women working for him now than before. It was almost certain that he sensed the growing danger, but he seemed to thrive on it.

In that respect, and perhaps no other, Carl Drew was very much like Andy Maltais. He seemed to draw a special power, a kind of stardom, that insulated him from the impending doom which was its source.

On the evening of February 29, Leap Year Day, Silvia, Joaquim, and Carey visited the home of Donald and Elvira Nolin, a third-floor apartment on Forest Street in Fall River. Since the previous May, the Nolins had been the foster parents to Karen Marsden's three-year-old son, JJ, under appointment by the court. The three detectives were there because they knew that Karen had stopped in at the Nolin apartment, as she often did, on the night she disappeared. They also knew she had come with Robin Murphy, also as usual.

The Nolins offered their visitors seats in the living room. Silvia began by asking what time Karen and Robin had arrived for that last visit.

Mrs. Nolin said, "Just about now, six-thirty."

He and Joaquim both had the same thought: if it was three weeks ago to the hour, that meant Karen must have joined up with Robin shortly after the two detectives left her at the door of the rectory of St. Mary's Cathedral. Silvia wondered if she had been able to talk with the priest, whether it was long enough to get whatever she had been looking for.

He asked, "Can either of you recall anything about that evening that might help us?"

Mrs. Nolin looked to her husband for affirmation, then back at Silvia. "Well, we both thought they acted peculiar."

"They were both a little high," Mr. Nolin said. "They were carrying beer bottles with them when they walked in, and they'd been drinking."

"Is that what you meant by peculiar?" Carey asked Mrs. Nolin.

"Maybe that was part of it," she said. "You know, Karen and Robin were inseparable, but this time Robin was acting different. I remember at one point I was in the kitchen while Karen was playing with JJ in the living room, and Robin came out and started saying—well—things that struck me as strange. At least, they were strange at the time."

Carey nodded, and Silvia smiled encouragingly.

"She began by saying she wanted to speak with me privately,

which was not something she had ever done before, and I wasn't sure what to make of it—I mean, you can say something about a person you don't want them to hear, and it doesn't have to be anything bad about them. But then she said, 'Karen is the way she is, and she's going to stay that way'—and I wasn't so sure."

"Meaning, Karen is unstable?" Silvia asked.

"That's the meaning I took from it, yes."

"That sounds like what she intended," Silvia agreed.

"Then Robin told me that if anything happened to Karen, we should keep the baby or give him back to the state."

Silvia wrote in his notebook as she spoke, stopping now and then to look up at her with more encouragement.

"I told Robin that we love the baby and have no intention of giving him back to the state."

"Did she say anything else?" Carey asked.

"When I told her that, she said, 'Good.'"

Mr. Nolin was sitting next to his wife, and he said, "Before they came here, they told us they had been at Robin's brother's house over on Park Street."

"Did you notice this too, Mr. Nolin—that Robin was acting peculiar?" Joaquim asked.

"A little—but I didn't see that much of Robin," he said. "The one I thought was being odd that night was Karen."

"How so?" Joaquim asked.

He struggled for the words to describe the impression. "She said things that sounded like we shouldn't expect to see her again. I thought that at the time—she's talking as though she's not coming back. One thing in particular—at one point, Jay called me Daddy, and Karen said to him, 'Do you love that daddy? Is that the daddy you want?' And Jay must have said yes—he did say yes—and Karen said, 'Well, that's the daddy you'll have; I want whatever you want.'"

Mrs. Nolin listened attentively, nodding as her husband spoke. "I think that's so sad," she said. "What do you think has happened to her? Do you have any ideas? Any leads?"

Carey said, "We know just about as much as you do. But we're trying hard to find out."

"There's one thing else that occurs to me that Karen said to us once," Mrs. Nolin said, tentatively. "It was on New Year's Day. We were sitting right here. She said, 'You'd both be surprised what's going on in Fall River.' She told us there was an occult gang, just like the one in California with Charles Manson. We'd seen on television about the murder of that girl last fall, but we said we hadn't heard about any gang. She said, 'They want me. That's why I'll be the next one to die.'"

Carey asked if she gave any details or mentioned any names, and they looked at each other and shook their heads. Mrs. Nolin said, "That was the only time she mentioned anything like that. It was hard to tell whether it was something to take seriously—but when she didn't say anything else about it, well—"

Silvia asked what else they could recall about Friday night three weeks ago.

Mrs. Nolin nodded again, sorrowfully. "In a way, the most disturbing thing of all that night was what Robin said to Karen as they were leaving the house: she told her she wanted nothing to do with her, that Karen was to go her way and Robin was going hers. Robin had to meet someone at eight-thirty, and Karen wasn't allowed along."

Silvia asked, "Do you remember the exact words? Or as close as you can get?"

Mrs. Nolin looked at a spot on the far wall, thinking. "'I gotta meet him,' I mean, 'I gotta meet somebody—at eight-thirty—out of town.' This was about eight o'clock, when she said it the first time. 'Let's go, let's go!'"

"'Him' or 'somebody'?" Silvia asked.

"That's just it, I'm not sure," Mrs. Nolin answered. "It's probably safer to say she said, 'somebody.'"

"Did Karen answer her?" Carey asked.

"Just to ask if she could go. And Robin said no. We both found it strange that Robin was trying to avoid Karen and seemed so mean about it. They were always together."

Mr. Nolin said, "Karen did say something else just before they left—which was about eight-fifteen. She told Jay she'd see him at Grandma's the next day—on Saturday. That's Karen's grandmother. Jay repeated what she had said, and Karen answered, 'I promise.' The next day I was sure something was wrong because Karen would never break a promise to Jay without a good reason and never without calling."

"So then they left," Silvia said, looking at both Nolins speculatively before closing his book.

Mr. Nolin said, "I asked if I could give them a ride where they were headed; I knew Robin was afraid she'd be late to wherever she was supposed to be at eight-thirty. But they said no."

The three detectives thanked them. There was handshaking all around. They left the Nolins' apartment at eight-fifteen—the same time Robin and Karen had left there three weeks before.

As Silvia walked down the stairs, he was still not able to shake off thoughts of his last view of Karen. Although they had left her on the sidewalk outside the vestry, his thoughts slipped into the dark interior of the church itself. He remembered from his own experience what it was like there in the dusk of winter, the vaulting windows opaque with gloom, the shadows blurring into shapeless darkness, the curl of smoke and the flickering light of the offertory candles, the empty pews wavering between visibility and the void. He hoped that the rectory held more light and warmth. He hoped she had found what she had been seeking.

The next day, Robin Murphy left her room at the Groveland Motel. Paul Fitzgerald was right behind her. They got into an unmarked vehicle of the Bristol County CPAC unit, and Fitzgerald turned the car briskly out onto the highway. Watching from across the street, Alan Silvia slapped the steering wheel of his own car in frustration. He had seen state police detectives move their witness before, usually for an appointment in court or for questioning in the DA's office in New Bedford. But this time Robin was carrying a suitcase.

Eventually, the district attorney's office got around to advising the Fall River Major Crimes Division that witness Robin Murphy had been relocated for her own protection, but they offered no clues about where she had been taken—except that it was outside the state.

The MCD surveillance of the Groveland Motel came to an end, but their investigation only intensified. Robin was still the key to the biggest case of their lives, and if the opposing team had stolen a temporary advantage, that was just in the nature of the game. The Fall River detectives were more determined than ever to stay on her trail.

TWENTY-ONE /**SEASONS OF THE HEART**

To some extent, Paul Fitzgerald had a choice of where he worked. The downtown CPAC facility was part of the district attorney's office in a modern, medium-rise building in the center of New Bedford. It was near two courthouses where Fitzgerald sometimes had to testify and in the closest possible proximity to the teams of prosecutors whom CPAC served. He spent a lot of time downtown because he had to, but he preferred the other location, on the second floor of the ramshackle wooden State Police Barracks in North Dartmouth. That was where Fitzgerald had worked before CPAC was created, and it felt more like home.

These days, he found himself downtown more often than he liked. The DA's office was putting together its case in the murder of Barbara Raposa. Fitzgerald and Lowney were running the investigation, which meant they were also in charge of the key witness for the prosecution. It was partly on Fitzgerald's advice that Pina had decided to send Robin Murphy into hiding, not so much to protect her against whatever uncertain fate may have befallen her friend Karen Marsden, but to anchor a loose cannon at a relatively safe distance from the scene of action. She was important to the case against Andy Maltais, but she was a volatile, risk-prone seventeen-year-old and they wanted to keep her out of trouble. Robin had a friend in Texas, so that was where they sent her.

She kept in regular weekly contact with Fitzgerald by telephone. The conversations were dutiful, dull, and usually short; one of the consequences of being that far from all the excitement was that she had very little to report. Robin also knew that there was no point at all in pumping Fitzgerald for information about what was going on back in Fall River. It was clear from the outset that the facts would flow in only one direction, and the state trooper offered no link at all to the life she had left behind. In the first days of her exile, Robin hungered for information more than ever, and she kept in contact with Sonny Sparda. But the length and frequency of those calls soon declined as Robin apparently settled into new routines.

March came and went, and winter went with it. In the park at Battleship Cove, buds began to reappear on the trees and the grass turned green again. There were fewer harbingers of the season just up the hill on the streets surrounding Harbor Terrace, but here and there a leggy, anemic forsythia struggled into flower and, in the odd window box, bulbs poked hopefully upward toward the warmer sunlight and the prospect of longer days.

Near the end of the month, Paul Fitzgerald told Robin she was coming home for a few days. Andy Maltais had gotten out of jail on $7,500 cash bail three weeks earlier. Maltais' lawyer, Robert Macy, wanted to ask her some questions. Fitzgerald told Robin the interview was set for the afternoon of April 9, but he agreed to leave some time on either side of that date so she could prepare herself and in case Macy felt one meeting was not enough.

Fitzgerald could expect Robin to have a mixed reaction to the news. She had met Macy before, at a hearing in the same case, and she hadn't liked him. Robin did not do well with adversarial situations, and she appeared to feel threatened by the fact that Macy was defending Andy. It was obvious that a big part of that defense would be to impugn Robin as a witness. On the other hand, the trip would bring Robin back to the area where she had been raised and where she had family and friends.

Fitzgerald met Robin at Logan Airport in East Boston on the afternoon of April 4 and drove her down to Dartmouth. This would not be like her previous term in protective custody, he told her. This time there would be no excursions to Harbor Terrace or downtown Fall River; she was under tight guard, and either Fitzgerald or Dan Lowney would be with her around the clock.

The interview began at three-forty in the afternoon, in the conference room of the district attorney's office in New Bedford. In addition to Robin and Macy, the meeting was attended by members of the DA's prosecution team, a stenographer, Paul Fitzgerald and other CPAC detectives.

Macy wasted little time with amenities: he established that Robin had waited until several days after Andy had been picked up for the murder, and then he asked her what had motivated her to go to the police at that time.

"The girl I was living with," Robin answered. "Sonny."

"Last name?"

"Sparda."

"She's a pretty good friend of yours, isn't she?" When Robin agreed, he asked, "Are you two lovers?"

"Yep."

He asked her if she had seen Sonny since her return to Massachusetts, and Robin said she had seen her on Sunday. She wouldn't say where the meeting had taken place or where she was staying, just that it was in Massachusetts.

"Okay," Macy said, changing course. "So, you know Karen Marsden?"

Robin said she did, but that she had not seen or heard from Karen since that night when she had failed to keep their date, two months before. "I didn't go back to meet her that day—I went back the next morning to see if she had been there."

Macy asked, when she talked to the police about Andy, whether she had gone to the state police or the Fall River police. She said Sonny had called the Fall River police, and they came down to the apartment. Macy nodded and asked, "Prior to that time, how were you making a living?"

"How was I making a living?"

"Yes."

"I was—Prostitution," Robin said.

"Was Karen Marsden doing the same thing?"

"Yes, she was."

"Barbara Raposa doing the same thing?"

"I have no idea."

"You knew her?"

"Yes, I did."

"Did you ever see her working the streets?"

"No."

"You know Karen was?"

"No."

For the moment, Macy chose to ignore the contradiction. He asked if Robin knew Dave Cowen. She said she did. Robin had told the police two months ago that it was because Barbara Raposa was seeing "that Dave Cowen" that Andy had said he was going to kill her. Robin told Macy that Cowen would take her and Karen dancing in Providence when the two girls were low on money, but that they were just friends. She had not seen him since she had gone to the police.

After establishing the relationship between Cowen and Raposa, Macy led her up to the evening of Raposa's murder. Once Barbara and Andy had gotten out of the parked car, she said, she had climbed into the front seat. Andy and Barbara were lying together on the ground behind and to the right of the car.

"Okay, so whatever you saw, you saw over your right shoulder?"

"Right," she agreed. "I would have to turn around to look at them, through the corner of my eye."

"About how far were they from you?"

"I'm not good at lengths. Little bit further than from here to the wall. I don't know."

Macy surveyed the distance to the end of the room. "Okay, maybe fifteen feet?"

"I don't know," Robin said impatiently, appearing to brush away the troublesome question with a wave of her hand. "I don't know length. I went to school, but I don't know, you know?"

There was a brief exchange between Macy and Fitzgerald to establish the distance she had indicated in the conference room. The lawyer then led Robin through her own activities within the car while the murder was taking place some fifteen feet away. "You looked from time to time, right?"

"Yeah."

"While you were listening to the radio?"

She shrugged. "I was in the car," she said, implying a limit to the number of things one can do alone in a parked automobile.

They talked some more about the landscape. Macy asked Robin how much she had had to drink that night. She said she didn't count, but she had been drinking for several hours. Macy was patient and methodical throughout. When he finished the review of her alcoholic intake, he leaned back in his chair.

"Now, as I understand what you said—let's see. If this happened in November, and you went to the police a week and a half later, as you said, after Andy was picked up, you waited quite a while to tell anybody about this."

"Yep," Robin said, appearing to imitate the lawyer's reasonableness and affability. "Andy didn't have no plan on telling anybody"— she took a deep breath—"except when Robin gets drunk, Robin has a big mouth. And she sat there and started crying, and nobody could figure out why, and—"

Macy raised his index finger, signaling her to stop for a clarification among the rush of words. "Robin, meaning you?"

"Yeah. I told the person why I was crying—she asked me why. And she told the cops."

"This person being Sonny?"

"Yeah," she said.

They covered what had happened next, following her meeting with the Fall River police. Macy asked if Carey and Silvia had next placed her in protective custody. "No, they let me stay where I was."

"Okay," Macy said, "but at that time, nobody knew Karen Marsden had been missing?"

Robin agreed.

Macy asked her who found out Karen was gone. She told him that they had made a plan to meet at the apartment of Robin's sister-in-law in Fall River later that evening and that Karen never showed up. "I went there to meet her, and she hadn't been there." Macy looked at her sharply; this contradicted what she had told the police about her movements two months before. Catching the look, Robin suddenly interrupted herself to backpedal out of what she realized she had just said. "Neither was I there, but neither was she."

Macy let it pass. He asked her what she had done next.

"I called up the grandmother to see if she had slept home last night; she said no. I called up my mother's to see if she had called, and nothing."

"Well, was it unusual for Karen not to have been in any of these places?"

"Sure was. She should have been with me."

Macy seemed puzzled. "Should have been with you—"

Robin rushed on. "She went to the corner—"

The lawyer repeated the stopping gesture with his hand. "What corner?"

"Bedford."

"There are lots of corners on Bedford."

Robin made the same gesture in return, impatiently. "The Hub pool hall, same difference—the whole area on Bedford Street."

Apparently by referring to Bedford Street so unspecifically, she meant the city's entire combat zone. In fact, the Hub was not on Bedford Street at all, but a block to the south, on Pleasant.

"So," Macy continued, "you decided she was missing?"

"Yep. We had no fights or nothing like that; she just got up and"— she opened her hand to show it was empty, like a magician—"no more."

Macy watched her without responding.

"She didn't take no clothes from her grandmother's. I had my mother talking to the grandmother. Maybe her grandmother just didn't want me to know anything—but that wasn't the case."

Fitzgerald knew from the Fall River police reports about Robin's conversation with Karen's grandmother, but this was the first time he had heard about Robin getting her mother to call as well. It was not something Karen's grandmother had remembered to tell the police.

Macy was also hearing it for the first time, but he listened without comment before he asked, "Why would you and Karen have a fight?"

Robin replied vehemently, "We didn't have a fight, that's what I'm telling you." She glanced around the table. It was a look that asked for allies, enlisting others to share her impatience at Macy's misinterpretation of what she had said.

"Were you that close?" the lawyer went on, unperturbed.

"Lovers, if you want to put it that way."

"I don't want to put it that way. I just want to know."

Macy asked Robin if Karen might have just walked out on everyone.

"Nope. I talked to Carol Fletcher, and Carol Fletcher said the last time she seen her that night was getting into the green Duster."

Fitzgerald, watching from the other side of the conference table, knew that Carol Fletcher had modified the story of the phantom car. Apparently, no one had told Robin.

Macy, seeming not to have heard either version, asked, "With whom?"

"A trick," Robin said.

"It wasn't anybody you knew?"

"Somebody that I knew," Robin said, then reconsidered. "But I don't know, I know him from seeing him going around the block."

"What did you know him by?"

Robin smiled thinly. "A cheap greenhorn."

"Why is he cheap?"

"He comes, like he just wants lays for fifteen dollars."

There were some laughs from the other end of the table. Macy smiled and asked, "What's the going rate?"

"To be honest with you—" Robin started, but the laughter interrupted her answer, and Macy repeated the question.

This time, Robin also repeated the question. "What's the going rate?"

Macy nodded.

"That's personal."

Still smiling, Macy suggested, "Sliding scale?"

"Yeah," Robin said, picking up the spirit of the exchange and trying to surpass it. "You got the girls from Providence, fifteen dollars. This girl from Fall River don't."

It was the third time Robin had spoken of herself in the third person. Macy asked her again, "This girl meaning you?"

"Me, and Karen too." She seemed impatient with his continuous need to clarify.

Macy asked her the going rate for sex with a girl from Fall River. Robin dodged the question for a time, then told him thirty dollars.

"Girls from Fall River are twice as good?" he asked, smiling.

"Got to be," she said, and smiled back.

When Macy asked if that was the price Barbara Raposa got, Robin was too smart to fall into the trap. "I don't know if she worked. I don't know."

For the next couple of minutes, Macy led Robin on a discussion of the Doreen Levesque killing and the disappearance of Karen Marsden. Robin said she thought Karen had also been murdered, a victim of the battle for control among Fall River pimps.

Speaking to the possibility that Karen was indeed dead, Macy said, "It's pretty clear that Andy didn't have anything to do with that. He was in the can at the time." When Robin agreed, he went on, "Now, you're afraid that the same thing that happened to Karen might happen to you?"

"Oh, yes," Robin said, "very easily."

"Those pimps in Fall River—"

But Robin saw the trap there as well, and again she evaded it. "The pimps in Fall River—and Andy."

Macy raised his eyebrows. "You are afraid of Andy?"

"Yessir."

Macy asked her why.

She thrust herself forward; it was the opportunity she had been waiting for. "I have known him for seven years," she said vehemently, "and any man that can pick up an eleven-year-old girl hitchhiking and want to fool around with an eleven-year-old girl has got to be a little sick." She hesitated, then sat back and crossed her arms, slightly subdued. "But I didn't think that at the time."

The lawyer tapped a pencil, bouncing the eraser end softly against the palm of his hand. "What did you think?"

"He told me that if I told anybody, I was the one that was going to get into trouble. He told me if I told my mother, that my mother was going to give me a beating and not think anything about this Andy guy—that it was going to be all my fault."

Macy looked sympathetic, but it was the expression of someone who was also trying to be reasonable and patient. "But you're still afraid of him. That's when you were a child."

"I'm afraid of him now because he's out."

Macy regarded her for a moment, taking in what she had said, the same expression on his face. He asked her quietly how old she was.

"Seventeen. I'll be eighteen in October."

"Aside from what he did when you were eleven, what makes you think he is guilty now?"

"Now?" she asked, her voice rising in astonishment. "He is! Really now, are you serious? I'm—if—" She began tripping over her words, her voice shaking with outrage. "He has an ejaculator and dildo in the trunk of his car—carries around pills to give to these girls and get them high and don't know what the hell they're doing—gives six-year-olds, gives them a pill—And he's not sick? He's normal? I mean, really, you know, is he normal?"

The more shrill Robin's voice became, the smoother and calmer Macy's sounded by comparison. "So that's why you think he's guilty—because of all these things?"

She slapped her hand on her forehead, her eyes wide. "He called me up one morning and said he was jerking off in the bathroom. 'Andy, what do I know, what do I care?' I told him." She leaned toward Macy, studying him. "Do you think Andy's guilty? You're Andy's lawyer—you don't think he's sick? You think he's really, really normal?"

Macy stopped playing with the pencil and laid it on the table. "Today, you don't have a chance to ask me questions; today, I ask you. Thus far—"

Robin was not about to be put off. "You want to talk about his psychological behavior, right? What do you think of riding around, jerking yourself off, as he does, with all kinds of people in the car?"

Macy asked, "Have you been with him when he does?"

"Sonny has, and a couple of other people," she said. "Carol Dias, David Roche. Sonny would never go in his car again—"

"You went in his car again," Macy reminded her.

"Yeah, because there was nothing that bothered me about him at that time. But I'd never go in the car with him alone—always some-one in that car with me—Carol Dias, Sonny, David."

"After November seventh, didn't you go with him? You'd call

him to give you a ride. He was pretty good about that."

Robin smiled with contempt. "He gave me a ride anywhere. But he'd expect a piece of ass afterwards—until he saw all the people I came down the stairs with, and brung into the car. 'Oh, shit,' you know? They're already there; that's his problem, not mine. Come down and give me a ride, and down come all these people."

There was some laughter around the table. Macy smiled. "And surprise, surprise, right? Poor Andy has to give you a ride."

Robin sat back and appeared to savor the reaction to her story. "Poor Andy ain't so poor."

"No?" Macy asked. "How poor is he? Does he have a lot of money?"

"I don't know. But there's this little girlfriend—"

Macy nodded, as though in encouragement. "How many little girl-friends does he have?"

"Here we go again. He's got—" Then she dropped it, veering back to the topic she had chosen before he interrupted. "It's approximately ten years now that she lives on the same street as him. I don't know if he still goes with her, if he's still seeing Kathy—she was thirteen."

Macy obviously had heard this story before, probably from Maltais. "She's older than that now."

Robin shrugged. "She's my age." She darted to the next thought, still a terrier but after a different rat. "He had Barbara, who I pawned off on him. Barbara started hanging around with Andy. Fine, I'm get-ting rid of him, he had Barbara. 'Andy, buy me a bag of grass.' And, if I wanted a six-pack of beer, 'Andy, give me a six-pack of beer.'"

"How old were you when this was going on?"

"No older than thirteen and a half. At the age of thirteen, I started going with somebody else. I started getting beatings from Andy for being out with other guys. He used to walk up and bang on the car window, saying I better get out of the car before the guy I was with got into trou-ble because I was a minor. I'd get out and he'd beat the shit out of me."

"What about you?" Macy asked. "You'd still call him back, and he'd give you beer, rides, and everything."

She laughed derisively. "I'm the biggest sucker in the world."

They spoke some more about Barbara Raposa and how Andy would supply drugs to Barbara and other people who wanted them. Then Robin mentioned the times that Andy had gotten her pregnant.

"How often was that?" Macy asked.

She glanced around the table to see the effect it was having on the others. "Approximately every other month."

"You got pregnant every other month by him?" The lawyer made no attempt to hide his amazement.

"Yeah. If you were going to bed with a guy every day, I think you'd get pregnant—" More laughter. "Not you, in particular, but any girl goes to bed with a guy constantly gets pregnant. He'd give me those white pills."

Macy asked what the white pills would do.

"They would jar up your womb and make you have your period—after I'd bounce off the bed a few times, sit on the end of the bed and fall off."

"So, all the times he made you pregnant, you never did have a baby? All these times, did the doctor tell you that you were pregnant?"

"No," she said.

Macy's face was blank. She looked back at him with an equally blank stare.

He turned to his notes and read for a moment, then looked up at Robin again. "On November seventh, you had a physical fight with Barbara, didn't you?"

"Yeah, because she hit me first. Punched me in the nose."

"And you punched her back?"

"Pulled in the back seat. Pulled her from the front seat to the back."

"You and she were fighting in the back seat. Who won?"

"Who won? Nobody. Andy broke it up. She was on top of me, though I don't like to admit that. I never lost a fight, but I was drunk—so that's a good excuse, most definitely."

"Could you beat her up if you weren't drunk?"

"Her head would go through the windshield."

Macy smiled and glanced at the district attorney, then back at Robin. "How would you have done that?"

"Barbara was only bigger this way than me," she said, cupping her hands like a bodybuilder and thrusting out her chest. "She wasn't bigger no other way."

For the record, Macy said, "You mean her chest—breasts—were bigger than yours?"

"That's about it. She was the same height, approximately—she wasn't any bigger than me."

"So you think, all things being equal, that you could have beaten her up?"

Robin cocked her head. "Yeah. Why not?"

"I'm asking you," Macy said, smiling. "I don't know any tough girls."

"Neither do I."

"You're tough. You want to put her head through the window."

Robin looked uneasy, as though she may have talked herself into a bad position. "She had no right to punch me in the face. That wasn't right at all."

They talked for the next several minutes about how Robin had come to know Paul Fitzgerald, through Andy's introduction after Thanksgiving. "Andy tricked us. He talked me and Karen into going with him to the North Dartmouth barracks because he said he wanted our help in finding Barbara. But the real reason was he told Paul Fitzgerald he had two girls who knew something about the murder of Doreen Levesque."

If she and Karen had been tricked, Macy asked, why did they continue to go back to see Fitzgerald on subsequent occasions?

"It was a form of self-defense. Someone told me Carl Drew and Carl Davis were going to kill us, and I figured it was a good idea to stay close to the police." The name of Carl Davis had come up before: he was a pimp from Providence who sometimes worked the Fall River area. "The day after Christmas, Drew and Davis were supposed to have people come down and rip the telephone wires out of the house and kill everyone in the house."

Macy's expression appeared to be struggling against an open show of skepticism. The story was right out of *Helter Skelter*. Besides, Robin obviously was speaking for effect, whether what she said was true or not. "Where did you hear that," he asked. "On the streets?"

"Somebody passed it along to me. Somebody called me up and said, 'Robin, get out of the house; they're coming over in a while.'"

The lawyer looked down the table at Paul Fitzgerald. "You've talked to Trooper Fitzgerald quite a bit? Have a lot of confidence in him?"

"I've got to," she agreed. "I have nobody else to trust."

"You trust Sonny, don't you?"

"Uh-uh. No, because she talks to Paul Carey. And he talks to the Fall River *Herald News*."

"About what?"

"About the whole situation. There was a lot of stuff in there that nobody else knew except him and his sidekick, Alan."

He asked her what the newspaper stories had said. She said they were about the two murders, about Satanism, about Karen's disappearance—and that they were all related.

"What did you say to the state police to persuade them to take you into protective custody?" Macy asked.

"I didn't persuade them, sir," she said angrily. "I explained what was going on, and I think that's enough said."

"About people ripping out telephone wires?"

"About people into Satan."

Macy considered this. "The same people whose names you have mentioned?" She nodded, and he added, "Not Andy?"

"Andy just started his 'Praise the Lord' bit a few months ago. I mean, before that, he used to go down and rap with Karen's grandmother, telling her that I was possessed by the Devil."

Macy looked at her in mock seriousness. "But you're not?"

"Yeah, I am, can't you tell? I can't wait, right?"

Macy smiled. "You can't wait for what?"

"To be possessed by the Devil." Her mood shifted, vacillating. She wanted to mock the question in order to ridicule Macy, but at the same time she could not resist the temptation to go for another big effect. "I was letting it bother me Christmas night—Christmas Eve—and I ended up getting rushed to the hospital. I had marks on my neck that weren't from my hand and nobody else's hand. But they told me at the hospital I had an asthma attack."

Macy nodded patiently, with polite interest. "What do you think was bothering you Christmas?"

"Somebody put a cross on my head, and it burned," she answered quickly. It was another set piece—the story of the crucifix burning the Devil—and she had obviously told it before. She was breathless and her expression was defiant, the look of someone who is going for the bomb but is uncertain what effect it will have on an adult audience. "Andy was there that night. David Cowen took me to the hospital."

Macy nodded, carefully ignoring the irony of his client being offered as a witness to his accuser's satanic possession. He returned to the question of which threat it was—Carl Drew, Carl Davis, Satanism, or Andy Maltais—that had brought Robin to accept protective custody. "Let me ask you a different way. There's no connection between them, is there?"

Robin had already said there was a connection between the two killings and the disappearance of Karen Marsden. But this was different; if she said there was a connection here, it would be effectively naming Drew and Davis as perpetrators along with Maltais. "No," she said cautiously, "not as far as I know."

"All right. But as far as you know, Drew and Davis are still out and not charged with anything?"

"They can't be charged," she said. "There's no proof of anything for that."

"Okay," he continued, "so they're not out on bail, and they're not being watched by anybody."

She nodded.

"And Drew's the guy you're really afraid of, right?"

"Andy's out now, and for me, that's a bigger scare," she said.

Macy remained patient. "Today is April ninth. Today, you're afraid of Andy? On the day you initially went to Alan Silvia, Andy was in jail, and you knew that, right? I think you said he'd been there about a week and a half."

She looked at him warily. "I read it in the paper."

"So it wasn't him you were afraid of then—it was these other guys."

Robin wouldn't budge. "Andy can still have connections through jail—I don't know, anybody—to have me done in."

He went over it yet again, and she still would not give up the contention that Andy Maltais was a danger to her and she was in peril while he was free. "You know, if you think the man is still capable of running around the street, more power to you. But if I show up dead—" Macy held up his hand, but Robin anticipated his objection and continued anyway. "I know, I'm in protective custody and I'm not around Fall River. The only way anything can happen to me from Davis or Drew is if I'm in Fall River. So if anything happens to me where I am now, it has to do with Mr. Maltais."

Macy dropped his hand in resignation and bewilderment. "How do you figure that?" he asked wearily.

"Maltais beat me before. 'You ever cross me, I'll tell your mother everything. She's going to give you a beating.'"

"That was when you were eleven," he said again.

She waved aside his remark. "Now!" she said emphatically. "When he was bringing me and Karen here and there, he'd tell us, 'Don't say nothing.'"

"When he was bringing you for rides and to find Barbara?"

She was vehement. "We never looked for Barbara. I told him once, I was going to call up his mother about the little girl that lived down the street. 'Andy, I am going to tell your mother about that; you shouldn't be doing that to a little girl.' You know what I mean: joints for a blow job."

The room was silent. Macy nodded slowly and looked back at his notes.

After a time he asked, "Who does know where you are?"

She thought. "My mother. Paul Fitzgerald. My brothers."

"And not Andy Maltais," he said.

"We hope," she said.

"Well, you haven't seen Fitzgerald talking to Andy? You trust him not to do that, don't you?"

She glanced sideways at the state trooper and said, "Oh, yeah."

The lawyer picked up his papers from the conference table and tapped them on their edge before putting them into his carrying case. "Let me ask you something. When you were in court last time, were you calling me names behind my back?"

The question came as a surprise to Robin, but she recovered quickly. "No, none. But I felt like I was going to choke you."

"Why was that?"

"You made me feel about this big," she said, holding up her thumb and index finger. "That I didn't know about—that I'm not from New Bedford."

Macy recalled the circumstances. He had thought Robin was holding back, and he had pressed her for details about her testimony at the time, details that required a knowledge of some of the New Bedford streets. Her defense was to go on the attack: she had responded in a way that suggested he was being unreasonable and mean. Now he studied her closely before repeating the question. "Is it true that every time I turned around, you were calling me names?"

Robin leaned back and returned his look, mockingly. "Stick the names at the end of my bed. I don't know what's at the end of my bed."

"So you did call me names, right?"

"Right," she said, contradicting her denial of a moment before. She glanced at the stenographer and grinned maliciously. "I can't even put it down."

"Yeah, you can put it down," Macy said.

"You were being an asshole with me."

"I heard you call me worse things than that when I turned my back—and a few syllables about Andy too."

Robin continued to stare, now openly contemptuous and no longer grinning, for several seconds after Macy turned his back.

Paul Fitzgerald leaned back in his chair and looked around the room, searching the other faces. Robin's performance was over, and he was interested in how it had been received. After a moment, the lawyers on both sides of the table began to gather their papers, the stenographer turned off the tape recorder, and the other CPAC detectives pushed back their chairs and stood up.

Only one other person at the table still had not moved. An assistant district attorney named David Waxler, sitting a couple of chairs beyond Pina, continued to study Robin Murphy intently. Still in his twenties, he had already won a couple of important murder convictions. Although no prosecutor had yet been assigned to the Maltais case, when the time came, Fitzgerald knew Waxler would be a likely candidate for the job.

TWENTY-TWO / CLEAVE THE WOOD

Late on the morning of April 13, George Dean was reading the Sunday paper in the kitchen with his wife when the telephone rang. Because he was fire chief for the small town of Westport, Massachusetts, there was always a possibility that any call could bring a problem, so Dean was relieved when he recognized Brian Field's voice on the line. A year earlier, Dean had subdivided some family property off Robert Street, on Devol Pond, and Brian Field had bought one of the lots. "How you doing, Brian?" Dean asked.

"Well, I'm not sure," Field answered. "I've been over at the land, brushing out a laneway"—he sounded tentative—"and I found something. You might want to take a look at it."

"Something like what?"

"Like a skull," he said.

Dean said he'd meet Field at the lot.

"I'm not sure that's what it is," Field cautioned him.

Dean said he'd meet him there anyway.

When he arrived, Dean could see from the road that Field had already returned to his work in the laneway, clearing brush. Dean parked the Fire Department pickup ahead of Fields's, then walked in along the new path. Field stopped his work, nodded a greeting, and said, "Sorry about getting you down here on a Sunday. I hope this is worth it."

"It's already worth it," Dean said. Until he had subdivided the land, this property had been in his family for well over a hundred years. "I love it down here."

They walked a few more yards, and Field pointed to the object he thought might be a skull. It was lying in some leaves next to a beech tree, about ten feet off the laneway. "Just where I found it. Hasn't been touched."

Dean hunkered down, careful not to get so close he trampled on any potential evidence, and examined it thoughtfully. "It does look like a skull," he agreed.

"Part of one, anyway," Field said. "No jaw that I can see. No teeth."

Dean nodded and continued looking. There was no flesh or hair either, but a thin membrane of what perhaps had been skin. "If it is a skull, it's facing down; we're looking at the stem."

"And it's not an animal," Field added. "The eyeholes are in front. There's no indication of horns."

"Nope, it looks human," Dean agreed, standing up. He looked at the forest floor in the area around them. "You didn't find any sign of the rest of him?"

"I haven't looked very far, but no."

Dean surveyed the area one more time, then said, "I guess I'd better call the police."

"Good God, George, what the hell did you sell me?" Field asked. They both laughed.

Dean walked out the laneway to his truck, and as he got in he remembered the Kodak Instamatic in the glove compartment. He took it out and walked back through the woods. "Whatever it is," he said to Field, "we might as well have a picture or two."

When George Dean got back to his house, he called Charlie Pierce, a Westport detective. Pierce was out, so Dean left a message. Then he told his wife and their three children what he had seen in the woods. Pierce called back a few minutes later, and Dean repeated the story to him.

The pickup truck was too small for the whole family, so when Dean returned with them to the site they went in his wife's car, with Mrs. Dean at the wheel and the three children in the back seat. As they turned into Robert Street, two Westport police cruisers were arriving at the same time; all three vehicles parked in a line ahead of Brian Field's truck. Dean said hello to Pierce and the other officers, then they all walked back to the laneway into the woods, toward Devol Pond.

Field, having apparently decided that the skull had already taken enough of his time, had again returned to his original task and was energetically cutting brush. Once more he put down his ax to show the new arrivals what he had found. Pierce took one look, then walked back to his car and called the police station.

At half-past noon, Trooper Michael Dusoe of the Bristol County

CPAC unit, having been notified by the state police in North Dartmouth, arrived at the scene. A few minutes later, a trooper from the Photo Bureau at the Middleboro State Police Laboratory appeared in another cruiser and began taking pictures. Bristol County Medical Examiner Paul DeVillers got there next. Dean, Pierce, and Dusoe stood by as DeVillers hunkered down, much as Dean had done an hour before, and looked closely at the object by the tree. The examination didn't take long; still without having touched it, the doctor looked up and told the detectives, "It's human."

Dusoe asked, "How long since death?"

DeVillers looked at the partial skull a moment longer, then put on a pair of rubber gloves and gently picked it up. "Very thin skin membrane," he said. "Can't tell much by that." There was a large hole in one temple, as though the head had been struck or dropped, and he peered inside. "Well, we still have some brain matter, and maybe a little blood. Considering the weather and the time of year," he said, thinking for a moment, "about eight weeks, plus or minus."

Pierce showed Dusoe a sock. "I found it over there," he said, indicating a place in the woods about thirty feet from the skull.

Dusoe took it and said, "There's got to be more."

Fifteen minutes later, when George Dean and his family walked back to the car, the narrow country road was lined with vehicles for at least a hundred yards, most of them police cruisers, and more were still arriving.

The Deans went home for lunch. After they ate, Dean and the two boys—Alan, fifteen, and Skip, thirteen—drove back down to search for the rest of the remains.

Partly because there were so many police vehicles on both sides of the road near Field's lot, and partly because of his lifelong familiarity with the surrounding terrain, Dean decided to go first to a laneway about three hundred yards down a narrow, muddy road called the Turnpike.

Little more than a path, the Turnpike ran off Robert Street for a mile or more through deep woods, emerging eventually to rejoin a public road called Narrow Lane. Dean knew that there was only one house on the Turnpike's entire length, inhabited by a single man. At one time, more than two centuries earlier, this wagon path had served as the main road between two of the region's principal farm villages and the high, gray stone walls on either side had bound open pastures. But now it was grown wild again, filled with scrub oak, soap plants, blueberry bushes, briars, a few beech and silver birch, lots of shiny-leaved holly trees, and littered with the criss-cross windfall trunks and the dark shapes of fungus-covered stumps. Off that rutted road, on the laneway where they now stood, Dean knew the police had often found burned cars that had been stolen from nearby New Bedford and Fall River. It seemed like a good place to begin their search.

He told the two boys to take positions about fifty feet on either side of him and to be careful to stay within his sight. It was still early enough in the year that there was little foliage, but there was plenty of ground cover—checkerberry, low-bush blueberry, occasional feathery runners of ground pine, plus field rocks and fallen branches—and he told them to go slowly.

Less than twenty-five yards in, the boy on his right called to him. Dean crossed over and looked down where his son was standing. At his feet, laid out neatly beside each other in a deliberate, symmetrical pattern, the decaying carcasses of three cats were receding into the forest floor. "Is this something?" the boy asked.

"It's something," Dean said. "Don't touch them."

They continued on, and the son on the left found something else. This time, it was clothing.

Blue jeans—turned inside-out, as though removed in an act of violence. Underpants. A woman's shoe.

The area where they lay had been cleared of its natural cover; the twigs, leaves, and low bushes had been crushed or brushed aside, as though heavily scuffed and trodden.

A row of gray stones, removed from the nearby wall, lay in a straight line that repeated the perfect geometry of the cats.

"What do you think?" the other son asked.

Dean looked beyond the clothing, nearer to the rocks, where the breeze was gently turning what appeared to be sheaves of winter grass. But it was not grass. More sheaves lay beyond, and on some, at their base, were strips of the same thin parchments of skin.

He shivered. "This is part of it too."

They walked quickly back to the lot and told the police.

Paul Fitzgerald was at home when Trooper Dusoe called him on a radio relay through the North Dartmouth barracks. Dusoe did not have much experience with murders, and he needed help.

"Where's the skull now?" Fitzgerald asked.

Dusoe said it was in a plastic bag in his cruiser. Dr. DeVillers had promised to contact Dr. Ambrose Keeley to arrange a forensic medical examination, but first the skull had to be taken to the barracks and put into evidence.

"And the hair?" Fitzgerald asked.

"Still at the other site," Dusoe told him. "Brown or blond. Probably female. Some indication of bloodstain. Mostly clumps with scalp attached. We haven't touched the hair or the clothing. I told Dean and his sons to keep looking for the rest of it."

Fitzgerald said he would get in touch with Dan Lowney, who was doing a shift at the motel guarding Robin Murphy. Thirty minutes later they met Dusoe in Westport.

By then, George Dean and his sons, along with the police who were now hunting beside them, had made further discoveries. About 150 yards to the northeast of the first find, they came upon another tangle of clothing. This time, it was a white jacket, a navy-blue turtleneck sweater, and a lighter-blue sweater, all twisted together and inside-out, apparently pulled off as violently as the blue jeans. A woman's silver Gruen wristwatch had caught by the strap in one of the sweater sleeves. It was no longer running.

Just beyond the sweaters and coat was another large clump of long, bleached-out hair, with skin and flesh at the base.

By now, the woods were filled with searchers. The entire Westport Police Department was there, plus firemen, state police detectives, troopers, technicians, paramedics. With each new arrival of investigators, George Dean was called upon to tell his story yet again, starting with the telephone call and up through his discovery of the latest clump of hair or article of clothing.

Near the middle of the afternoon, a single rider turned onto Robert Street on a Harley Davidson motorcycle. He was wearing leather pants, and his jacket was heavily ornamented with patches and decals—for beer, for spark plugs, for a local bikers' club. Dean had just reemerged from the woods and was standing beside a state police cruiser up near the start of the Turnpike, talking with several of the searchers from his fire department. He looked down the road from time to time between answers, curious to see how the police at that end were going to deal with the intruder. To his mild surprise, he saw one of the Westport policemen point down toward the Turnpike, sending the rider in his direction. A moment later, the man on the Harley pulled up in front of the cruiser.

The rider smiled at Dean. "You found the skull?"

"Not exactly," Dean said. "But I was here pretty early on."

"You found the other things," the rider said. "And you know the area."

Dean nodded.

The rider pulled the bike off the road in front of the cruiser, turned off his engine, and pushed down the kickstand. He got off and walked back around into the roadway, where Dean was standing with the other volunteer searchers. "I know you've done this a few times by now, but would you tell me just how this happened? What you found, where you found it?"

A couple of the firemen were studying Dean in the same bemused way as he himself had watched the policemen down the road a moment earlier, obviously wondering how he was going to handle it. Dean smiled back at the motorcyclist. "Sure," he said. And he told the story one more time, from the start.

Every time Dean had told the story before, none of his other audiences had been interested in hearing about the cats. But this time, when he got to that part, it was different. "Where are they?" the biker asked, obviously excited.

"Over there," Dean said, gesturing down the Turnpike in the general direction of the laneway and the woods; he was gratified at the reaction, but curious as well. "What do you think they mean?"

"I'm not sure. We have a case in Fall River that could be related. Maybe a couple of cases."

Dean was uncertain what he was hearing. "Are you a police officer?" he asked.

"I'm a Fall River detective," the man answered. "Sergeant Paul Carey, with the Major Crimes Division."

The two firemen who had been watching glanced at each other, then quickly shifted their gaze to the ground.

Dean led Detective Carey down the Turnpike to the break in the wall where the stones had been moved and then beyond, to where he and his sons had found the cats.

A few minutes later, four of the state troopers followed the same pathway through the woods, stopping for brief rituals at the successive places of discovery—of each of the various articles of clothing, of each of the clumps of hair and flesh. Because Dusoe had been there before, he led the way. At every station of their journey, Dan Lowney would survey the setting thoroughly and make notes. The trooper from the

Middleboro labs would photograph the artifacts just as they were found. And when they were done, Paul Fitzgerald would pick up each item in turn, with the greatest of care, and place it in its own evidence bag.

Fitzgerald took no notes. For almost all his life, once he had seen or heard something, he didn't forget it. His mother was like that too. It was more than a trick memory. The most trivial details seemed permanently available. He could recall the birth date of a witness he had interviewed fifteen years before, or the day of the week when a certain thing had happened, no matter how small or long ago. Or what someone was wearing at a particular time, even months earlier—details he might not even consciously have noticed at the time they were being recorded in his mind—down to the buttons of a coat, the pattern of a sweater, the precise color of a person's hair.

He didn't have to try hard; it was a detective's perfect natural gift, and the memories came unbidden.

As they came now.

"You told us Karen Marsden is in Ohio," Lowney said, referring to a comment Robin Murphy had made a few days before.

Robin was lying on the motel-room bed, idling through the pages of *People*. The detective's remark was deliberately ambiguous—possibly a question or perhaps a challenge—and she flipped another page before glancing up at him. "If you're asking me where in Ohio, I still don't remember," she said, and turned back to the magazine. "I just know she has friends there."

Lowney watched her for a moment, then slid open the closet door, arranged his jacket on a hanger, and sat down in a chair by the draped window. His relief had just left, and the pages of the Sunday *Boston Herald* were strewn around the motel-room floor beside the chair. Lowney looked down at the paper, deciding which section to pick up first.

Robin put aside the magazine a second time and asked, "Why?"

The trooper shrugged, as though to say the remark had not meant anything and the subject was not worth pursuing. "It's your last day, that's all." He picked up part of the Sunday paper and started refolding it.

Robin regarded him warily in silence, then said, "Yeah, and thank God."

Lowney, still smoothing and recreasing the newspaper, didn't offer a response.

During the ten days that Robin Murphy was in Massachusetts, Lowney and Fitzgerald had taken turns guarding her at the new motel where she was sequestered. Fitzgerald had been with her all of Saturday, and now Sunday was Lowney's turn. Another trooper spelled him when Fitzgerald called Lowney to join him at Robert Street, but the replacement had gone back to the barracks as soon as they had returned.

Robin had no idea why Lowney had left for those couple of hours, and she had been told nothing about events taking place in Westport. Because they suspected Robin's story about Karen being in Ohio was an attempt to mislead them, they had made the decision to keep her from learning what had been found off Robert Street for as long as possible.

Both Lowney and Fitzgerald were certain that the clothing in the woods belonged to Karen Marsden; by itself, however, the clothing did not prove murder. The skull was another matter: they were sure that it too was Karen's, but they also knew that establishing the skull's identity might turn out to be far more complicated, and perhaps even impossible, unless the rest of the body could be found and identified by matching fingerprints or dental records. In the meantime, it was remotely possible that Robin might tell them something new about Karen being in Ohio, something they could use to prove she deliberately had been misleading them.

But either the suggestions about Ohio had been ingenuous, or Robin was instinctively smart enough not to rise to any of Lowney's bait. The subject of Karen Marsden's whereabouts did not come up again.

On Monday morning, Dr. Paul DeVillers called Dr. Ambrose Keeley and described the grim discoveries of the preceding day.

"What happened to the body?" Keeley asked.

"Well, that's a good question. The police found some clothes, and they think they have the murder site, several hundred yards from where the calvarium was recovered," he said. A calvarium is a partial skull, usually with no lower jaw. "But they're still looking for the rest of it."

"No teeth, I gather?"

"No teeth. Nothing below the eye orbits."

"How did the calvarium get so far from everything else?"

"Your guess is as good as mine. Dogs, maybe; it's wild country, and there are plenty of strays in the area."

Keeley thought for a moment. "I'll do whatever you say, but would it make sense to wait just a bit, in case the search turns up anything else?"

DeVillers agreed. The two doctors scheduled the autopsy at St. Anne's for the following afternoon.

That same Monday morning, Fitzgerald picked up Robin at the motel in an unmarked cruiser and drove her to Logan Airport. During her stay in Massachusetts, Robin had complained to Pina that her exile on the outskirts of Dallas was lonely, so she had been given permission to take a girlfriend named Pam Coady along when she returned to Texas.

Pam Coady was a high-strung but relatively quiet girl of twenty, and she appeared to have no connection with any of the three killings. The expenses of Pam's trip were added to the cost of protecting Robin and were paid by the district attorney's office. After all, Robin was the star witness in the Commonwealth's case against Andy Maltais and was emerging as a possible key in the Levesque case as well. Pina was willing to go to unusual lengths to keep her sweet.

TWENTY-THREE / **PROFESSIONAL COURTESIES**

Lieutenant Kaegael read through to the end of the report, not saying a word, then turned back to the beginning and read it over again. Alan Silvia stood in front of Kaegael's desk, watching the movement of his eyes, waiting for a reaction, and he lifted one hand in impatience, then let it drop, when the lieutenant started over.

"Take it easy," Kaegael said quietly, still reading. When he reached the end a second time, he laid the pages carefully on his desk, then looked up at the young detective.

Silvia looked back, trying not to let his impatience show as exasperation.

Kaegael asked, "Did Sonny Sparda go along with this?"

"If you mean, did she hear what we heard, yes," Silvia said. "And if you're asking whether she gave her permission for us to listen in, yes again." When the lieutenant still looked at him questioningly, Silvia added, "Whether that makes it legal or not, I don't know."

Kaegael thought for a moment longer, then looked back down at the report. "Well, this turns the whole thing over."

"Yeah," Silvia agreed. "It does."

The lieutenant picked up the report and handed it back to Silvia. "Bring it this afternoon," he said. Then he added, "But keep it in your pocket until I tell you."

The detectives of the Major Crimes Division of the Fall River Police Department had been meeting regularly with their state police counterparts since the previous fall, after the body of Doreen Levesque had been discovered under the bleachers at the Diman playing field. At first, most of those meetings had taken place at the MCD offices in Fall River because the crime had occurred in that jurisdiction and the state police detectives were willing to make the trip as an accommodation

177

to the home team. But as the agenda of those meetings grew, first to include the Raposa killing and then again with the discovery of the skull in Westport, an additional jurisdiction became involved, more people attended, and with increasing frequency the location was shifted to Bristol CPAC headquarters in the office of the district attorney in New Bedford.

That afternoon, Alan Silvia settled into a chair beside Lieutenant Kaegael, patted his jacket pocket to make sure the report was where it should be, and looked around the conference table. Across from him, Chief Rene Dupré of the Westport police smiled his customary cheerful greeting. Beside Dupré, Charlie Pierce pored over a long, typewritten list, preparing himself for any questions from the district attorney about the evidence recovered from the woods near Devol Pond. Tom Joaquim and then Paul Carey were seated to Silvia's right. There was a vacant chair beyond them and then Paul Fitzgerald and Dan Lowney. Fitzgerald returned Silvia's nod and asked, "How's it going?"

"Good," Silvia said. He liked Fitzgerald and Lowney, but today he was being careful.

At the other end of the room, a door opened and Ron Pina entered with Ray Veary, two more CPAC detectives, and a secretary. After everyone else was seated, Pina and the secretary remained standing at the end of the table as the DA counted heads.

One of the detectives said, "Mine was the baked stuffed lobster. I hope you didn't forget again."

Pina grinned. "The way this is growing, we should be thankful for the sandwiches." He told the number to the secretary, who left the room as Pina took his seat.

The meeting began with some brief comments by the district attorney on events that had taken place since they had met the week before. The secretary returned with a tray of sandwiches in waxed paper, and they were distributed around the table. As Pina unwrapped his, he looked over at Lieutenant Kaegael and said, "Okay, what have you got for us from Fall River?"

Alan Silvia was watching the DA, but when there was no answer, he turned to his left. Kaegael was sitting with his hands folded on the table, the sandwich still in its wrapper, and although he was looking right at the district attorney, he gave the impression that he had not heard the question.

"What have you got?" Pina asked again.

Kaegael waited a moment longer, then asked the district attorney, "What have *you* got?"

Around the table, the chewing slowed or stopped. Heads turned warily in the direction of the acting captain of the Fall River detectives. Beside him, Alan Silvia spread his hands flat on the smooth tabletop and studied his fingernails.

Pina looked around the table for some clue to what was going on, then back at Kaegael. "C'mon," he said a third time, "what have you got?"

To Silvia's amazement, Kaegael suddenly pushed back his chair and rose to his feet, angrily slapping down a manila folder and pointing toward the CPAC detectives at the other end of the table. "Who are these people to come into the Fall River jurisdiction," he demanded, his face flushed, "and take an informant that we've been developing for over a year and scoop that witness without even coming to the people who are investigating the case?"

Kaegael was referring to an incident that had occurred the day before, when two CPAC detectives had picked up Sonny Sparda without advising the Fall River police and taken her to Westport to look at the presumed murder site. The state police were within their rights: although the witness lived in Fall River, the murder had taken place in a different jurisdiction and technically was not a Fall River case. But CPAC had been high-handed with Robin Murphy, and this touched a painful nerve, reminding the local police once again that they stood lower in the law-enforcement hierarchy and reinforcing their suspicion that the CPAC detectives viewed them as inferior in other ways as well. Silvia knew Kaegael had been angry when he learned of the violation of protocol—everyone in the MCD had been angry—but he was astonished to see what he now was doing about it.

Kaegael had joined the Fall River Police Force before either Alan Silvia or Tom Joaquim had been born. In almost everything else Silvia had ever seen him do, their acting captain was the most civil of civil servants, a rules man who was careful of authority to a fault, an habitual oiler of even the most slightly troubled waters. But today, apparently because he realized how seriously the incident had affected the morale of his detectives, and bolstered by the knowledge of what was in Alan Silvia's pocket, he rose up to challenge the chief law-enforcement officer in the county.

Pina rose as well. He glowered across at the veteran detective, and for a moment it appeared as though the two men were preparing to do physical battle. It ended when Pina, still without replying, slapped the remnant of his sandwich onto its wrapper and strode from the room. Perhaps it was a retreat to get his own temper under control.

More likely it was a kindness to the older man, disengaging before Kaegael could do himself harm.

After a moment, the lieutenant sat down again. No one at the table said a word, but when Silvia glanced briefly to his right, he saw that the other Fall River detectives were now sitting straighter than they had before and he sensed that both Joaquim and Carey were suppressing smiles. A minute or two later, Pina came back into the room and took his seat as well. "Okay," he said, "let's get on with it."

Kaegael too appeared to be sitting taller than before and to have his anger under control. He turned to Alan Silvia, nodded, and said, "Now."

Silvia reached into his pocket and removed the report. As he read it to the others in the room, he looked up now and then, partly for dramatic effect, but also to check the faces around the table for reactions. He came to the place where the report quoted what Robin Murphy had whispered into the telephone. At that point, he paused slightly longer than before, this time looking directly across at the district attorney.

Pina was listening carefully, his hands folded before him, watching the tabletop, taking in every word. He looked up, waiting for Silvia to continue. His young face was slightly flushed, but his expression gave away nothing.

The events that led to Silvia's report began on the evening of March 2, the day after Fitzgerald checked Robin Murphy out of the motel, when Carey, Silvia, and Phelan had dropped in at 5 Harbor Terrace to interview Sonny. She started out by telling them what they already suspected: the last time she had seen Robin was in this apartment two days earlier, on the afternoon and evening when Robert Bohun had come in to baby-sit.

While Sonny was talking, Carey asked questions and Silvia took notes. Phelan, seemingly distracted, walked about the living room. After a few minutes he wandered down the hall toward the kitchen at the rear of the apartment.

"What about Karen?" Carey asked.

"I asked Robin how she killed her," Sonny said.

Silvia quickly flipped over a new page in his notebook and continued scribbling.

Carey said, "Her exact words, as close as you can come."

"'I did it with my hands. It's slower that way. Using a gun is too fast.'" Sonny took a deep breath and continued. "I asked Robin, 'Didn't she scream? How could you do it?' And Robin said, 'She didn't say a word. She just cried—and that pissed me off all the more.' Then she said, 'It will take the detectives two years to figure it out.'"

When she stopped, Carey watched her for a moment longer, then nodded. "Okay."

As Silvia stood up, he asked, "Any idea where Robin's gone?"

"Texas," Sonny answered.

"How do you know that?" Carey asked.

"Texas," Sonny said again.

They thanked her and left. Once the three detectives were back in the car, Phelan asked Silvia for his notebook; he wrote down the area code 214 and a seven-digit number which he had memorized from a scrap of paper in the kitchen of Sonny's apartment. When they returned to the division, Carey dialed Information for area code 214. The exchange on the slip of paper turned out to be in Addison, a suburb of Dallas.

The friend with whom Robin—and now Pam Coady as well—stayed in suburban Dallas was named Cheryl Uretsky. During Robin's earlier stay, before her return to Massachusetts for the interview with attorney Macy, Robin had spoken frequently with Cheryl about Karen Marsden. Cheryl knew that Robin and Karen had been friends and that something terrible had happened to Karen, but Robin had always stopped short of saying just what that something was. It was possible, Cheryl thought to herself, that the reason Robin did not say anything was because she did not know any more than she had already told. This rationale had gained support on one occasion when Cheryl overheard Robin call Karen's grandmother in Fall River to ask her if she had learned anything new about Karen's disappearance.

On April 14, the night of Robin's return to Dallas, Cheryl overheard another of Robin's telephone conversations, this time a call from Sonny Sparda. When Robin hung up, she was trembling. "The cops have found Karen's skull," she told Cheryl.

Unsure what this information meant for Robin, Cheryl waited for her to say something further. Instead, Robin walked nervously back and forth, talking more to herself than to Cheryl, repeating what she had just heard from Sonny as though she were trying to understand it. "They found it yesterday," she said. "They had it yesterday, and they didn't tell me—"

For lack of anything better, Cheryl asked, "That's all they found? A skull?"

Robin either did not hear the question or chose to ignore it. She picked up the telephone again and dialed eleven digits; a moment later, Cheryl realized that Robin had called home and was speaking to her mother. This time, the conversation was short, and when Robin hung up she still looked apprehensive but somewhat relieved. "They have a skull," she said. "But they don't know whose it is."

Robin's relief was short-lived. On the following night, Sonny called again. Cheryl heard only one end of the conversation, and at first she thought Robin and Sonny were having an argument. Robin's voice was vehement, even shrill, as she kept repeating what she had been told by her mother the night before. "They still don't know. There's no way they could know."

But apparently Sonny was just as insistent at the other end and would not be moved. From what Cheryl could understand from Robin's side, the police had found Karen's clothes. And the skull had been positively identified as well.

This time, when Robin hung up the telephone, she looked sick.

The next person to overhear one of Robin's telephone calls, just a couple of nights later, was Pam Coady.

Pam had turned out the lights in the bedroom and had been lying for a long time with her eyes shut, breathing shallow, sleeplike breaths, hardly moving at all. Now and then Robin would say something to her from another place in the apartment, and Pam would just lie there in the dark and not answer. She wanted to be somewhere else, but there was no place for her to go.

It was still early. Robin had started that afternoon with beer and pot, and now that she was popping Valiums, things were getting worse. They were not in Cheryl Uretsky's apartment. Earlier that day, Pam and Robin had driven to visit a friend of Cheryl's named Mike Minnick, and after a while Robin had gotten so high, Pam wanted to get away from her and had retreated to the bedroom. When Robin was strung out, being with her was like trying to dodge a high-tension wire that was gradually losing its insulation, blowing unpredictably in the wind, sparking on everything it came near.

From behind her closed eyelids, Pam listened to Robin talking with the others, mentally tracking her movements through the apartment, hoping the tension would subside, hoping she would ground herself and drain off her dangerous energy. But it didn't seem to be working out that way. She was still drinking, still smoking dope, still knocking down the pills. Her voice was getting louder and her angry, raucous laughter more frequent.

Fall River, where the Quequechan River goes underground. *We'll sit in a circle. There will be some praying and chanting. If you let yourself into it, you'll be able to feel Satan in the room.*

Carl Drew. *What the cops were really mad about was, here's this new guy that's moving into town, and I just moved right into Bedford Street and started taking over.* (From the files of the Massachusetts State Police.)

Charlie's Cafe.

At 7:00 A.M. two women jogging on the outdoor track at Diman Vocational High School discovered the body of a girl believed to be between the ages of 14 and 19. (Reproduced from a clipping.)

Doreen Levesque. *Dear Jesus, thank you for everything you've done for me. Someday I would like to be with You in heaven.*

Pier 14 in the early 70s.

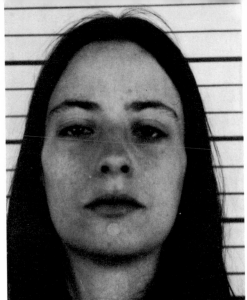

Karen Marsden. *I'm a good person. . . . God w[ill] help me.* (Photo courtesy of the Massachusetts State Police.)

Robin Murphy. *I'm not going to jail for something I don't know.*

New Bedford Standard-Times

Andy Maltais, with Paul Fitzgerald on the right. *I think I'm going to wait for the Big Guy to show up before I say anything.*

I saw her last night and she looked awful . . . South Main Street, walking in that direction.

Paul Fitzgerald at the Westport site. *What haven't you told me?*

It's not an animal. The eye holes are in front.

Photo by George Dean

Robin Murphy. *I am so sick of getting myself in trouble, it's not even funny.*

New Bedford Standard-Times

Carl Drew (left) and Carl Davis (right), just before
arraignment.

More searchers at Devol Pond.

Robin. *I happen to shoot my mouth off when I get high.*

Andy Maltais in court. *I used to be with Satan. Now I'm with God, and God is with me.*

Drew in court. *No one has ever knocked me off my feet.*

Alan Silvia (right) with attorney John Birknes. *We worked like hell; our motivation was the exhilaration of knowing we were doing the right thing. But part of me was lost in the process.*

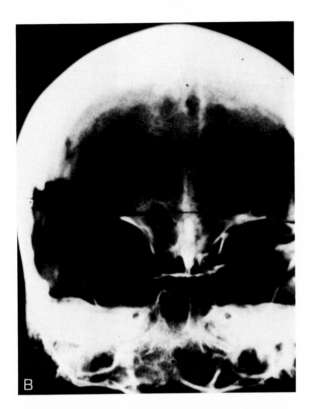

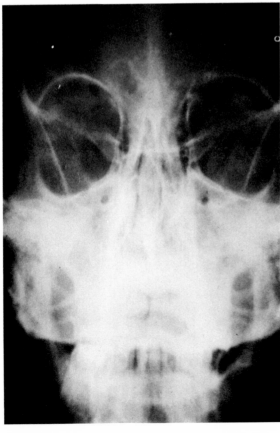

Frontal X-rays submitted in evidence.
(Photos courtesy of Dr. Douglas Ubelaker

On the advice of his lawyer, Carl Davis declines to testify.

Pamela Coady.
I don't want to remember nothing,
don't you understand?
(Reproduced from a clipping.)

New Bedford Standard-Times

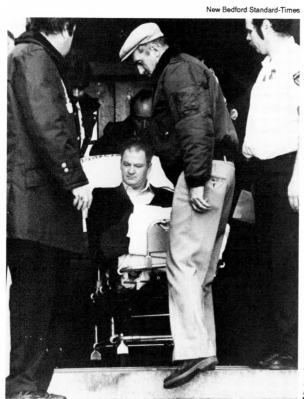

Andy Maltais. *I could see just enough.*
It was dark. She was drugged.
She was saying, "Andy, forgive me."

'Boy gives Drew good news about the Levesque case.

New Bedford Standard-Times

New Bedford Standard-Times

Villie Smith. *I never knew any of these people. I think this was a joke.*

Pier 14, boarded up, March 1981.

What was happening tonight, Pam realized, had really been building up for the last nine days, ever since they had arrived in Texas, starting with that first telephone call from Sonny Sparda. Pam was pretty sure that Robin's mood had nothing to do with Andy Maltais, who was supposed to be the reason Robin was in protective custody, and as far as Pam could tell it had very little to do with Carl Drew either. Robin's growing tension was connected in some way with the skull that had been discovered in the woods in Westport and which Sonny said the police had identified as Karen Marsden's.

After a time, although her eyes were still shut, Pam could sense that Robin had come into the bedroom. There was a brief space of silence, then she heard her voice, just above a whisper. "You asleep, or what?"

Pam continued the rhythmic breathing and didn't move. A moment later she heard the bedroom telephone being lifted from its cradle and then the sound of dialing. Pam turned, rearranging herself on the bed as though in deep slumber, and faced the wall. From the number of digits, she could tell it was long distance.

Now that Pam realized there was a telephone in the bedroom, the thought came to her that she could use it to call Cheryl Uretsky as soon as Robin was finished. If Robin wasn't ready to go home yet, maybe Cheryl could come up with a way for Pam to get back to the apartment by herself.

As Pam was sorting through the possibilities in her mind, from across the room, something from Robin's murmured conversation intruded on her thoughts.

"I did it for you," Robin had said to the telephone. Her voice was very tense and low, shaking with the drugs, almost tearful.

Involuntarily, Pam opened her eyes and looked at the blank wall beside the bed. She sensed the meaning of Robin's words even before she heard the rest of it. The carefully measured breathing stopped in anticipation of what was coming.

At the other end of the line, in the kitchen of her apartment in Fall River, Sonny Sparda leaned forward, also trembling, and read the scribbled writing on the pad that had been slid across the countertop before her. When she spoke back to the telephone, fighting to control her voice, she repeated those words as they were written.

"Did what?"

"Killed Karen," Robin said.

Sonny ran her fingers through her hair, trying to think of what to answer. After a moment, she said, "Yeah."

"I love you so much, Sonny," the voice on the wire whispered back.

"Yeah," Sonny said again.

"That's why Karen's dead," Robin said. She seemed to be pleading for some further acknowledgment, for understanding, perhaps even for approval.

Sonny looked at the two Fall River detectives who were standing in the kitchen beside her, their heads bowing to the same earpiece, to be sure they had heard. Alan Silvia glanced up for an instant and nodded emphatically, then lowered his head again to continue listening.

"They'll never figure it out," the voice on the telephone was saying. "I did it the same way Lizzie Borden did it."

Silvia made a slight, inquiring gesture. Sonny hesitated, then asked, "What do you mean?"

"I took off all my clothes," Robin said.

Silvia recalled the movie in which Elizabeth Montgomery, playing Lizzie Borden, had undressed before killing her father and stepmother in order to avoid getting blood on her frock.

Beside him, Tom Joaquim wrote another question on the pad.

The conference room was absolutely silent when Silvia finished reading his report; even the chewing had stopped. Kaegael sat impassively, his hands folded before him, looking across at Pina. Silvia carefully refolded the paper and returned it to his pocket.

It was the district attorney who finally spoke, and when he did he was looking at Paul Fitzgerald and Dan Lowney, his voice low and steady. "Get her back up here."

A nearly immediate result of the afternoon meeting in New Bedford—and possibly, to some degree, of the confrontation between Lieutenant Kaegael and the district attorney—took place that evening. After scrupulously notifying the Fall River Police Department, Fitzgerald and Lowney visited Sonny Sparda at Harbor Terrace and followed it with a long conversation with Robin Murphy's mother.

Then, just before ten o'clock, the two state troopers walked into the offices of the Major Crimes Division. Both of them had reservations about what Silvia had told the DA that morning—Lowney in particular suspected the report of the telephone conversation had been colored by Silvia's enthusiasm—and they both felt that the Fall River detectives had made a big mistake in reporting to the chief law-enforcement officer of the county about what amounted to an illegal wiretap—but they were there under orders, and they gave away nothing of these misgivings. Alan Silvia greeted them with a welcoming grin, feeling like Mohammed when the mountain first began to move. The state police were still in charge, but the loftiness and long-festering adversity appeared to be coming to an end. A few minutes after they arrived, Paul Fitzgerald placed a telephone call to a number in Texas.

When Robin Murphy got on the line, Fitzgerald identified himself and told her the district attorney wanted her to come back to Massachusetts.

There was a pause, then Robin said, "Okay." It was tentative, as though she expected the trooper to tell her something further about what was in store for her.

But Fitzgerald was absolutely neutral, offering nothing. "I've made reservations for the twenty-ninth."

"Yeah—" she said, sounding even more hesitant.

"I'll meet you at Logan," Fitzgerald told her. "Same as before."

There was a long pause. Robin said, "Look, I've been—" She stopped, then started again. "There's some things I haven't told you."

Fitzgerald's tone didn't change. "What haven't you told me?"

"Some things," she repeated. "About a lot of stuff."

The detective waited for her to say more, but now she was the one who let the silence run on. When he realized nothing further was coming, Fitzgerald said in the same businesslike voice as before, "The twenty-ninth is next Tuesday. Have you got a pencil?"

"I know it's Tuesday," Robin said. There was an edge in her voice, but she sounded subdued, even depressed. "Hold on a minute; I'll get one."

As he waited, Fitzgerald looked up and saw one of the Fall River detectives signaling him from the door to the adjacent office, telling him in pantomime that there was another telephone call. Fitzgerald put his hand on the mouthpiece and asked who it was.

"Carol Fletcher," the detective said. "From the West Coast. Tacoma."

Dan Lowney had been sitting at the next desk, and he jumped up to take the call.

At the same moment, Robin came back on the line; Fitzgerald gave her the arrival time and the flight number and reaffirmed that he would meet her when she got to Boston.

"Look," Robin said again. "About that stuff—"

Fitzgerald decided to help her a little. "You mean, the things I haven't heard about."

"That's right. I'll tell you when I see you," she offered. "Next Tuesday."

"That'll be good," Fitzgerald said.

A moment later, after he hung up, Fitzgerald walked into the next office where Lowney was still talking on the telephone with Carol Fletcher. Carey, Joaquim, and Silvia were in there as well; together they waited in silence for that call also to come to an end.

"We'll come out to see you," they heard Lowney say. "We'll want to ask you some questions."

Lowney paused to listen, and then he answered, "Well, an assistant DA—probably that would be Ray Veary. Paul Fitzgerald. Me. And someone from the Fall River Police Department—" Lowney looked inquiringly at the three MCD detectives. Paul Carey pointed to himself, indicating he would be the one to go. "You know Sergeant Carey?" Lowney asked.

The conversation lasted a few minutes more, and Lowney agreed to get back to Carol the next day. When he was through, he placed the handset on its cradle and looked at the other detectives. "It doesn't rain but it pours."

Alan Silvia shook his head. "This isn't just chance," he said. "Both Robin and Carol have been talking with Sonny Sparda. I'll bet we'd find a call to Texas on Sonny's phone bill for every time we've talked to her since Robin went south."

"And tonight, to Tacoma, Washington," Joaquim added.

Fitzgerald shrugged. "Maybe—it might have been Sonny, or tonight it could have been Robin's mother who called Carol—or even Robin herself. Whichever, it doesn't seem to be doing any harm." He looked at his partner. "It sounds like Carol and Robin are both getting their memories back."

Lowney said, "Carol went to Tacoma because she says she's in fear for her life."

"Sounds familiar," Carey said.

"Carol knows what happened the night Karen Marsden was killed. She's ready to tell."

Alan Silvia said, "Every time Carol Fletcher gets ready to tell, she gives us a different car and a different description of the driver. She can be a little time-consuming."

"Not now," Lowney said. "This time, she's giving us four names. Carl Drew. Carl Davis. Robin Murphy. And herself. They were in Carol's car, and Carol was the driver. She says that on the night of February 8, they all drove Karen over to Westport, and Robin and Carl Drew killed her."

PART TWO

//

TWENTY-FOUR / **GOLGOTHA**

One of the first American murder trials involving the identification of a skeleton in court took place in Boston in 1849, before the science of forensic anthropology had a name. The victim was Dr. George Parkman, a wealthy patron of the Harvard Medical School. The killer was Professor John W. Webster, of the Harvard Medical School faculty. The murder took place in Webster's Medical School office. The expert witness whose testimony sealed the killer's fate was Jeffries Wyman, another anatomist who happened to be Webster's department head at Harvard. This was not a crime that required any of the principals to travel a great distance.

Professor Webster had borrowed some money from Dr. Parkman and, when the doctor asked for repayment, Webster invited him to step into his office, where he killed him. He then cut off Parkman's head, hands, and feet. School was out at the time, so Webster threw the extremities into the laboratory furnace and dropped the rest of the body down his office privy. It may have been that he expected the torso to wind up eventually in the Charles River, whose less-than-pristine waters flushed the privy, but when and if that happened, he was certain that identification would be impossible.

But the dismembered portion of Dr. Parkman's body never got as far as the Charles. It was discovered where Webster had left it, and a pair of unfortunate Boston policemen, lowered into the hole on ropes, brought it back up into the laboratory. The partially burned bones of the head, hands, and feet were retrieved from the furnace. To Professor Jeffries Wyman fell the heroic task of reassembling and closely examining this evidence and then testifying in court that they were all originally one. On the strength of that testimony, Professor Webster was found guilty and hanged.

Some forty-five years later, Harvard University began offering courses in physical anthropology. George A. Dorsey received his doctorate in American Archaeology and Ethnology in 1895—the first such degree conferred by Harvard based on its new anthropology curriculum—partly in recognition of his work at the Chicago World's Fair the previous year, where he had assembled an exhibit on human skeletal anatomy. It was because of Dorsey's exhibit at the Fair that the term "physical anthropology" first came into use. The term was coined to distinguish the science of the study of human skeletal remains from the broader science of cultural anthropology, which was the study of the context in which the original owners of ancient skeletons had lived.

Two years after receiving his degree, Dr. Dorsey too became involved in a spectacular murder case.

What the Parkman killing did for the Harvard Medical School, the trial of Adolph Leutgert did for America's sausage industry. In 1897, Adolph, a wealthy meat merchant, killed his wife in their Chicago home, drove the body in a carriage at night to the family factory, and dumped her into a processing vat with 375 pounds of potash. While waiting for the corpse to dissolve, Leutgert was apparently overtaken by fatigue; he was found by an employee in the morning, sleeping in his office. His tenderizing technique worked so well that the vat had overflowed during the night, and the floor was covered with a gray, greasy foam. Adolph headed home and in due course reported his wife missing.

A few days later, his wife's brother heard about the incident at the plant and arrived there with the police. By then the vat had been drained. More in frustration than in the hope of finding anything, one of the officers scraped with a stick at the congealed sediment in the bottom. Eventually, he uncovered four tiny pieces of bone. He set them aside, unsure if they were large enough to mean anything. Then he scraped some more and found Mrs. Leutgert's wedding ring.

These discoveries set the stage for the first great forensic duel of its kind, between Dorsey, the physical anthropologist, testifying for the prosecution, and an anatomist from the Northwestern University School of Medicine for the defense. Dorsey stated that the four bones, each so small that together they barely filled a bottle cap, were human. The anatomist claimed they were from a small animal. Either way, the publicity was bound to reduce the consumer demand for sausages in the city of Chicago.

It is hard to know whether Dorsey's side won the case because of the lucidity of his presentation or whether the anatomist lost it for the defense when he fell into a lawyer's trap and identified a monkey's leg bone as coming from a dog. The result of the trial and the reasons behind it, however, were of little consequence to Dorsey. He went to court to testify in the area of his expertise, which he did as conscientiously as his scientific knowledge and skills allowed. The defendant's innocence or guilt were not within that area, and the outcome of the trial was not his responsibility either.

In contrast to that professionalism, and despite the jury's acceptance of Dorsey's testimony, his courtroom adversary chose not to play by the same rules: In an 1899 meeting of the Medico-Legal Society of Chicago, the anatomist who had been routed in court staged a rematch before their peers, ridiculing Dorsey's identification skills and attempting to discredit the new science. It must have been painful; there is no evidence that Dorsey ever worked in the field of forensics again. Nevertheless, the standard of scientific detachment he exhibited at the Leutgert trial is an important part of his legacy to the profession he helped create.

In 1903, another young physical anthropologist, Ales Hrdlicka, became the first curator of that discipline on the staff of the Smithsonian Institution's National Museum of Natural History in Washington, D.C. An immigrant from Bohemia as a boy, Hrdlicka had served on a number of important research expeditions under the aegis of New York's American Museum of Natural History while still in his twenties, and when he came to Washington at thirty-three his star was rising fast.

In 1910, Hrdlicka was named head curator of the Division of Physical Anthropology of the National Museum. In 1918 he founded and became the first editor of the *American Journal of Physical Anthropology,* and some years after that he founded the discipline's first professional society. Under his stewardship, the Smithsonian Institution's National Museum archive of human skeletal remains grew to include the skulls and bones of more than thirty thousand individuals, from the earliest Africans and ancient Egyptians right up to twentieth-century Americans.

Meanwhile, Hrdlicka himself became famous for his studies in support of the Asiatic origin of American Indians, for his anthropologic survey of Alaska, and for his work in skeletal measurement and the evolution of man.

In the middle 1930s, this combination of scientific brilliance and the world's largest reference collection of human bones attracted particular interest, albeit in the most circumspect possible manner, from the museum's new neighbor across the street, the Federal Bureau of Investigation. Hrdlicka consulted with the FBI from the time the bureau moved its laboratories into the Department of Justice Building in the Federal Triangle, but he never published on the forensic side of his work and only rarely discussed it, even with his colleagues.

In the romance between science and crime detection, the great barrier to open matrimony was the Victorian question of class; science was still an elitist art, while police detection—Sherlock Holmes notwithstanding—was considered by many to be just the opposite. Although a growing amount of police work was conducted at the back door of the Smithsonian and a handful of other museums, virtually nothing was published in the field of forensic anthropology by any scientist until just before the start of World War II. It was the dark side of scientific query, and while it served a useful social purpose, it was not yet a discipline in which any serious scientist was willing to build or risk his professional reputation.

Hrdlicka's only student was T. Dale Stewart, who had come to work for the museum as a very young man in the 1920s. With Hrdlicka's encouragement, Stewart earned a degree in medicine from Johns Hopkins in order to improve his skill as a physical anthropologist, and in 1942 he succeeded his mentor as curator of physical anthropology. When Hrdlicka died the following year, the FBI began bringing their bones to Stewart. He was surprised to discover how much forensic work his reticent predecessor had been involved in.

Over the next twenty years, Ales Hrdlicka's sole protégé not only assumed the master's mantle as the American dean of physical anthropology, but he led the way in liberating the forensic side of the science from the constraints and secrecy of an earlier age. As in many other aspects of life, a major agent of that change was the war; for physical anthropologists, the identification of victims, often from fragmentary skeletal remains, became a new patriotic duty.

But the forensic side of the science came out of the closet for another reason as well. With the rapid rise of technology, the culture gap between the gathering of scientific knowledge and its practical applications in everyday life began to disappear. What this meant in anthropology was that the past began to catch up with the present; the original high principles of the discipline remained intact, and the feared taint of exploitation, sensationalism, and commerce began to fade away. After a prolonged, embarrassed, and awkward courtship, anthropology and the law were finally headed for a public wedding.

One of Dr. Stewart's earliest forensic cases involved military remains, delivered in a cardboard box by two FBI agents in 1942, but they were not a product of the war.

The relics had been found in an abandoned well on a farm near Quantico, Virginia. Stewart concluded from his examination of the bone fragments that the victim had been a white male of about twenty-eight, around five-feet-ten-inches tall, probably left-handed, and afflicted with periodontal disease, a bone loss around the teeth. Because the FBI had also retrieved some military buttons from the same site as the body, they headed over to the Quantico marine base to see if anyone of that description had dropped from sight a decade or more before.

What they found was the fifteen-year-old record of an ex-marine who had been suspected of being a bootlegger and had disappeared, presumably in a hijacking incident, in 1927. A suspect had been identified by the police, but no arrest had been made because of the lack of a body.

Even in cases involving the most compelling combination of motive and circumstance, police and government prosecutors are extremely reluctant to arrest or indict a suspect in a murder case unless it can be proven that the victim is indeed dead. Literature, almost all of it fiction, is filled with tales of amnesiac housewives or impulsive travelers who return after prolonged absences to discover that the police have dug up some dog bones in their backyard and on the strength of that evidence have hanged the village idiot for murder. And in the odd instances when that scenario takes place in real life— as it did in upstate New York in the 1940s, when the presumed murder victim returned home, totally unaware of all that had transpired since her disappearance eight months earlier, just in time to stop the scheduled execution of her handyman—they tend to reinforce any subsequent jury's natural impulse toward the presumption of innocence.

But that is not the only reason prosecutors are reluctant to bring a suspect to trial without a body. Under the constitutional protection against double jeopardy, a murderer who is acquitted because no body has been found cannot be retried once the corpse turns up. In virtually every trial involving testimony by a forensic anthropologist, the central issue—even ahead of the defendant's guilt or innocence—is either how the victim died or whether the alleged victim is really dead.

The bones from the well in Quantico provide an excellent case in point. The ex-marine's file established his height within a half inch of Stewart's estimate, although the anthropologist was two years over in his assumption of age. The missing man's mother confirmed that her son was left-handed and that he had come home from his last dental examination with a diagnosis of pyorrhea. Fifteen years after the killing, the suspect was arrested, tried, and convicted of murder.

In 1962, Dr. Stewart became director of the National Museum, and his forensic work came to a stop. That same year, he named J. Lawrence Angel to be his successor as curator of anthropology. Angel also succeeded to the open acceptance of forensic anthropology by the scientific world and the general public which Stewart had helped bring about. Angel was middle-aged when he took the new job, and he brought no forensic experience with him to the task. But he had a natural gift, was quickly able to transfer his scientific skills to forensic applications, and even refined some important new techniques for the identification and evaluation of human skeletal remains.

Moreover, he felt right at home in his dual role. "It is the anthropologist," he said, "who gives skeletons a voice, whether they cry out for justice or help us resurrect the human past." That was the kind of thing the FBI and police departments around the country loved to hear. They sought the Smithsonian's services often and openly, and an admiring press began referring to Angel as Sherlock Bones.

April 15, 1980: Another day and a half of searching had turned up no further evidence beyond what Brian Field and George Dean found in the woods Sunday the thirteenth, so on Tuesday afternoon DeVillers and Keeley conducted the autopsy on the partial skull found near Devol Pond.

They met in the basement of St. Anne's, where Keeley had examined the body of Barbara Raposa just three months before. Silvia and Fitzgerald were also there, along with an ID man from Fall River. The physicians unwrapped the calvarium and laid it on the same table where the previous autopsy had taken place. This time, they didn't have much to go on. No teeth to match with dental records, nothing of the face.

DeVillers wrote on a pad as Keeley turned over the skull, "Anatomic diagnosis in lieu of remainder of body." He drew a line and below it added, "Calvarium with left lateral crush injury."

Keeley picked up the skull and peered into the hole in the temple where DeVillers had looked when he first examined it in Westport. "The specimen consists of a calvarium containing meningeal membranes and brain," he said. The meningeal membranes form a natural barrier, like a sac or a bladder, that insulates the brain from the inside of the skull.

"The facial bones are completely absent," Keeley continued, laying a metal ruler against the fracture as DeVillers wrote. "The skull shows an oval defect in the left temporal and parietal areas which measures three inches by 3/4 inch. Brain protrudes, and the bone fragments around the periphery appear to be deviated inward."

The ID man took pictures. Keeley rotated the calvarium in a full circle, examining it closely, then laid it on the table and stepped back to allow DeVillers time to catch up with his words. When the medical examiner nodded, Keeley said, "The external color of the skull is brown, and there are adherent tree leaves. No external soft tissue remains."

Keeley turned to the built-in desk behind him and opened a drawer. He removed a stainless-steel instrument shaped like a large question mark, then turned back to the table and picked up the skull again, in his left hand. DeVillers put down his pen and unzipped another evidence pouch, similar to the clear plastic bag in which the skull had been transported from Westport, and held it out for his colleague. Keeley inserted the steel device into the hole in the left side of the calvarium; by alternately prodding with the surgical tool and tipping the fracture downward, he coaxed the brain and meningeal tissue through the hole in the skull and dropped them into the pouch. DeVillers zipped the bag shut and laid it on the table.

Keeley peered into the now empty skull. "The fracture goes all the way around to the right frontal base," he said. "And—there it is—"

"Hematoma," DeVillers said, anticipating.

"A large subdural hematoma," Keeley confirmed, "about five millimeters thick, over the right parietal area."

Two days later, Paul Fitzgerald drove his unmarked Massachusetts State Police cruiser into the drive-through entrance to the headquarters of the Federal Bureau of Investigation in Washington. A messenger was sent down from the Evidence Control Center, and the trooper was accompanied to the third-floor offices of the FBI laboratory. There he was introduced to the center's head, a man named Myron "Mike" Shulberg. Fitzgerald briefly described the case to him and delivered the skull, the brain, the hair, and eighteen other items recovered from the site in Westport, along with a letter of conveyance. He stayed a few minutes longer to make sure there were no further questions, then returned to his car and started the long drive back.

Shortly after Fitzgerald left, an FBI examiner named Alan Robillard was glancing through the laboratory log of incoming work and saw the new case from Fall River. "Hey," he said aloud, and rushed down the hall to see if this one had been assigned. "My hometown," he told Shulberg. "What do you say?"

Robillard, thirty-four, had grown up in the Flint, a tenement district around Lafayette Park, graduating from Durfee High School in 1963, then went on to study textile technology at Southeastern Massachusetts University (at that time called Durfee Tech). Just after graduation in 1967, he entered the Marine Corps, where he became a pilot, and joined the FBI in 1976. Because the principal examiner in a case of this sort was very likely to be called upon to testify in court, Robillard jumped at the chance to return to the city where he had grown up. He no longer felt a part of Fall River, but going back as a witness for the FBI would be a kind of triumph.

Moreover, Robillard already knew Dan Lowney in the Bristol County CPAC unit, as he had done the hair work on a previous case, the murder of Doreen Levesque. Robillard also knew Lowney's partner, although not as well, and when he recognized Fitzgerald's name on this latest case he was annoyed that he had missed him.

As a general rule, the assignment of each case entering the Evidence Control Center depends on the principal nature of the evidence. If the majority of specimens were documents, the case probably would be assigned to the Document Section; if it were mostly blood, it would go to Serology; and so on. Since most cases involve more than one type of evidence—a document, for example, may contain a bloody fingerprint and therefore fall into the provinces of Documents, Serology, and Identification—the decision on its primary assignment often required some degree of subjective judgment. But this was different. Shulberg knew immediately which case Robillard was asking for, and he shook his head. "Sorry, Al, this one goes to Fred." It involved bone, and in any case with bone the policy on primary assignment was ironclad: it was given to Fred Wallace.

Wallace, who headed the FBI's Hair and Fiber Unit, was the designated liaison with the Smithsonian Institution.

Fred Wallace's first task was to carefully sort through the articles in the carton to make sure everything on the Bristol County evidence list was properly accounted for. Then he commenced a procedure known as Q-ing and K-ing the items: a Q number was assigned to articles of questionable origin, and a K number was given when the origin was known. Although almost everything in the box carried a strong inferential link to a particular suspected victim, under the laws that govern evidence, that connection was still questionable until it could be proven scientifically.

He wrote Q1 on the intake sheet, and beside it he wrote "Skull."

Although the Q and K numbers are assigned by the FBI, the description of all incoming evidence is taken from the labels supplied by the referring police agency. Q2 was described on Fitzgerald's list as a coat. Q3 was a sweater. Q4 was another sweater. Successively, Wallace assigned Q numbers to the rest of the items in the box. A brassiere. Panties. Two portions of sock. Another sock. The jeans. Two mittens. A shoe. Five pieces of fabric. Six clumps of hair with attached scalp and dried flesh. A comb. A soap dish. The clear plastic bag with what was left of the brain.

There was only one K, and that led back to a Q: the blood sample which had comprised the hematoma was known to come from within the skull.

When he completed relabeling the exhibits, Wallace's next job was to distribute the assignment to different examiners throughout the laboratory. In addition to the primary tests in Hair and Fiber, this particular job called for auxiliary examinations in Serology and Identification. In cases where one specimen goes two places, the fingerprints are done last because tests in that unit involve the use of chemicals which could compromise or possibly ruin the examinations conducted elsewhere.

He took the clumps of hair into a closed room and laid out the six evidence bags, starting with Q15 on the left and running to Q20 on the right. He then opened each bag in turn, carefully shook and brushed out all the debris from the hair onto a piece of brown paper, and placed the paper in a pillbox which he labeled with another Q number. When the contents of each successive evidence bag had been cleaned in this fashion, he took the bags to another room and mounted sample hairs from each strip of scalp onto a series of glass slides, which he also labeled in turn.

Microscopic examination of human hair cannot establish with certainty whether any two specimens are from the same source, but by comparing observed characteristics with their known frequency, it can supply a precisely measured degree of probability for such a match. Probability and proof are two different matters, especially in a court of law. The only proof available through this method of inquiry is negative in nature: in instances where the two hairs exhibit demonstrably different characteristics, the examiner can state with certitude that they are not from a single source.

Wallace's initial examination of the hairs from the evidence bags indicated a high degree of probability that they were all from the same person, which is just what he expected. He read in the letter accompanying the samples that additional evidence would be coming in another few days. He set the slides aside for eventual comparison with hairs which the police in Massachusetts would attempt to collect from a brush belonging to the suspected victim, Karen Marsden.

When Fred Wallace called the Smithsonian, he was told that his contact there was not available. Dr. Douglas Ubelaker, the curator of anthropology who had three years earlier succeeded Larry Angel as the FBI's bone man, would be back the following week. Wallace made an appointment, marked the date in his diary, and put the skull aside as well.

On April 25, 1980, when Fred Wallace and another FBI agent arrived at the Smithsonian with a box containing the skull from Fall River, Dr. Douglas Ubelaker had been chairman of anthropology less than four months. At thirty-three, he was one of the youngest department heads in the history of the Smithsonian and only fourth in the line of forensic anthropologists since that position had come into existence three quarters of a century earlier. But he had been with the Smithsonian for nine years, since shortly after receiving his doctorate from the University of Kansas, and despite his youth he had managed important archeological digs in the Midwest, in Maryland, and in South America and had refined several new techniques for extracting from bones valuable information about past peoples. Like Hrdlicka, Ubelaker had ties to Czechoslovakia; his grandfather, Johann, had come to America from Moravia at about the same time Hrdlicka arrived on these shores. Working alongside both Larry Angel and Dale Stewart, Ubelaker also had provided expert analysis in a number of cases from the FBI and other agencies and along the way had become a diplomate of the American Academy of Forensic Sciences. Wallace had worked with him on several of those prior assignments.

Wallace set a box on the table in the middle of Ubelaker's laboratory, opened it, and removed the skull, still in its evidence bag but now tagged with the FBI's Q number. "This one's from Massachusetts. I think you're going to find it a bit of a challenge."

Ubelaker took the bag and turned it over briefly in his hands. Through the plastic he examined first the supraorbital ridges and the mastoid process of the skull. "It's female," he said. "I don't know about the time since death—there's not much soft tissue." He set it down again in the box.

Wallace also gave Ubelaker a folder with a memorandum of conveyance and the report from DeVillers and Keeley, who had autopsied the skull ten days before in Fall River. "We're hoping for a positive ID," he said.

"Naturally." Ubelaker was soft-spoken, and he smiled quizzically. "If this is all you have, you know a positive ID is unlikely."

The other FBI agent tapped the folder with the autopsy results. "There's a picture of the missing girl—"

Ubelaker looked doubtful, and he put his hand on the folder to stop the agent from opening it. Five years earlier, Larry Angel had identified the skull of a murder victim solely from a photograph, and the case had received a lot of publicity. He had been able to do it because there was a slight misalignment in two of the front teeth, which Angel had matched exactly with a picture of the victim smiling. But neither Angel nor anyone else in the Smithsonian had done it before or since. And in the present case, there were no teeth, no jaws, nothing of the face below the brow line.

There was an additional reason Ubelaker did not want to see the photograph at that point. Since he had first started in forensic work, he had made a practice of carefully avoiding anyone else's opinion of the material he was given until after he had completed his own examination. He did not want to risk tainting his observations by unconscious acceptance of someone else's assumptions about what he was seeing—and if the skull carried a Q label, then a photograph was just such an assumption. "I wouldn't expect too much," he said. "Even if we get into reconstruction, there's not an awful lot to work with. Most of a person's face is below the brow ridges, and that's the part we don't have." He glanced surreptitiously at his wristwatch. He had squeezed in this meeting in the middle of running a two-day symposium on studies of the Plains Indians at the Smithsonian, and it was about to start up again. "I will look at the picture, and I'll give you an opinion. Are you in a terrific rush?"

Wallace shrugged. "We've still got a way to go at our end. There's a fair amount of other evidence."

Moving aside the box with the skull, Ubelaker looked at his calendar. It was an extremely busy time for him. Once the symposium ended, he was committed to work on several manuscripts from it in the days ahead. Another book-length publication, on the Ayalan burial site on the south coast of Ecuador, had just gone to press. All this was on top of sorting through his new responsibilities as head of the department. "I don't know what we might get into, especially if we decide to do something with the photograph," he said. "It may be a couple of weeks—"

Wallace thought for a moment, then nodded. "Fine."

Ubelaker pushed the box across the counter to a young woman assistant, and he passed her the folder. As he walked toward the door with the two agents, he said, "You know what would be a whole lot better than a photograph?"

Wallace turned when he was in the hall. Behind him, in stacks that reached almost to the ceiling and stretched far into the distance, were the drawers containing the Smithsonian's reference collection of human skeletal remains. "The teeth? The mandible? The rest of the body?"

"Maybe even better than all that," Ubelaker said. "An X-ray. A medical X-ray of the skull, taken while the subject was alive."

TWENTY-FIVE / MISSING PARTS

In the two weeks since the discovery in the woods off Robert Street in Westport, the surrounding area was the subject of almost continuous search. Teams of state and local police daily trudged the woods. Divers from the state police and the Westport Fire Department scoured the bottoms of Devol Pond and nearby Sawdy Pond. Every septic tank and dug well in the area was opened and searched. George Dean even supervised the draining of two small swamps, which were pumped dry and systematically raked across their bottoms.

The effort to find the rest of the body culminated on the Sunday after the calvarium skull had been delivered to the Smithsonian. Led by the Massachusetts State Police, more than one hundred volunteer searchers, mostly from area police and fire departments, made a massive sweep through the woods, progressing methodically in a grid pattern, turning rocks, prodding with rods for soft soil beneath the surface, checking under every shrub. Teams working with police dogs specially trained to find dead bodies crisscrossed ahead of the volunteers.

The effort produced no other hair or bones, no more of Karen's clothing, not a single new piece of related evidence. As on the first day, the only real proof that a crime had occurred was what remained of the faceless head. And even there, the connection between the partial skull and the disappearance of Karen Marsden was only circumstantial; however strong the inference, there was still no proof that the calvarium was hers or that the skull was related to the clothing.

But legal proof is one matter, and nearly certain probability is another. The police knew that the clothing was Karen's, and they remained convinced that the murder had taken place at or near the site marked by the rocks, where they had recovered the blue jeans and most of the hair and scalp.

The distribution of the other items of evidence, in a northerly course through the woods, suggested the killers had approached with their victim from that direction, tearing off her clothing as they went and possibly dragging her by the hair. If that had been the case, then the supposition which had taken George Dean and his two boys to the laneway off the Turnpike in the first place was partially incorrect. The vehicle had not been parked on that laneway, but further down Robert Street, perhaps in a cleared triangle where a road branched off to Devol Pond about three hundred yards from the presumed murder site.

It was also problematical why the partial skull was found at an even greater distance from that site and in yet another direction than the path of the clothes. When a decaying body begins to fall apart—in the language of forensics, to disarticulate—it is not uncommon for the head to separate from the neck and roll downhill from the rest of the body. But the condition of the remaining soft tissue suggested that decay had not yet progressed to the point where such a separation would have occurred naturally. And even if it had, the ground where the calvarium was found was relatively flat, so there was no way it could have rolled more than a few inches. The most generally accepted theory remained the same as on the first day: probably it had been picked up near the place where the jeans and shreds of scalp were found and carried down Robert Street by a ranging dog.

As for the total absence of any other remains, a second theory began to emerge, collateral to the first. The head had been separated from the neck during the commission of the murder. Because of the remoteness of the location, the victim's remains could have lain undetected in the woods for a considerable time after the crime, perhaps even several days. During that period, before the killer or killers returned to dispose of the body, the head could have been carried away from the site.

But these were all suppositions and useful only as far as they guided the judgment of the police in deciding where to look next. Even before it became apparent from the grid search that the woods were unlikely to yield any more clues to what had taken place there, the focus of expectation had shifted to the two young women who had come forward as witnesses to the killing.

Paul Fitzgerald and Dan Lowney met Robin Murphy at Logan Airport in the early afternoon on the Tuesday after the search and drove her directly to the district attorney's office in New Bedford. This time,

Robin flew alone; her friend Pam Coady was so terrified by what she'd overheard in Dallas that she packed and returned to Massachusetts ahead of her.

At four that afternoon, in the now familiar conference room of the DA's office, a CPAC detective lieutenant read Robin her rights.

"You understand what he said?" Pina asked. He was standing across the table from Robin, watching her intently. "You have a right to a lawyer if you want. If you cannot afford one, the court will appoint one for you."

"It's okay," Robin said, smoothing her hair back from her face and frowning in what seemed to be impatience with his attention. "Everything is fine."

Pina was not to be put off. "You're not on drugs or anything like that?"

Robin shook her head. "No."

"So you are aware of what he just said to you? Voluntarily, you want to make a statement?"

"Yeah," Robin said, looking apprehensive but resigned.

Pina sat back, satisfied that he had done everything he could to defend the record they were about to create against the most obvious avenues of attack if their witness changed her mind at some future time. He looked over at Dan Lowney and another trooper named Robert St. Jean, who would be asking most of the questions. "Okay," he said.

Despite what they knew of Robin's telephone conversation of a few nights before with Sonny Sparda, Pina had instructed the detectives to follow the same sequence as the events themselves and not to jump ahead. This was normal procedure in an interrogation; it developed the case logically from the beginning, and if the transcript of the interview became evidence in court, it would provide a lucid, accessible document for the jury.

But in this case, there was an even more compelling reason for Pina's strategy. So far, they knew that Robin was anxious to give the impression she was cooperating in all three murder investigations and because of this she was testifying without an attorney. If the police told her what they now knew, it would alert her to the fact that she had become a suspect in the death of her best friend, and her apparent cooperation was likely to end on the spot. They already had her testimony on the Raposa murder, so this time they started off with the killing of Doreen Levesque. Lowney began slowly, asking her what she remembered from the night of the killing.

As she had done frequently in her interview with Macy three weeks earlier, Robin began her response by repeating the question. "Why do I remember that night?"

St. Jean said, "Any reason that sticks out—"

"I was with Carl Drew that night."

The troopers waited for her to say more, but she looked back at them as though she had delivered an important fact and now wanted some form of acknowledgment. She was far more guarded than she had been in previous interviews, a certain sign that she was now aware that her situation had become more tentative. After a moment, St. Jean smiled and said, "Okay—"

"That's why I remember that," she said.

"In Carl Drew's car?" St. Jean asked, trying to draw her into a narrative.

"Yeah," she said and smiled back at him, giving nothing.

Across the table, Pina seemed more impatient with the interrogator than with the witness. "Ask where she was."

Before St. Jean could do so, Robin turned to the DA and said, "We picked up Doreen Levesque from Bedford Street."

Dan Lowney was alarmed at Pina's intrusion; if the witness revealed something material to the case in response to one of the DA's questions, Pina could find himself in the embarrassing position at the trial of being called as a witness for the defense. Partly to cut off any further prompting, Lowney asked, "How did you know Doreen?"

"Because she was prostituting up there," Robin said, shrugging as though the question were obvious. "And I knew."

St. Jean asked if Doreen worked for anyone in particular, by which he meant a pimp, and Robin said she worked for no one. He then asked if Robin had ever talked to her.

"Yeah, just to stop, you know, on my bike," she said, reminding everyone in the room, perhaps consciously, that she was still less a woman than a child, "and smoke a joint with her, whatever."

"That particular night, you were with Carl Drew?" St. Jean asked, returning to the time of the murder.

She pushed back her hair again and nodded. "Carl Drew and a black man named Willie."

In response to St. Jean's methodical questions, offering nearly nothing at her own initiative and forcing him to extract the information from her one small fact at a time, Robin outlined the events of that evening up to their meeting with Doreen Levesque. After Robin got into Drew's car on either Pleasant Street or Bedford Street, they drove around for a time, then picked up Willie in the Highlands area, near Ruggles Park.

Robin described Willie as about Carl Drew's height, average build, with "short, kinky, black man's hair" and wearing black sneakers. The only other thing she could recall was that he lived with a white girl called Cookie—a blond girl, with glasses—Robin didn't know her by any other name either.

When Willie got into the car, Robin said, Carl drove around the corner, down Rock Street, up Pleasant, then across on a side street to Charlie's Cafe. After checking out the intersection, he turned and started slowly down Bedford. Between Charlie's and the next corner, which was Ninth Street, they saw Doreen Levesque standing on the sidewalk.

Carl pulled up to the curb and asked her how she was doing. Doreen shrugged; Drew had a reputation for violence, and although he got along well enough with other pimps, she knew he had a very different attitude toward free-lance hookers. But this time, Drew did not seem to have anything particular in mind. They traded pleasantries, and after a while he asked her if she wanted to join them for a couple of joints.

Doreen was smart enough not to be put off by the apparent friendliness of the offer; she looked into the car to see who else was with him. Recognizing Robin, she thought about it for a moment, then got into the back seat, beside Willie.

As they drove around the town, smoking and looking at the sidewalk sights, Carl asked the same question St. Jean had just asked Robin: was Doreen working for anyone?

Doreen had half expected the question. She said she was on her own and that she liked things better that way. That was not the answer Drew wanted to hear, and he told her she had to work for someone, that she "couldn't afford" to work the street on her own. Doreen disagreed. There was some yelling. Without pulling over, Drew turned around and slapped her in the face with the back of his hand, then turned back to his driving.

Robin said that Doreen started to say something more, but Drew told her to shut up. He watched her in the rearview mirrow; blood was starting down her chin from a cut on her lip. She began to weep. Drew told her to stop.

St. Jean asked, "Did she?"

"Well, she sort of kept it quiet." Robin did not let down her guard with the interrogators, but it was obvious she was gaining confidence from their concentration on the actions of the others rather than on herself. "She didn't stop crying, but, you know, she wasn't saying anything else. She was just listening to him."

By this time, Robin said, they were on Stafford Road, on the south side of the city and away from the bars and bright lights. Drew turned left, and a few minutes later they were driving in darkness down Eagleton. Doreen said, "How about heading back to Bedford Street?"

Drew did not answer. Instead, he turned to Robin. "You in any hurry to get home?"

"Nope, not me. I'm fine."

He kept on driving.

After another block, Robin said, Drew looked into the mirror again and spoke to the back seat. "So you're sure you don't want to go to work for me?"

Doreen was clearly frightened, but she shook her head and stubbornly returned his glare.

Drew turned the car up over the curb and off the road. Robin looked out the window to the right and saw that they were at the Diman, the vocational technical high school on the northeast edge of Fall River. Drew drove across an unpaved area near the school's playing field and finally parked beside the dark shape of the bleachers.

Robin said that Drew got out of the car and opened the rear door. Doreen refused to get out, so Drew told Willie to help him. Together, Drew and Willie picked her up and carried her away from the car. Drew warned Doreen not to call out, and although she resisted them, she remained silent as they carried her into the deeper shadows under the stands.

Lowney interrupted Robin; he had visited the murder site and was familiar with the area she was describing. "That's pretty well lighted down there. Could you see under the bleachers where they took her?"

Robin replied quickly, "There wasn't light—"

Lowney persisted. "The back part of the bleachers—"

"Where we were wasn't light," she said sharply. "The parking lot was light, but not the field, not where we were. It wasn't lighted. Uh-uh."

St. Jean knew the area as well and tried to steer the interview back to the narrative of events leading up to the killing. "The parking lot is on the right, and the bleachers—"

Robin was not about to be diverted, not with this detail still at issue. She cut across his words. "Yeah, but it wasn't lighted where we were, uh-uh."

"All right," St. Jean said, holding up his hands to put an end to what Robin apparently saw as a threat to her credibility. She took a breath and leaned back. When it appeared she had let go of it, St. Jean said, "You saw them carrying her away?"

"Yeah," she said. She glanced darkly at Lowney, apparently still smarting from the challenge.

"How far did they carry her?" St. Jean asked.

"From the car to the bleachers." She sounded impatient at the need to repeat what she had just told them.

The detective lieutenant who had read Robin her rights tried to help. "Maybe the length across this room—"

"Here we go again with distances," Robin cut in. "I don't know."

Still conciliatory and calm, the lieutenant asked, "Could you tell what went on, what happened after they got her out of the car?"

"I didn't see anything," Robin said. She turned angrily back toward Lowney. "Okay? I didn't see nothing."

Lowney nodded. "Did you hear anything? Did Doreen at any time yell?" Robin had covered that already, and she raised her hands in frustration and looked away. Lowney let it pass and asked, "How long were they gone?"

"Ten minutes, about that—they weren't gone that long." She seemed placated by his change in the direction of the questioning. "And when they came back, I asked Carl where Doreen was. He said, 'You don't really want to know.' And I said, 'Okay, I don't. Fine.'"

The detectives and the district attorney all looked at her without speaking for a moment, and then Lowney asked, "You never saw or heard anything?"

Robin pursed her lips and shook her head vigorously. "Not until I saw it in the paper."

There was silence around the table. Then Paul Fitzgerald, who had said nothing to Robin since the interview began, leaned forward.

"How did they tie her up?"

"I don't know," she said, pushing the hair back from her face and looking the detective straight in the eye.

"Where did they get the things to tie her up with?" Fitzgerald asked.

"Carl had things in the trunk," she said, then cut herself short. Perhaps she realized her story was beginning to sound too much like what she had told this same audience about Andy Maltais and the death of Barbara Raposa. "He didn't go in the trunk," she rushed on, "but as far as I know, they could of had something underneath his front seat." She smiled nervously and shrugged, as though to indicate she was as bemused as anyone about the answer to Fitzgerald's question. "I don't have the privilege of going in Carl Drew's front seat. I might get my arm broke."

The district attorney asked if Drew or Willie had brought anything belonging to Doreen when they had returned from under the bleachers to the car.

"I think Willie had some articles that belonged to her," she said.

"Like what? Do you remember?" Pina asked.

"Shoes and stuff like that," she said. "In their Satan thing, that's what they do—they take the belongings of the person. If they get any spots or blood from that person on their clothing or anything, they have to burn it."

"Did you see any spots of blood on their clothing?"

"No."

"Were you looking?" Pina asked.

She shook her head, and again the hair fell across her face. "Uh-uh," she said, emphatically.

The lieutenant said, "But you did see the shoes that Willie had?"

Robin seemed less certain. "Willie had something"—she hesitated, then finished indecisively—"that was her shoes."

"Could you describe what he had? What color? How many?"

"Let's see—" She appeared to strain at the recollection. "I can't be exact." She lifted her hands in surrender. "No, I couldn't." She smiled ruefully at the detectives and the DA. "I don't want to give you no wrong details."

"You're pretty sure it was Karen's shoes?" the lieutenant asked, unaware that he had used the wrong name when he had meant to say Doreen.

"Yeah, something that belonged to her," Robin answered, unaware as well.

Pina changed the subject. "Do you know Willie's last name?"

"Willie?" she asked back. "No, I don't."

"Last names don't mean anything to you?"

"Nope," she agreed amiably, "they don't. I know it was Willie that lived with Cookie."

"Do you know where he lives?"

"With Cookie," she repeated.

After a few questions by Fitzgerald and others, St. Jean returned to the question of the shoes. What had made Robin think Willie had them when he got back into the car?

"They took Karen's shoes," she said.

"But you don't know if they took Doreen's shoes?" St. Jean answered. It was not so much a question as it was to establish the fact that they were talking about Doreen Levesque, not Karen Marsden. It was as though he had nudged her with an electric prod.

Robin put her hand to her forehead to push back her hair, but she held it there, tense with anxiety, as she tried to sort out the confusion between the names. How long had she been saying Karen? Had she let anything else slip without noticing it? "I don't know. I don't know what it was," she said. "I am saying shoes."

Then, as though the lapse had been theirs and not her own, she added impatiently, "I know what they took off Karen."

Fitzgerald and St. Jean took turns asking Robin about what else had happened during the ride to and from the place where Doreen Levesque was killed, looking for facts that could be checked and details that could be verified. Had she seen anyone she knew during the two hours they drove around the city together before the murder? Robin was sure she had, but she couldn't remember. Did anyone see her? She said it was likely. "If I was a prostitute on the corner, I'd stare at every car that went by." But again, she couldn't recall a single name.

St. Jean asked if Robin had any conversation of her own with Doreen during the long ride.

"Carl was talking to her." She shrugged, as though it were obvious that under those circumstances there was no possibility of interrupting.

"You were with her for a two-hour period. You didn't talk at all?"

She shook her head. "Carl talks mostly."

St. Jean asked, "Why?"

Robin looked at him without comprehension. "Huh?"

"Why?" he repeated.

"Why?" She surveyed the others around the table, then turned back at St. Jean. "If the man ever looked at you, you wouldn't want to say nothing either."

"You were afraid of him?" he asked. And when Robin nodded, he asked again, "Why?"

"He worships Satan."

St. Jean asked her to repeat her answer.

"He worships Satan."

St. Jean brought Robin back to the conversation she had with Drew when he and Willie returned to the car.

"I asked him what happened to Doreen, and he said, 'You don't want to know.' And I said, 'You're right. I don't want to know.'"

"Why did you ask?" St. Jean prodded.

Robin looked away quickly, then back at the detective. "Because I just wanted to know."

"Did you think he was going to tell you?"

"I thought he would," Robin said. "And even if he would of then, I swear to God I wouldn't of said nothing."

St. Jean returned to his best question. "Why?"

"Because I don't know how many people there are to his little crew. All's I know is what he told me and what other people tell me: I know he worships the Devil, and I know a couple of other people who do it with him—Carl Davis and Willie. They told me he's involved with the Satan Avengers—people from New Hampshire; other people are telling me he's the one who started that—I don't know."

The lieutenant asked, "What do you call them? Satan Avengers?"

"Yeah," she said. "Worshipers of the Devil."

The lieutenant was looking at her with his head tilted, as though unsure whether to ask the next question. "If you had seen something that night, would you tell us now?"

Robin shrugged. "Yeah."

He looked reassured, and smiled at her. "Okay. I just want to make sure we understand you."

St. Jean leaned toward her and tapped the tabletop with his finger for emphasis. "You realize how important it is that you tell us the whole truth?"

"Yeah," Robin said again, louder this time, looking as though she couldn't decide between being offended or amused at their insistence. "And nothing but the truth. Whatever."

No one at the table showed any reaction to her show of nonchalance. Still speaking in a calm, reasonable voice, St. Jean said, "We don't want you to add anything that isn't there or didn't happen."

The frown on Robin's face darkened. Her voice dropped, trembling in frustration and scorn. "That's why I'm telling you what I'm telling you."

There was no reaction to this new show of vehemence either, but this time Robin seemed to sense that she had overreacted and that she might now appear to be protesting too much. She leaned back in the chair and looked at St. Jean sullenly from under a veil of dark hair.

St. Jean returned the look without giving away a thing. He seemed to have no comprehension of why she might be angry.

Flustered and ill at ease, she again brushed the hair from her face, turning toward Paul Fitzgerald, whom she knew better than anyone else in the room. "Okay, are we done yet?"

"No," Fitzgerald said, equally as impassive as St. Jean. "Not yet."

St. Jean brought the questioning back to what had happened after the killing. They reached the point where Drew dropped off Willie at Charlie's Cafe, agreeing to pick him up later. Fitzgerald asked, "Why was he going to pick up Willie afterwards, instead of dropping you off first?"

"Why are you asking me?" Robin said. "Ask him—"

"Did he say?" Fitzgerald persisted.

Robin thought for a moment. "Carl wanted to see what *I* was going to say. After he dropped Willie off, he said, 'You don't know nothing, right, Robin?' I said, 'Right.'"

The detectives asked Robin whether she thought this was a threat. She said she did. The lieutenant asked her if she had ever seen Doreen again.

"No, I didn't," she said. "I saw her picture in the paper, and my mother asked me if I knew her. It was—I don't know—a week later."

Lowney said, "There must have been talk on the street the next day or the day after."

She shook her head. "I don't know about then. I rode my bike by. If I don't see somebody, I'm not going to stop and talk to them—I am just going."

"Were the girls talking about Doreen?"

"I don't know."

Fitzgerald said, "It was on the radio all day, and in the newspaper, about the body they found that day. Did that mean anything to you?"

"The next day?" She looked surprised.

Fitzgerald nodded. "Really."

The lieutenant added, "On the radio, TV, certain newspapers: a girl's body had been found there."

Robin looked from one detective to another, her face neutral. "I don't know nothing about that," she said, "until her picture was in the newspaper."

Dan Lowney leaned forward. "Weren't you curious? To find out what happened to her?"

Robin pursed her lips again. "No. I never wanted to know what happened to her. Nothing." She shook her head, thought for a moment, then looked up at Lowney. "Dan, I am so sick of getting myself in trouble, it's not even funny."

She sounded like a rueful truant, as perplexed by her behavior as they were, throwing herself on the mercy of her audience. Lowney did not respond. No one responded, not even with a smile.

"Did you ever tell anyone else about what happened that Friday night?" St. Jean asked.

"Uh-huh. I told Karen."

"Why did you tell Karen?" Fitzgerald asked. "That was after you came to the barracks with Andy?"

"Because she knew something was fishy. She was thinking of going up to Cookie's house to get some of her clothes. I told her not to, and she said, 'Willie said it was all right.' And I said, 'Yeah, but you can't trust Willie.' And I explained to her why. I told her that girl was found dead."

The lieutenant asked, "In your mind, you think they killed her?"

"In my mind, I know."

"Did Karen know Doreen was dead?" Fitzgerald asked.

Robin looked at him in a way that said he already had the answer; back in December, Karen had spoken with him about the killing at least a dozen times. "Yeah," she said, guardedly but with an edge in her voice.

"Why did she think Carl did it before you told her?" Fitzgerald asked.

Suddenly she looked trapped and started answering the question before he was finished. "I imagine Carl had mentioned to her about it," she said quickly. "In fact, I remember Karen telling me Carl had threatened her about the girl under the bleachers. 'You'll be found the same way.'"

The lieutenant held up his hand as though he were directing traffic. "Run that by one more time."

Robin slid down in her seat, seeming to cringe. "Carl told Karen that she would be found the same way."

"Why did he threaten her?"

"At the time, she wasn't with Carl." Robin meant that Drew was no longer Karen's pimp. She sat up a little straighter in the chair, thrusting out her chin with the smallest hint of pride. "She was with me."

"Recently, Robin," Lowney asked, "have you told anyone else about this?"

Robin hesitated uncomfortably. "Yeah."

"Who?"

"Pam Coady."

St. Jean asked, "Why did you tell Pam Coady?"

She raised her eyes to the ceiling, then shook her head in wonderment and chagrin at how she had come to do such a foolish thing. "Because I happen to shoot off my mouth when I get too high."

Pina asked quietly, "Anyone else?"

"No," Robin said. She was slumped back in the chair, her elbow on the armrest and her hand at her forehead, looking at the tabletop.

After a moment more, in the same soft voice, Pina laid out the next card. "Did you ever tell anyone named Sonny?"

Robin looked up sharply, trying to hide her panic. "There *was* somebody else," she said in a rush, as though the idea had just come to her.

St. Jean asked, "What's Sonny's real name?"

"Maureen," she said, shaking her head again.

"Maureen what?"

"Maureen Sparda." Robin made a tight mouth and clenched her right hand into a fist below the table, still shaking her head in a show of disbelief at this new evidence of betrayal. It was not possible to tell if she was angry with Sonny or with herself.

"When did you tell her?"

"Sonny?" she asked, fighting for time to organize her thoughts.

St. Jean did not even bother to nod, but waited patiently.

"When I was gone away," she finally said. She unclenched the fist and let her hands lie open on her lap. "I talked to her over the phone. Couple of weeks ago."

Fitzgerald asked, "Before you came back or after you came back?"

When she appeared not to hear it, St. Jean said, "What made you tell Sonny?"

"What made me tell Sonny? I think I told you." Robin looked nervously to either side of her. "I happen to shoot my mouth off when I get high."

"You were high when you told Pam," St. Jean said, "and high when you told Sonny?"

"Yeah," she said, dropping her eyes again.

"That's on—"

"Valium," she said. "Or—I tried to OD on whatever they were. I ate them, and I ended up talking that night."

"That's the only reason you told them?" St. Jean asked.

"Yeah," she answered. She brushed back her hair and looked around the table. "Otherwise, I would of never opened my mouth."

The district attorney watched her for a moment, then leaned forward and in the same quiet voice as before, he asked, "How about a fellow named Bobby?"

This time, instead of being alarmed at the DA's participation, Lowney was annoyed. He glanced across at his partner, but

Fitzgerald's attention was resolutely on the witness and he did not look back.

"Uh-huh, Bobby Bohun," Robin said helpfully. Her eyes betrayed the briefest possible hint of anxiety, but it was gone in an instant and then her face showed nothing.

"While he was at Sonny's house?" Pina finished.

"No," she said emphatically. "Because I never talked to Sonny about that in Sonny's house. I talked to her about that over the phone."

For the time being, the CPAC detectives and the district attorney agreed they were finished with questions about Doreen Levesque. Pina then asked Robin if she wanted to change her earlier testimony about the death of Barbara Raposa. Lowney sat back in resignation. Robin said she did not.

"Did you in any way do anything to Barbara Raposa?" Pina asked.

"Nope—just what I did to her in the car. She hit me, and I hit her back."

"Did you ever hit her with a rock?"

"Uh-uh."

Dan Lowney said, "Was Karen there, Robin?"

She looked at him warily. "You mean was Karen there that night? Uh-uh."

Pina asked, "Was Carl Drew there that night?"

She shook her head again. "In fact, I just found out a few days ago that Carl Drew knew Andy. I didn't know that—I just found that out."

Pina repeated the question. "Was he there that night?"

"No," she said, dismissing the question so she could return to her own agenda. "But Carl went to talk to Andy sometime last week—I don't know what about. He told Sonny, 'Robin is going to get stuck for this, not us.'"

"Okay," Pina said, acknowledging her answer and disregarding the rest. "Just wanted to know."

Robin was not to be put off. "That's why I wasn't going to say nothing to her," she went on, referring to her telephone conversation with Sonny. "I am not going to jail for something I don't know."

This time, Pina responded. "You understand that I hear a lot of things, Robin."

She looked at him from under her eyelids, then shrugged in acknowledgment.

"So I'm going to ask you questions, okay?"

She shrugged again, and looked away.

But Pina was not finished. He said, "Nothing you want to change on that story for Barbara Raposa?"

She did not look back at him. "No."

The DA studied her for a moment more before he said, "Okay."

Finally, after more than an hour on the Levesque case, they came to the matter of Karen Marsden. Led a step at a time by the CPAC detectives, Robin gave them their first eyewitness account of what had taken place the night of February 8.

Robin said that at about eight o'clock that evening, she and Karen had walked down from the Nolin apartment on Forest Street, where they had been visiting Karen's son, and started hitchhiking on South Main. They were picked up, and Robin rode as far as the corner of Pocasset, where she got out and started walking over toward Harbor Terrace, while Karen continued in the pickup truck to Bedford Street.

Before Robin had gone very far on foot, she said, Carl Drew and another pimp named Carl Davis drove by in a rental car that belonged to Carol Fletcher. They told Robin to get in. A short time later, they found Karen Marsden on Bedford Street, and they told her to get into the car as well. With Davis at the wheel, they crossed over through Tiverton, Rhode Island, and then down to Westport. In a deeply wooded area beyond Family Beach, Davis pulled off the road and parked.

St. Jean asked, "Who was in the car at that time?"

"Me, Karen, Carl Drew, and Carl Davis."

The lieutenant held up his hand again. "Was Carol Fletcher in the car?"

She shook her head. "Not in the car."

Pina asked, "She never went to the scene with you?"

"No," she said.

His voice still quiet and steady, Pina persisted, making certain he was understanding all the facts correctly. "She never went to Westport with you?"

"No," Robin said again. She looked curiously at Pina, pursing her lips.

"Go ahead," the lieutenant said, as though the matter were of no consequence. "Keep telling us."

Robin hesitated a moment longer, then began again. "Carl Drew told me to get Karen out of the car. I just looked at him. 'Robin, take her out of the car.'" Her voice was low and menacing, as she acted out Carl Drew's role in addition to her own for the district attorney and the detectives. "So, I took her out of the car by the hair"—she looked at the faces around the table, knowing at least part of what they knew about what had been recovered at the murder site. "Because she wouldn't get out of the car," she said plaintively. "And Carl did make me hit her a couple of times, and I did—" She continued searching the faces at the table and raised her voice as though in anger. "Because, if I didn't, then I would be laying on the side of her."

The interview continued for another three quarters of an hour, the police and the district attorney leading her through this account as methodically as the one that had gone before. Carl Drew, she told them, had forced her to pull out Karen's hair. Then, she said, Carl Drew broke Karen's neck and cut off her head. And after a time, one of them kicked the head into the woods. She said they poured gasoline on the body and burned it until there was nothing left. There had to be a scar on the forest floor from the fire, she told them, but she couldn't point to the place on the district attorney's aerial photograph where the burning had taken place. It was too dark. She could not recall.

Robin continued answering their questions about her story. Throughout the interview, the detectives and Pina were constantly mindful that if Robin became too threatened, their conversation could come to an immediate end. They listened carefully to each response and asked her more questions, leading her painstakingly on, but determined as they did it not to break the fragile pact between them.

They were also careful to avoid giving away any of their own reactions. Because on at least one major point, and probably on several, they knew she was lying.

At ten minutes to six, they agreed to stop for dinner.

At eight-thirty that night, Pina, St. Jean, and Detective Brian McMahon returned with Robin to the conference room and interviewed her for an additional forty minutes. In that second session, the questions were limited to the murder of Doreen Levesque. Robin's answers remained the same except in one important exchange. McMahon asked, "Is there anything else that you can remember about that night that you haven't told us?"

"No, sir," Robin said. Then she added, almost as an aside, "I was pretty well—however you want to say—half in the bag, or whatever."

McMahon recognized the comment as a positioning statement, one that suggests guilt by denying responsibility. He immediately asked her again, "Did you take any part in the beating of Doreen Levesque?"

"No," Robin said. She hesitated, then said, almost as an afterthought, "Not that I know of."

"Did you tie her or assist anybody in tying her?"

"No," she repeated. And again, she added, "Not that I know of."

McMahon had to proceed with extreme caution. He was sure she was on the verge of implicating herself as a participant and not just as an observer. But first, Robin needed to establish this new notion that she was too high to remember. "Did you take any part in the murder of Doreen Levesque?"

"No."

"You're sure?"

"No."

"You're not sure?" His tone was patient, understanding, almost soothing.

"All right," Robin said, leaning forward and her voice rising. "I'm sure I didn't bash her head with a rock. I'm sure I didn't punch her or do anything like that to her—she was a friend of mine. But as far as tying her up or anything that would, you know, not really make me feel that I was involved"—she leaned back and turned her palms up in a gesture of uncertainty—"it's possible, because I really don't remember."

McMahon looked over at the district attorney.

Pina looked briefly back at him, little more than a glance. But as he did, he offered the detective the slightest inclination of his head. McMahon had done a good job.

Forty-eight hours later, on the other side of the country, Dan Lowney, Paul Fitzgerald, Paul Carey, and Assistant District Attorney Ray Veary sat down with the second eyewitness in a suburb of Tacoma, Washington.

Lowney read Carol Fletcher her rights. In addition to getting her recollection of what had taken place that night at Westport, the interrogation team hoped for some insight into why Robin Murphy had denied three times that Carol had been present at Karen Marsden's murder.

One possibility was that Robin was trying to protect her friend.

Another was that Robin was afraid of what Carol knew and was simply trying to protect herself.

In the first full week of May, after the interrogation team returned from Tacoma, the Bristol County district attorney's office reached a decision to charge Carl Drew, Carl Davis, and Robin Murphy with the murder of Karen Marsden.

As a witness in protective custody, Robin had been held under close confinement, if only in a motel, since her second return from Texas the previous week; the state police were with her night and day, and the possibility of escape, if it was even in her mind, was nearly nonexistent. Drew was in custody as well, having been sentenced to fifteen days in the Bristol County House of Correction on an unrelated matter just a few days before. While the warrants and other paperwork followed their bureaucratic—and relatively leisurely—course, the investigation continued on the street and elsewhere.

At 11:00 A.M. on May 7, Dan Lowney met with Leah Johnson at the Dartmouth barracks. A twenty-three-year-old black prostitute who worked for Carl Drew, Leah told Lowney she'd come up from New Jersey just a few weeks before, had met Drew in Charlie's Cafe, and that same night had moved in with him to his apartment on Pleasant Street, across from a bar called the Sword and Shield.

Leah appeared extremely nervous; when Lowney asked her why, she said she was afraid Drew would have her killed for talking to the police. He reminded her that Drew was in jail, but it appeared to have little effect.

Lowney had heard that Leah carried a buck knife that Drew had given her, and when he asked her for it she took it from her pocket and laid it on his desk. The detective picked it up and turned it over in his hand; it appeared to be the same kind of knife that the police in Fall River had borrowed from Drew and examined three months before, right after Karen Marsden had been reported missing. Lowney said he wanted to keep it for testing as possible evidence.

"I'm going to be in enough trouble if he finds out I'm here," Leah said, "in fact, more than enough. You keeping that knife's going to make things a lot worse."

"I don't plan to go down to the jail and tell Carl I have it or where I got it," Lowney said.

"If he finds out you have it, he's not going to have to ask where you got it," she said. "He's not stupid."

Lowney opened the knife, examined the blade, then folded it again and placed it in his desk drawer. He looked back at Leah and gestured toward her left hand. "That's a nice-looking ring."

She looked down, then reflexively covered her left hand with her right.

"Let's see it." His tone was friendly, but firm.

Reluctantly, she held it toward him. The stone was a solitaire diamond.

"Where'd this come from?"

She hesitated a moment, looking desperate, pulled her hand back, and covered it in her lap. In a small, resigned voice, she said, "Carl."

Lowney watched her questioningly. "What are you bothered about?" he asked her. "You still look scared."

"You know—" She changed her mind. Perhaps it was not a good idea to tell policemen what they knew. She looked down at her hand forlornly, then said, "I been told this ring was Karen Marsden's."

The detective waited for more, and when nothing came, he quietly asked, "Where'd you hear that?"

"Sonny. Up on Harbor Terrace."

"Sonny saw the ring and told you it was Karen's?"

She nodded miserably and continued looking at her lap.

Lowney held out his hand. "I can tell you if it is soon enough."

She looked up to see that he expected her to give him the ring, but she made no move to respond.

"Just for a couple of hours," the detective said.

"If I did that," she said, "Carl would have me killed for sure. I told you too much already."

"Leah, Carl Drew is in jail—"

But she stood up from the chair, and the hand with the ring was thrust deep in the pocket of her jacket. "I told you too much already," she repeated and rushed out of the office.

Lowney remained seated at his desk, listening to her footsteps running down the wooden stairs.

The next morning, May 8, Dan Lowney was in the Fall River District

Court receiving authorization for search and seizure of Leah Johnson's diamond ring.

By 10:00 A.M. the same morning, a warrant of another kind was obtained in the New Bedford District Court. It charged Robin Murphy with the murder of Karen Marsden on or about February 8, 1980.

And in Washington, at the National Museum of Natural History in the Smithsonian Institution, Dr. Douglas Ubelaker removed Q1, the calvarium skull, from its plastic evidence bag, laid it carefully on the black-topped table in his laboratory, and began his examination.

The murder warrant was served on Robin at four o'clock that afternoon. She was arrested by state police detectives at the motel and taken to the barracks in Dartmouth for fingerprinting, then locked up for the night in the New Bedford Police Department.

On May 9, the Bristol County grand jury returned indictments against Robin Murphy, Carl Drew, and Carl Davis, and District Attorney Pina swore an affidavit in support of his request for a warrant on Drew, citing Drew's indictment by the grand jury for the killing of Karen Marsden and stating that Drew "participated with others in the pre-arranged, ritualistic slaying of the victim and the dismemberment of the victim's body."

Drew was arrested in the Bristol County House of Correction at noon and delivered by the Sheriff's Department to the CPAC headquarters in the district attorney's office in New Bedford. At twelve-thirty he was interviewed briefly by Dan Lowney and Paul Carey, who came in from Fall River. Then Drew and Robin Murphy were arraigned in the Bristol County Superior Court.

Robin and Drew were led into the courtroom separately, each in handcuffs. Robin was dressed in a red down vest over a black sweater, jeans, and hiking boots. A large gold loop ring swung from one ear, and her ponytail lashed her shoulders as she wept uncontrollably during the reading of the charges against her.

Drew, dressed in an open-collared white shirt and jeans, glowered at the press, the judge, the lawyers, and at Robin Murphy. But there was no sign of tears. Except for anger and a sense of suppressed and lofty outrage, he showed no emotion at all.

Both pleaded not guilty. The judge ordered Robin Murphy to be examined by a court-appointed psychiatrist to determine her ability to stand trial. Both were held without bail.

That afternoon, the district attorney held a press conference. One of the reporters asked whether rumors of a satanic cult were accurate.

In the past, Pina had not been anxious to seize publicly on that particular dimension of the case. It was dangerous. A number of stories had already appeared, mostly describing the police investigation in the Freetown Reservation and mostly originating with the Fall River Police Department. There had also been a front-page exposé on Silvia and Carey having attended the satanic meeting in Sonny Sparda's apartment. That story clearly had not come from the police, but from someone else who had been there and who had called the newspaper in the hope of embarrassing the detectives enough to keep them away from Harbor Terrace. Satanism was lurid, and the Fall River police had discovered that lurid could cut two ways.

It could cut two ways for the district attorney as well. Pina was enough of a politician to recognize the publicity potential, and he was enough of a lawyer to understand the risk of pretrial prejudice. He weighed his answer carefully. "The cult is not unbelievable. There may be some substance to it—there's a strong possibility. I'm not a disbeliever of anything right now."

Like Drew, Carl Davis, twenty-four, was already in jail at the time of the murder indictment, serving a thirty-day sentence in the Plymouth County House of Correction for assault and battery. He was arraigned later than Drew and Murphy. When he appeared in court, the press noted he was wearing a thin goatee and a mustache very similar to Carl Drew's. Like Drew and Murphy, he was ordered held without bail.

At ten-thirty Saturday night, Alan Silvia received a telephone call from Dan Lowney, who told him about the warrant on Leah Johnson and asked for his help in recovering the ring. As soon as Silvia hung up, he and Tom Joaquim headed up to Bedford Street. They looked in Charlie's Cafe, Pier 14, along the sidewalk, and on street corners, but to no avail.

Five days later, Leah Johnson contacted Lowney again, through an informant, and surrendered the diamond ring.

Karen's grandmother could not remember having seen the ring before. But when it was shown to a friend of hers who knew Karen very well, it was positively identified as having belonged to Karen Marsden. The friend said she had seen the solitaire diamond on Karen's hand as recently as a few days before she disappeared. She had worn it all the time.

TWENTY-SEVEN / ALIBI

C arl Drew's memory was far from his strongest asset. He had trouble recalling the dates or even the months of some of the landmark events of his recent life, such as when he first met people, or the time spans when he had lived with certain women.

His recollection of the night of February 8 was a notable exception. He claimed he was in Fall River the entire evening, and he recalled in considerable detail exactly where in town he had been, what he was doing, and the people and events he had seen during the period when Robin and Carol said he was in Westport, killing Karen Marsden.

This wealth of detail was all the more remarkable for its triviality: almost nothing he recalled was outstanding or even, on the face of it, deserving of recollection. He had played pool. He had visited two bars and had stood on the street corner outside one of them and smoked a joint. He had seen people passing on the street. He had spent most of the evening, although intermittently, in the company of his then current girlfriend, Margarida Revorido. They went home together early— early for them—when the bars shut down at one o'clock. Carl Drew's alibi described an unexceptional evening in the kind of detail most people forget within minutes. And it made pimping sound dull.

Drew first told his story when Silvia and Carey interviewed him on February 10, just forty-eight hours after the night in question. Two and a half months later, after his arrest, he still recalled the nonevents of that evening with the same precision as when he had first told them and had even improved the details in one important respect. While he had been smoking the joint on the sidewalk, he was talking with a friend who could verify that he was there. The friend was Carl Davis.

During those early days and nights in February when Drew's story was still fresh, Carey, Silvia, Joaquim, and other detectives of the Major Crimes Division had attempted to verify his alibi in the course of their conversations with dozens of possible witnesses who had been in the Bedford Street area during the time in question. Some of them recalled having seen Drew during the early part of the evening, and a couple thought they had even seen him late at night, but no one seemed sure. Part of the problem was that Drew was a Bedford Street regular, and nobody could say with certainty whether he had been in any one place at a given hour during a particular Friday night. Another part of the problem was that for almost everyone, whether Drew was there or not didn't really matter: the recollections comprising his alibi were not landmark events, or even events of much interest, and the details of that night were as ephemeral as most of the other aspects of Bedford Street life.

One exception was Drew's girlfriend, Margarida Revorido. Her recall of the night of February 8 was nearly as precise as Carl's. She had been interviewed several times by the Fall River police and the CPAC detectives when the Karen Marsden case was still a missing persons investigation and again after the discovery of the Westport skull.

A few days before Carl had been picked up and jailed for parole violation—essentially a technicality which allowed the police to hold him until they developed their case more fully and he could be formally charged with murder—Margarida had been arrested on separate charges related to prostitution. The police knew that Carl and Margarida had already had plenty of time to rehearse their stories over and over, but by separating them now, they reduced the possibility of future collaborations if new facts emerged which might require adjustments in Drew's alibi.

In the normal course of making the case against Drew, the CPAC detectives were instructed by the DA's office to interview Margarida more formally. On the twenty-first of May, Dan Lowney and a stenographer from the Bristol district attorney's office drove up to Plymouth, where she was being held in the County House of Correction.

Margarida knew why they had come, but for the record Lowney said they were there to talk about Carl Drew's connection with the murder of Karen Marsden.

"I don't think he could do something like that," she answered. "Four years I've been with him."

The detective asked her if she had known Karen.

"Yeah. She was always all right to me. She came to the house last summer. Carl and I broke up in July or August, and then got together in November or December of last year."

"Was she afraid of him?" Lowney asked.

"No." Margarida had a soft voice, but spoke earnestly, and her expression suggested the idea was preposterous.

"Not at all?"

"No. She used to talk about her boyfriend. She didn't love Carl—but she loved him as a friend."

"Was she working the streets for him?"

Margarida nodded and said, "Yeah," as though Lowney's question confirmed the relationship she had been trying to describe.

"What happened when she stopped?"

She held up her hands in a gesture of bewilderment. "He never forced her to do nothing." Then, pointing her hands toward herself, she added, "He never forced me to do nothing; he never threw me out of the house."

This was pretty much what Lowney had expected to hear. "Never laid a hand on you," he said, trying hard to avoid sounding deliberately ironical.

"He didn't *do* that," Margarida said even more earnestly. "And he didn't do those things to Karen."

"Do you remember the first Friday night in February?" Lowney asked.

"No, I can't remember."

"The night Karen disappeared?"

The eighth had been the second Friday of the month, not the first. When Margarida realized Lowney's error, her face brightened. "Carl was with me," she said decisively. "Down to the Pier."

"You recall that Friday night?"

"Yeah," she said. "I told a lot of people he was with me."

"How do you remember?"

"I was home all day," she said. "I called down to the Pier about seven—I didn't have no car or anything. Carl was always playing pool, all night long. He wouldn't of left there without telling me, because he knew I'd bitch."

He asked her if she had seen Karen or Robin. She said she had seen each of them that week, perhaps even the previous day, but not together.

"What's so special about that particular Friday, that you remember seeing Carl then?"

"We were together and the bar closed and we went home. On Friday night, Karen was by herself and I saw her, and I went inside the bar and I told Carl and he said, 'Fuck her.' He didn't care. That Friday, he didn't leave the bar." She hesitated, then quickly corrected herself, "We went to Charlie's—and back to the bar."

"Was Carl Davis there that night?"

She nodded, and said Davis had been down at the Pier. She thought Drew and Davis had played pool together, then had gone out to the sidewalk to smoke a joint. When they returned, Drew told her they had seen Karen drive by with Carol Fletcher.

Lowney took it all in, and when she had finished he gave her a long, thoughtful look of appraisal. "Did you talk to anybody about this night? Did you talk to Carl Drew?"

"No," she said.

"Did Carl Davis get a message to you?"

"No."

"What about Sonny?"

She acknowledged that she had spoken with Sonny Sparda on the telephone and had received a letter from her during the past week. She said Sonny had expressed faith in Drew's innocence and had told her Karen had been on drugs.

Lowney listened with increasingly obvious skepticism. "Are you making an alibi for Carl Drew?"

"No," she said, with the same expression as before, indicating the absurdity of the suggestion. "Every night, he was always with me."

"He never left you?"

"I was always checking in with him. I was never gone more than ten or fifteen minutes. I stopped and let him know I was there. He was shooting pool."

"That night, was Karen with Carl?" Lowney asked, meaning, was Drew still her pimp.

"I'm not sure," she said.

"Was she working?"

"Yeah."

"Was Carol Fletcher working for him?"

"I can't tell. He had a whole bunch of girls that he knew."

He asked about Robin, and she told him that Robin worked for herself. He asked again if Karen Marsden was working for Carl, and this time she said she did not think so, repeating that Drew never forced her to do anything.

"Did Carl Drew ever use Carol Fletcher's car?"

"He used to walk or call a taxi. Ever since we went back together, he didn't bother about too many people because he knew I'd bitch."

"Carl told me he was living with Karen until the end of January. Was he?"

She thought for a moment. "No. We were together for Christmas and New Year's. He made a mistake. His mind is screwed up."

"Carl told me that, and other people told me that," Lowney pressed. He leaned toward her. "You could be wrong about that Friday night."

"No," she said decisively, holding her ground without pulling away from his physical proximity. "After we went back together, he was always with me—not only that Friday night. When I'd go down to my mother's house, I'd call and make sure he was still there, and I'd stay away only about a half hour."

Lowney showed no reaction, but moved on to other topics. He asked if she had ever seen Karen with a diamond ring. She said she had not. He asked her about the shoes.

"I heard all about the shoes," she said, shaking her head in denial. "Two pairs of boots—that's all I have at home."

Lowney asked what she had heard about the shoes and from whom.

"That the shoes I had was Karen's. Sonny told me, when Carl was locked up, Saturday or Sunday." She reflected for a moment. "They were like brother and sister. I was never jealous of her; she was the only one."

"There was no reason to be jealous," Lowney said.

"Did you know Doreen Levesque?"

"No," Margarida said quickly, then took it back almost as fast. "Maybe I did. I never bothered with her. Carl was with a lot of girls when I wasn't with him."

"Why did he let you go out on the street? Did he stop you?"

"He didn't tell me," she said defensively, then quickly added her standard disclaimer. "He didn't force me."

"What about the money you made? Did you turn it over to him?"

"Yeah. He'd buy the groceries and pay the rent. If I wanted anything, he gave it to me. I was only making about seventy or eighty a night—I was too afraid to stay out."

"Were you afraid of Carl?"

"Yeah, I am afraid," she said. Lowney noted the shift to the present tense and looked quickly at the stenographer, who nodded without looking at him, holding onto her concentration, the transcription keys clucking softly beneath her fingers. Margarida continued, "But I'm not afraid of him like Karen and Robin are."

"Why are they afraid?" he asked.

She shrugged. "I imagine because he is a man."

"Did he beat on you?" Lowney already knew from others that Drew beat her frequently, but he was curious to see if his question produced a denial.

Margarida smiled obliquely and shrugged. "Most of the time, I deserved it."

The detective looked at her speculatively, without answering.

"He broke my nose on the barges. I was drinking and making a fool out of myself, acting like a bitch. I was drunk and he smacked me—and I wasn't mad because I know I deserved it." She looked across the visitors' room, reflecting. "He needs help."

Lowney still said nothing. When she glanced at him, he looked back at her without any sign of response.

"I can't do more for him than I've done." Her eyes wandered across the room again. "He never talked about God—and now all he talks about is God." She turned back to the detective, as if in anticipation of his next question. "He doesn't go to seances. And he never talked about the Devil with me."

Lowney listened noncommittally. "Why were Karen and Robin so afraid of him?" he asked again.

"I don't know. It had to be for something he never did to me."

"Maybe he never told you everything."

Margarida smiled, half pleading and half in despair. "I asked him so many times, and he sweared to God that he didn't do it." She shook her head in frustration at her apparent inability to convince the detective of Drew's innocence. "And he never talked about God as much as now."

Lowney remained impassive. He took her back once more over the events of the night of February 8. As before, she confirmed that she had never been away from Drew for more than twenty minutes at a time.

"Why that Friday night?" he asked her at the end. When she looked at him without comprehension, he said, "What's so special about that Friday night that you remember?"

She held his eye for a moment, and she looked as though her mind were racing desperately over a long, familiar course; then she leaned back in the chair and looked away. "Nothing special," she said weakly, shrugging again. "We were there until the bar closed."

"You were there every bit of the time with Carl Davis?"

She said that Davis had not been there all the time, just Drew. Lowney said Drew had told him Davis and he were together the entire evening. Margarida looked at the detective defensively, as though she had been challenged. "I tell you the truth."

"Did he tell you to say this?"

"No. I swear to God, no."

"You're the only one that says he was there."

"If he left and went back, that is something I didn't see."

"They were gone for quite a while. Did you see Karen that night with Carol Fletcher?"

"Yeah, earlier; Carl told me."

"Carl Davis and Carl Drew went with them," Lowney said.

"How?" she asked. "They just went outside and were smoking a joint."

"They went into the car," Lowney said. "How long were you gone?"

"Never more than fifteen or twenty minutes," she said. Then, seeing the skepticism on his face, she went on to explain why she reported back so faithfully. "Because one time a guy really screwed me and had a knife to my throat."

Lowney's expression did not change. "Are you willing to take a lie detector test?"

She sank back in her chair. "Yeah," she said, and looked sullenly across the room.

"Didn't you see them get into the car with Karen and Carol?" he persisted.

She would not look at him. She appeared to be weighing what she said against the possibility that there were other witnesses. Her hands were lying open in her lap, and she moved them slightly in a small gesture of concession. "Maybe when I left," she said almost inaudibly. "I don't know."

"You're not sure?"

Her eyes moved to the transcription machine; the stenographer's hands were poised over the keys, waiting for her answer. "I don't know," she repeated plaintively.

"He could have gone?" Lowney pressed.

She slumped further down in the chair. She was trapped between the rock of her loyalty to Carl Drew and the hard place of self-interest. When she finally answered, it was almost in a whisper. "Could have."

"If you have to testify," Lowney went on mercilessly, "would you say you are not sure?"

She nodded. "I am not sure."

"You are in love with Carl and trying to cover for him, aren't you?" Lowney said.

As Lowney spoke, Margarida's eyes went back to the stenographer and then down to the paper that was slowly unrolling from her machine. Suddenly, as if she were just then realizing the significance of the record that was being made of their conversation, she sat upright in the chair, clasped her hands together, and turned toward Lowney. "I am not covering for him. I don't want to ruin my life because of him. I've got kids, you know. I'm not lying about anything: he was outside with Carl Davis. If he did get in the car, I didn't see it. I'm not trying to protect him. I'm not trying to protect him. I don't know how to lie. I have my kids, and I'm thinking about myself."

"You are in love with him," Lowney said. It was not an accusation, just a statement of fact.

They talked some more, and Margarida showed Lowney the letters she had received from Drew since she had been in jail. The detective weighed the small stack of letters in his hand, then gave them back to her. "Did he write to you before he was locked up?"

"Yeah." A piece of printed paper, different from the letters, protruded from one of the envelopes, and she pulled it out for Lowney to see. It was an offering card; at the bottom was printed the name of a church in Fall River. She held it toward the detective tentatively, like a talisman of uncertain power.

"Look." Her dark eyes were swimming. "He sends me prayers."

The numerous brown head hairs of Caucasian origin present in Q15 through Q20 exhibit the same individual microscopic characteristics and, accordingly, probably originated from one individual. Most of these hairs were forcibly removed from the scalp. The remaining hairs are broken at the basal end.

The first FBI report on the evidence arrived back in Massachusetts on Monday, the second of June, at the Bristol CPAC office in the North Dartmouth State Police Barracks. The letter containing the report was directed to Sergeant Dan Lowney. Although Paul Fitzgerald had made the initial delivery, Lowney had made a follow-up trip to Washington on May 10 with the buck knife he had taken from Leah Johnson, several rocks collected at the murder site, some hair curlers found nearer to Devol Pond, hair samples from Karen Marsden's hairbrush, and a strand of the hair removed by Carl Drew from his own scalp when Alan Silvia had interviewed him on February 10. Lowney read the report and passed it on to his partner.

While the report was far from conclusive, both Fitzgerald and Lowney knew enough about forensic analysis—about what it could do and what it could not do—that they were not disappointed with the FBI's findings. Fred Wallace's summary could not tell them with certainty, for example, that all the clumps of hair were from a single source and that the source was Karen Marsden. But by demonstrating that the hairs retrieved at the murder site were consistently of a kind, there was a high-enough degree of probability that they were from a common source to meet the test of reasonable doubt.

The report went on to say that the same combination of characteristics was present in the hairs in Q32, which had been removed by state police technicians from a hairbrush known to belong to Karen Marsden and supplied by her grandmother. And they were found to match the hairs which were imbedded in Q25, Q27, and Q28, the rocks recovered at the murder site. Taken together, the report offered a strong inferential case that the hair was Karen Marsden's and that the rocks had been used to kill her—or at least to smash her skull. It was the kind of inference an assistant DA would feel comfortable presenting in court.

One finding in the report, however, was somewhat troubling.

Specimen K2 consists of a single brown head hair of Caucasian origin that has been forcibly removed from the scalp. This single hair is dissimilar to the hairs present in Q32.

Lowney and Fitzgerald knew that K2 had been taken from the head of Carl Drew. A call to Alan Silvia revealed that Drew had yanked out the hair himself when the police had questioned him and requested a hair sample in February. On the basal end of that strand there was evidence of blood; in the hands of Drew's defense attorney, that portion of the report could create a problem.

The FBI laboratory also indicated that there were cut marks, as though from a knife blade, in the white jacket that had been recovered in the woods. No blood and no stains were found at the sites of the cuts, and there was no indication that they had been made by the buck knife. This finding—or lack of a finding—was predictable: because of where the jacket had been discovered in the woods, the state police detectives had assumed it was stripped from Karen before she was killed, so it was unlikely the cut marks were related directly to her murder.

Attached to the FBI letter was a memorandum from Dr. Douglas Ubelaker at the Smithsonian Institution, reporting on "one human skull."

The bone is well preserved, with considerable dried soft tissue still present. The upper portion of the cranial vault has been separated.

The small size of the mastoid processes and supraorbital ridges and general morphology suggest female sex.

Age at death is difficult to determine from the skull alone. However, the lack of union of the cranial sutures and general morphology suggest the individual was a young adult, probably between the ages of 15 and 35 years.

Since only a partial skull is present, no reliable estimate of racial affiliation, weight, or living stature can be made.

The presence of dried blood and soft tissue on the remains suggests that death occurred recently. Since most of the soft tissue was removed prior to this examination, an estimate of the actual time since death is not possible.

Comparison of the skull with the submitted photograph is not productive, since most of the facial bones are missing.

Paul Fitzgerald read Ubelaker's memorandum through to the end. The detectives had hoped for a positive ID, but they also knew the odds had been against it, and they had not expected anything more than they got. Fitzgerald laid the report back on his desk.

A few days later, the FBI returned the skull to Massachusetts. One of the things the FBI told Dr. Keeley was that Ubelaker believed even a calvarium skull could be identified by comparison with medical X-rays. Soon afterward, Keeley heard about that same technique from another source: Dr. William Sturner, chief medical examiner for the state of Rhode Island, spoke with Assistant District Attorney Waxler about this case and also suggested such a matchup was theoretically possible. Dr. Keeley decided he could use a little help; he put the box with the skull in his car and drove down to Providence.

Dr. Sturner, forty-four, was widely regarded as one of the most knowledgeable forensics specialists in the country; he taught at Brown University and Harvard Medical School, was published widely, and had just been named to the editorial board of the *American Journal of Forensic Medicine and Pathology.* Equally important, both in Providence and in a previous position as assistant medical examiner in New York City, he had performed autopsies on nearly a thousand homicides and had testified in over four hundred court cases.

After being shown into Sturner's office, Keeley placed the box on his colleague's desk and took off the lid. "In your opinion, what are the odds that this particular skull could be identified by comparing X-rays?"

Sturner examined the calvarium and then told him that the answer depended almost entirely on the existence of medical radiographs taken while the owner of the skull was alive. If such pictures could be found, he reiterated that the technique was available for establishing identity by that means. He showed Keeley a book entitled *Modern Legal Medicine.* "There's a whole chapter on identification by sinus X-ray patterns," he said. "In fact, I went to court myself with just such a case five years ago."

Keeley was interested in the technique, but he was skeptical about the likelihood of finding a comparison radiograph. "Except in the dentist's office, most people never have the occasion for an X-ray of their heads."

Sturner was an energetic, enthusiastic man, much more inclined to try to find solutions that to contemplate why something might not work. He turned over the skull, then stood up. "Let's take one right now."

A few minutes later, the two physicians examined the result. The image on the film was unlike anything either of them had ever seen. While the frontal sinus in a normal skull is shaped like a butterfly, the lacework bone pattern above the brow ridge in the picture showed only a smudge where the right wing should have been. Sturner looked at Keeley and smiled. "Now that's the kind of condition that can cause a medical problem."

Keeley held up the X-ray and nodded. "It's certainly unique."

"If I were you, I'd check every hospital, clinic, and private practitioner in the area where Karen Marsden lived. I'll bet anything she had sinusitis, and it was bad enough that she went somewhere for help."

As he put the skull back in its box and prepared to leave, Keeley contemplated the task Sturner had set for him. "That sinus pattern certainly raises the odds," he agreed. He smiled but still looked doubtful.

"Sure it does. That's the spirit."

Keeley started across the room, the box under his arm. At the door, he turned to shake Sturner's hand. "This would be a lot easier if they'd been thoughtful enough to leave some teeth."

Sturner put on a long face and nodded solemnly. "These were not thoughtful people."

TWENTY-NINE / **BRAIN CHEMISTRY**

Very few written words are awaited by their intended audience with such eagerness—not to mention high hope and dreadful fear—as the opinion of a psychiatrist in a murder trial. The psychological evaluation of Robin Murphy, ordered by the court at the time of her arraignment, did not actually take place until early June. John D. Snell, M.D., a psychiatrist from the Boston suburb of Needham, visited Robin at the Massachusetts Correctional Institution in Framingham on the fifth. He completed his report two days later, and Bristol County Superior Court Judge Robert Prince received it on the twelfth. It immediately became the object of heated and highly public contention.

Andy Maltais' attorney, Robert Macy, filed a motion for discovery, ostensibly to review the report in order to find out whether Robin was competent to stand trial. At the hearing, however, Macy addressed another purpose. "It is important for Mr. Maltais to know if there is anything in the report that would challenge her credibility."

Clearly, if Robin were found incompetent to stand trial for one murder, she would hardly be an acceptable witness to the guilt of Macy's client in another. This same logic was apparent to the attorneys representing Carl Drew and Carl Davis.

Judge Prince heard all three requests and denied them each in turn. "I am not prepared at this time to make the report available to the defense counsel. I will defer that decision to the trial judge."

In neither the Raposa nor the Marsden murders had a trial judge been appointed. This meant that among the many other things Maltais, Drew, and Davis could hope for in the long months ahead was that their chief accuser would be found incompetent—or even better, hopelessly insane. Their lawyers warned each of the defendants against building such castles in the air. But the prospect of such a dramatic turnaround was compelling.

If they could have seen the report when it was issued, they would have invested their hopes for salvation elsewhere.

The patient is a short woman, appearing somewhat older than her stated age of 17. The usual Lamb warning was given, the patient indicated that she understood, and she was entirely cooperative with my examination. She gave a history of a severely sexually abused childhood, of engaging in prostitution since age 11, and at intermittent attempts at psychiatric treatment for several years. She expressed extreme fear that she may be killed by acquaintances who know that she had been cooperative with the District Attorney on another murder case, and she firmly insisted that she is innocent of the murder with which she is charged, having been "set up" by these same persons. She specifically begged that she not be sent to the Plymouth House of Correction, for she feels certain she will be killed if she goes there.

She was oriented in all spheres. Her interpersonal contact and rationality were good throughout. I found no evidence of psychosis or serious mental illness. She understands the nature of the charge against her, and the possible consequences. She showed an adequate grasp of courtroom procedure, and could adequately describe the functions of the judge, jury, district attorney and defense attorney. She shows good ability to cooperate with her lawyer in her defense. It is my opinion that she should be found competent to stand trial.

The report was no better news for Robin than for the others.

As the patient insists that she did not commit the crime with which she is charged, my opinion with regard to her mental capacity at the time of the offense does not imply any opinion as to whether she performed any specific acts, but only an opinion as to her probable mental state during that time. It is my opinion that, at the time of the offense with which she is charged, the patient did not lack the substantial capacity to appreciate wrongfulness of her conduct, nor did she lack substantial capacity to conform her conduct to the requirements of law. Although the patient described taking alcohol, marijuana and mescaline around that time, I do not believe that the effects described can be considered to constitute a lack of substantial capacity as used in the law. I believe, therefore, that the patient should be found criminally responsible if it is shown that any act of hers at that time was criminal.

While Dr. Snell had been preparing his analysis of the state of Robin Murphy's mind at the time of the Karen Marsden murder, the FBI was conducting a similar enquiry, although necessarily by other means, into what had been going on in the head of her purported victim during the same period. The FBI's supplementary report arrived in Dan

Lowney's office at the end of the same week Snell's report arrived in Superior Court.

These tests completed the FBI laboratory's assignment from the Bristol CPAC in the matter of Karen Marsden, Homicide. On the blood samples from the skull and clothing, tests were inconclusive: the samples were human, but too limited in amount for purposes of grouping.

The following three compounds, however, were found to be present in specimen Q23, the brain that had been removed by Drs. Keeley and DeVillers from the calvarium skull: 14.9 mg percent of acetone, which could have been a by-product of natural decay following death; 0.05 mg percent of phentermine, which comprised slightly more than a trace of a nonprescription asthma medicine; and 0.01 mg percent of phencyclidine.

The third element was more widely known by its street name of Angel Dust.

THIRTY / **CHARACTER REFERENCES**

As the investigation gathered momentum, the general belief that Carl Drew would not return to the streets grew with it. And the detectives began to hear things they would never have heard otherwise.

There is probably no loyalty more ephemeral than the kind that is based solely on fear. Whatever other emotions continued to bind Margarida Revorido to Carl Drew, whether love or a sense of deserved punishment or both, the bonds that had connected him to many of the other women on Bedford Street began to loosen in the days after his arrest. Drew's arraignment, and his removal from the scene which he had dominated, may have created a temporary vacuum, but it also shifted the power balance, for a time at least, in favor of the detectives of the Major Crimes Division and of the Bristol CPAC. In place of a choice between obeying Carl Drew or suffering a beating or worse, the police investigation offered a far more attractive menu to his acquaintances and former associates: righteousness, the common good, self-preservation, liberty, and revenge.

One of the early voices in the growing chorus was Cookie, the woman who lived with the black man whom Robin Murphy implicated in the murder of Doreen Levesque. Acting on the advice of CPAC, Alan Silvia and Paul Carey had located Willie, whose last name was Smith, in the vicinity where Robin said she and Drew had picked him up on the night of the Levesque killing. In the course of digging further into Willie's involvement in that case, Lowney and Fitzgerald learned that Cookie had worked for several months previously as a prostitute for Carl Drew, and they brought her into the New Bedford CPAC office for an interview.

Cookie told the police that her legal name was now Mildred Mindle.

"I got married May first to this jerk," she explained. "What a mistake. I've never been with him since the day we got married. He went home to his mommy."

The two detectives smiled.

She then told them how she had come to make a friend of Karen Marsden and about her stolen car and the episode with Drew. Sergeant Lowney asked what Karen's reaction had been when she learned that Cookie had gone to work for her pimp.

"Karen wasn't happy. She told me not to do it. But she knew how I am when it comes to my kids. She sort of figured the way I did: like, what could I do, you know?"

"Did you feel you were set up?" Lowney asked.

Cookie looked at him thoughtfully, then shook her head. "Not really. I guess I was a little naive."

"When did Karen mention to you that she was in fear of Carl Drew?" Fitzgerald asked.

"September," she said, then corrected herself. "She told me when I first started working for him: watch him, he really shoots up, and when that happens, he's in a bad mood. And whatever he says to do, you say, 'Yes, Carl, I'll do it, Carl.' So that's the way it went."

Lowney asked, "Did you ever hear Carl threaten to kill Karen?"

"Most definitely," she said, "when I was living on Seabury Street. Carl forced Karen to go into stores and rip things off, and he used to make me go with her. This is why I can't go to Harbour Mall in Fall River anymore. He made us rip off clothes and stupid stuff and take them down to Bedford Street and sell them at half price. Karen didn't want to—she wanted out of the whole thing. But he used to say to her, 'You do it. If you don't want to fuck around anymore, you're going to steal.' So we did. Dartmouth Mall, Swansea, every day, every mall, one after another."

Fitzgerald repeated Lowney's question. "You heard him threaten her?"

"It started in late September, early October," she said. "She was scared to rip stuff, and he'd go, 'Either you start making your quota or I'll kill you.' You had to turn over to him so much money: if you can't make your quota, then he's going to bust your face in. Karen wasn't ripping near her quota, so he started threatening her to work the streets; he'd say he was going to kill her—either her life or her quota. She said, 'Why don't you kill me and get it over with? You're going to kill me anyway.'"

She told them that the last time she had seen Karen Marsden was the week after Thanksgiving.

Karen Marsden had left Cookie's life, Fitzgerald realized, at just about the same time that she had entered his, the week that Andy Maltais had come to the North Dartmouth barracks to talk about the killing of Doreen Levesque.

Lowney asked if Cookie had ever heard anything about a satanic cult.

"Carl used to say he was the leader of it," she answered. "He could get people to believe—you know, he had hypnotic eyes, and he could get a girl to do what he wanted. All of them have been in love with him. I never loved him, but he used to say, 'You will before it's over.'" She looked reflective. "It's not over yet."

She told the detectives how another girl who worked for him had informed on her to the police, and she was arrested on prostitution charges. "Carl was pissed. He said he was going to kill her for it—tie her to a tree to be sacrificed and pour warm blood from a live goat all over her face—tie the goat above her neck and let the blood and guts, whatever, run all over her. They'd make love to her while she was tied like that, whatever they wanted to do while she was tied: hit her with baseball bats or with the blood by her, you know, orsifice."

"Orifice?" Lowney asked, helpfully.

"You say it better than I do." She grinned self-consciously. "I know how to spell them. I don't know how to pronounce them too good."

"When was this?" Lowney asked, bringing her back to the topic.

"October." Her face lit up and then quickly darkened as she remembered something else. "He'd be high on heroin, and one time, he goes to me, 'I wouldn't kill you right away.' I go, 'What would you want to kill me for? I don't do nothing bad.' He said, 'That's why I wouldn't kill you right away. You give good head.'"

That part of the story did not go over the way she had expected, and there was an awkward hiatus as Lowney said, "To each his own" before looking away in apparent embarrassment.

For the first time in the interview, Cookie suddenly became angry. "No, not to each their own. That's how I prevented my face from getting busted a lot of times, I'll tell you. I had to do anything to be on Carl's good side. I was so terrified—"

"Why did you think Carl would kill you?" Lowney interrupted. "Did he ever threaten you after you got your freedom?"

"He told me not to fuck with him," she said, still vehement. She was trembling, not so much in anger at Drew as in resentment at her sense that what she said was being discounted by the detectives.

Lowney shook his head. "Why would he be afraid of you?"

"Maybe because I could testify he was a pimp. I'd be putting myself in trouble—"

The detective was still not persuaded. "Being a pimp is a long way from being a murderer."

"Not really," she shot back. Hearing Lowney say what he did, she suddenly realized that was the whole point: the two things were not that far apart at all. Cookie looked back and forth between the two detectives, searching their faces for some indication that they understood what she was trying to tell them. "Not really," she said again, more insistently than before.

Another girl who eventually found the courage to speak with the police about Carl Drew was a Fall River prostitute named Nancy. Nancy was in jail at the time Lowney got word that she had something to say, so he took a stenographer with him and drove up to visit her in the Plymouth County House of Correction.

"I hate him," she said. "I got a broken nose from him. He threatened me. 'If you don't work for me, you'll have to look around your back.'"

"When was this?" Lowney asked.

"Last year—June. He told me if I called the cops, he'd kill my nieces."

She told the detective the assault and threat had occurred in the Sword and Shield, across the street from Carl's apartment, and that she had gone to the hospital. Three days later, she saw Drew again. He warned her again about going to the police. "I go by your house," he said. "I know where you live and I know where your nieces are—and I will kill them."

The threat against the children of Cookie Powers had occurred in June as well. Apparently, Drew had found a sales pitch that worked and had decided to stick with it.

Nancy said she avoided him after that and started working in Boston instead of Fall River. She never went to work for Carl Drew. But until now, she had never gone to the police either.

Even Leah Johnson, the girl who had been so frightened of Drew's vengeance that she had at first refused to let the police examine the solitaire diamond ring he had given her, became emboldened by news that the court continued to deny him bail. Each time she came back to answer questions in the North Dartmouth barracks or in the CPAC office in New Bedford, she recalled a bit more about her brief relationship with Drew in the days just prior to his arrest.

And finally she told them everything.

Leah said she had heard things in the street, and they worried her. So one night she asked Carl about the girl who had lived there before her, the girl who had disappeared.

Leah and Carl were lying on the bed in his apartment, smoking dope and taking other drugs. There was nothing threatening about the way she asked, but Drew didn't answer at first, and she wondered dreamily if she had struck some kind of a nerve or invaded a private realm. When he finally did start to speak, it was not about the girl. Instead, he started telling her about his father.

They lived on a farm in New Hampshire. Drew's parents had divorced, but his father had a powerful personality and his mother stayed in the area, never able to disconnect—so Carl was equally as trapped as his mother in the orbit of his father's influence. When Drew was still a young boy, just entering his teens, his father had taught him to slaughter animals. It was a job Carl said he hated, but the more he objected to doing it, the more his father pressed: he made the boy hold the killing knife, to bleed the pigs or chickens; he made him drink the dying animals' blood; and, what Carl hated most of all, he forced him to go down into the slime and suffocating stench of the slaughter pit where the waste was stored and bring up the hides and hooves in a wheelbarrow for rendering.

One time, Drew told Leah, there was a fire in the barn, and a horse was burned to death. His father told Carl to cut up the body and drag it to the pit. The boy was revulsed by the sight of the dead carcass, but his father was unyielding: he put an ax in his hands, pointed to the wheelbarrow, and told him to get to work. When the boy backed away, the father kept pace with him, shouting at him to do as he was told, slapping him repeatedly in the face. He backed him to the edge of the pit, and before Carl could catch his balance and save himself, he fell in.

Leah did not know what to say, and she listened in silence. When he finished the story, Drew lay on the bed beside her, propped up on one arm, and exhaled a long column of smoke toward the ceiling.

Then Drew answered her question at last, as though it were a natural extension of the story he had just finished. He turned toward her, Leah told the police, his eyes half shut in reverie, and proceded to describe, in the same detail and with the same drugged detachment, how he and three other people had gone into the woods of Westport just a few weeks earlier with the girl who had lived there before her—Karen Marsden. And he told Leah how they had slaughtered her.

Although Carl Drew, Robin Murphy, and Carl Davis had all been indicted for the same murder and seemed at their arraignments to be headed for a common fate, each had a different lawyer, each was implicated to a different degree, and each would eventually choose a different avenue of defense. On July 23, when attorneys for all three defendants appeared before the bench in Bristol County Superior Court, each was there on a separate matter. The paths had already begun to diverge.

Carl Davis's attorney was there to request the court to set bail so that Davis could be released from custody until the time of the trial. The request was refused.

Carl Drew had been denied bail earlier, and he was there with his court-appointed attorney, John Birknes, to petition the court's permission for a polygraph test in connection with the killing of Karen Marsden. The judge warned Drew that if he failed the test, even though the results were not certain to be accurate, it could be held against him in court. Drew said he was willing to take the chance. The motion was approved.

Attorney Kenneth Sullivan was also successful in his petition on behalf of Robin Murphy. He said he needed help in locating witnesses who could testify in her defense. And although his client had been ruled competent to stand trial, Sullivan requested a more comprehensive psychological examination into her probable mental state at the time of the murder. The court approved up to $1,000 each for a private detective and a psychiatrist.

Finally, Ron Pina told the court that all the state's evidence in the case had been presented to the three attorneys and that they had twenty-one days to advise his office on the nature of their defense.

*   *   *

A short time later, Robin changed her story about the killing of Doreen Levesque. Although she had repeatedly denied it under oath, Robin now admitted that when Carl Drew and Willie Smith had dragged Doreen from the car and into the darkness under the bleachers that last night of her life, another witness besides herself had been present at the murder.

"Son of a bitch," Silvia said to Joaquim. They had just checked into the station at the beginning of their shift when they learned that Robin had placed Karen Marsden at the Levesque killing. "Robin has given the DA her motive for murdering her best friend."

"She's also just given him Carl Drew's motive," Joaquim said. "That's all the DA is going to see in this. Nobody over there wants Robin—she's just a helpless little seventeen-year-old kid. They want big, bad Carl Drew."

Silvia looked out the rain-streaked window at the grayness of Bedford Street, feeling impotent and sensing something new and sinister in this turn of events. He could not predict where they were going, but he suspected that Robin had given up an obvious truth in exchange for the chance to create an even bigger lie. "Everyone already knew Karen Marsden saw the Levesque murder; she practically told us as much last winter. The only reason she didn't spell it out was because she was protecting Robin, her best friend. So how does Robin repay her? By cutting off her fucking head!" He slapped his flat hand against the desktop so hard it hurt. "And now Robin's going to find some way to turn this whole goddamned thing around, to make it look like somehow Robin was protecting Karen. Jesus H. Christ!"

Joaquim looked out at the rain for a moment as well. "Maybe and maybe not." He shrugged. "Anyway, she hasn't done it yet."

"C'mon, c'mon," Silvia said angrily, "on the best day of her life, Robin never protected anyone but Robin."

Pending the outcome of the psychiatric examination, Sullivan submitted Robin Murphy's plea in the murder of Karen Marsden: not guilty, by reason of insanity.

"And if that doesn't work," Silvia said on hearing of the plea, "she can throw herself on the mercy of the court as 'almost an orphan'—because all of her friends are either dead or in jail."

The process of law, sometimes swift but often not, seemed to descend to a state of near dormancy during the month of August and into September. But the change of pace was largely an illusion. The responsibility for the case was simply—and inevitably—passing from the hands of the police into the hands of the prosecutors. The new team on the field was running just as fast as those from whom they had taken the baton. But the cadences of the judicial process, which is governed by order, are different from those of police work on the street.

Meanwhile, the three defendants in the Karen Marsden murder sweated out the dog days of summer in their prison cells, planning their individual strategies, each anxiously aware that his or her former allies were now potentially his or her most dangerous enemies. Which of them, if any, would survive the process ahead depended on how successfully that alliance could now be disowned, on whether the betrayal of their criminal partnership could still be bartered to advantage, and on which of them could gain a decisive moral advantage over the other two.

At the end of September, Robin Murphy's petition for a separate trial was approved by Judge Eileen Griffin in Superior Court.

Robin had broken further from the pack. Silvia, Joaquim, and Carey could do little more than watch nervously from the sidelines as she widened her lead.

But the growing gap may have been illusory. Just seventy-two hours after the splitting of the trials, Assistant District Attorney David Waxler, who had been assigned by Pina as prosecutor, announced that the cases against all three defendants in the Marsden murder might warrant the state's invocation of the death penalty. The original hounds of justice were no longer leading the chase, but it was clear that their replacements were still on the scent and pressing hard.

Birknes, Drew's lawyer, said he was "confused and irritated" by Waxler's announcement to the press and left open the option of asking for a change of venue for the trial based on unfavorable publicity.

Carl Davis's attorney said, "I prefer to try the case in the courtroom." He refused further comment.

Kenneth Sullivan was far more vocal in behalf of Robin Murphy. He said he would file a motion asking Waxler to specify the evidence in support of any request for the death penalty and that if Waxler refused, "I will ask that the state be prevented from invoking the statute at the trial."

Sullivan also announced that he intended to send a letter to the district attorney in connection with the trial of Andy Maltais. "I think Robin should have immunity," he said, "or she should not testify."

A week later, when the second psychiatric report on Robin

Murphy had been completed, Sullivan withdrew the plea of insanity. The report, he said, "showed no basis to support that defense."

Things seemed to come to a standstill during the period between Thanksgiving and Christmas. Then, on December 29, a Bristol County grand jury commenced a "John Doe" investigation into the conspiracy to murder Karen Marsden. Carol Fletcher was called as a witness. She refused to testify, citing her Fifth Amendment guarantee against self-incrimination. But a week later, on January 7, 1981, her lawyer cut the deal that everyone had been expecting. In exchange for her testimony against the other three suspects, Carol was granted immunity from prosecution for Karen's murder.

The Fall River detectives took a pragmatic view of the grant of immunity. There was no evidence that Carol had been involved in either the Raposa or Levesque cases. By striking its deal with the one participant in the Marsden murder whom the police did not consider dangerous, the prosecution eliminated Robin Murphy's best remaining hope: escaping by the same exit.

The Marsden murder was not the only case at issue for Robin, however. One week later, she made a far more complicated—and costly—deal of her own.

Before Robin's deal was struck, when it still appeared she would have to face trial, it had been the intention of her attorney to employ what had come to be known as the Patty Hearst defense: he would contend that she had been under the control of a more powerful personality and could not be held responsible for what she did at the time of the Marsden killing. But there was no precedent for that defense in Massachusetts law, and it began to look too risky. For one thing, while Carl Drew was an undeniably powerful figure, it soon would become obvious to any jury that Robin had a very strong personality of her own. And while Patty Hearst had started out as a victim, Robin had not. On the contrary, Robin had already admitted to being present at the Raposa killing, a case which did not involve Carl Drew in any way. "If there's a Patty Hearst in this whole thing, it isn't Robin Murphy," Alan Silvia told Tom Joaquim. "My vote would be for Andy Maltais."

"Your vote doesn't count," Joaquim said. "Besides, Patty Hearst was a woman; that defense would never work the other way around."

"How about Adam? He claimed a woman made him eat the apple."

"Yeah, and look where it got him."

Virtually on the eve of the trial of Andy Maltais, Sullivan struck a bargain with District Attorney Pina for Robin to testify on the murder of Barbara Raposa and to testify at any subsequent trials connected with the murders of Doreen Levesque and Karen Marsden. In exchange for that testimony, Robin would be granted immunity in the Raposa and Levesque killings and would be allowed to plead guilty in the Marsden case to a reduced charge of second-degree murder.

"Her agreement to cooperate in these cases is the only reason the Commonwealth has agreed to lessen the charge," Waxler told the press.

Both first- and second-degree murder convictions in Massachusetts carry an automatic life sentence. A second-degree conviction is subject to eventual parole. First-degree murder is not. Robin would be eligible to appear before the parole board in fifteen years, in 1996. Her assistance in the three murder trials, District Attorney Pina announced, would be weighed heavily at that time.

At two-fifteen on the afternoon of Wednesday, January 14, Robin appeared before the same judge who had signed Carol Fletcher's immunity agreement the previous week. Waxler read a summary of her involvement in the murder of Karen Marsden, as Robin listened impassively. She was then sworn as a witness, the judge led her through the summary again, and she acknowledged that the facts as given were correct.

A few minutes later, the clerk read the automatic life sentence. Robin's eyes were vacant. When she turned from the bench, she sighed deeply—perhaps with regret, but almost certainly with relief. The bargain Robin had struck meant she would never stand trial and therefore could never be convicted of murder in the first degree in any of the three killings.

"She'll be out before ninety-six," Silvia said, shaking his head in anger and disbelief. "This is just *bullshit*." But when the police turn a case over to the DA, they also give up the right to comment on it in public. Unlike Waxler and Pina, the Nighters had lost their access to the press, and Silvia's only audience was the other detectives in the Major Crimes Division, most of whom already shared his view.

"She'll be out before ninety-six," he said again, "and every friend she ever had will be dead or in jail." He ticked them off on the fingers of his left hand. "Barbara Raposa, Doreen Levesque, and Karen Marsden, then Andy Maltais, Carl Drew"—Silvia switched to his right hand—"Carl Davis, Willie Smith—everybody she was close to and a couple of guys who were unlucky enough to be in the vicinity. They

all go away forever, and Robin is on the street again before she's goddamned thirty years old."

Andy Maltais finally came to trial in the third week of January. On
taking his seat, he placed a Bible and a colored picture of Jesus Christ
in front of him on the defense table. The judge ordered them removed
before the jury came into the courtroom.

By the end of that week, largely on the testimony of Robin
Murphy, he was convicted of first-degree murder in the death of
Barbara Raposa and sentenced to prison, with no possibility of parole,
for the rest of his life. Andy walked back to the defense table,
removed the Bible and the picture from the drawer where he had
stored them, and clasped them to his chest as he was led from the
courtroom.

Margaret Charig, a reporter who had covered the murder for the
New Bedford *Standard Times*, approached Maltais' attorney as he was
packing his briefcase. "I've been wondering all through the trial, Mr.
Macy—what kind of a car did Andy Maltais drive?"

Macy was smarting from the loss, and he continued collecting his
papers, obviously weighing the question before deciding whether or
how to answer. He latched his briefcase and looked at her with guarded puzzlement.

"Robin said she was sitting in the front seat," the reporter went
on, "listening to the radio, while Andy was out in back of the car,
killing Barbara."

Macy still did not say anything. With obvious forbearance, he
hefted the briefcase by the handle, waiting for her to get to the point.

"And Robin also said that while she was waiting in the car, Andy
went to the trunk and took out the bag with his sex paraphernalia."

Macy pointedly set the briefcase down again on a chair. Instead of
answering, he looked across to the prosecutor's table, where several
other reporters were still interviewing David Waxler.

"On most cars, you can't open the trunk without a key."

Macy glanced back at her, nodded distractedly, and checked his
wristwatch.

"And on most cars," she continued, "you can't play the radio
unless the key is in the ignition."

At last he looked directly at her and held her eye, as though suddenly he had understood the point she was making. "Most cars," he
said.

"That's right, not all cars. But wouldn't it be worth checking the one they were in that night to see which kind it was? It won't necessarily vindicate Andy, but it may tell whether Robin was lying about being in the car, listening to the radio, when the murder happened."

Macy looked at her a moment longer, then picked up the briefcase again. He walked away from the table without answering.

On February 2, Carl Davis's attorney succeeded in separating his client from the remaining defendant in the murder of Karen Marsden. Davis would be tried at some later date. The last cord binding any of the three original defendants had been cut.

When Carl Drew finally came to trial in just another four weeks, he would be on his own.

THIRTY-TWO / **DIGGERS**

Whereas when Fred Wallace developed heart trouble, Mike Shulberg was faced with a dilemma. As head of the Evidence Control Center, Shulberg was responsible for the assignment of cases within the FBI laboratory, and several months earlier he had given all the hair and fiber work on the Karen Marsden murder to Wallace, not only because Wallace was in charge of that section, but because he was the bureau's liaison with the bone man at the Smithsonian. With the trial in that case just a few weeks away, it was now apparent that Wallace would be in no shape to travel to Massachusetts. The law required that an expert witness could testify only to matters of which he had direct knowledge, so the evidence would have to be resubmitted by the Massachusetts State Police and Shulberg would have to assign another investigator to the job.

Then he remembered that someone in Hair and Fiber had come to him about this assignment when it had first come in—someone who had grown up in Fall River, where the case originated. This time, because of the new circumstances, Shulberg would be able to give him the assignment. He picked up his telephone and called Alan Robillard with the good news.

Across the street, in the Smithsonian's National Museum of Natural History, Dr. Douglas Ubelaker was facing a dilemma of his own. He was carrying his new administrative responsibilities as department chairman as well as an unusually heavy academic workload: finishing off several papers related to his work in Ecuador, at the same time he was deeply involved in editing a collection of essays from the symposium he had organized the previous April in honor of John Ewers and Waldo Wedel. In the midst of this, his burden was increased by an unusually large cluster of forensic referrals, mostly from the FBI, involving cases in Montana, Georgia, Wyoming, Connecticut, and California.

Although the FBI assignments all involved mortal crimes, and usually by living people, they were handled with the same absolute objectivity and with the same scientific techniques as Ubelaker's analyses of remains from the most distant past. But if the intellectual approach was the same, he was never able to free himself from an awareness that the ultimate goals—even the spiritual nature—of these assignments were poles apart from those of his labors in academia. On the scholarly side, the object was the expansion of knowledge of the human condition. On the forensic side, it was usually the illumination of mortal folly.

Ubelaker's labors in connection with the Ewers/Wedel symposium, celebrating the careers of two great scholars who had dedicated their lives to science, provided a case in point. Their accomplishments, and the symposium held on the eve of their retirements, represented the epitome of what it meant to Ubelaker to be a scientist: to freely pursue the life of the mind, to achieve insights to nature and the hidden past that were previously obscure or unavailable, and, finally, at the end of a brilliant, productive career, to be warmed by the accolades of admiring and grateful colleagues.

It was along this same path, and with luck to that same good end, that Ubelaker contemplated his own career in science. His work in Ecuador, for example, which had begun eight years before, had already yielded valuable new insights to the health, physical characteristics, and ways of life in cultures which had flourished and vanished long before the arrival of Columbus. That was not all it yielded; through his first dig there he had met the young Ecuadorean archeology student who became his wife.

One of the papers he was currently writing dealt with an excavation on the Santa Elena Peninsula of Ecuador known as the Las Vegas Complex, the largest early mortuary site to be found in the New World, where some two hundred skeletons dating back nearly eight thousand years had been recovered. The paper examined the lives of a hunting and gathering people who inhabited the area prior to the invention of ceramics and before the rise of agriculture. It even touched on a mystery and what may have been the oldest record of a romance in the Western Hemisphere: a young couple, apparently in their late teens, was found buried together with their arms lashed around each other. They were beneath several large rocks which had been placed on their grave but above no others, in a site which became known locally as Los Amantes, or the lovers.

The forensic case Ubelaker received from the FBI at the end of February, just five days before he was scheduled to testify in the Drew trial in Massachusetts, provided a telling contrast to the romance of his fieldwork. On Palmara Island in the Pacific, an old munitions dumping site from the war years that had since been abandoned by everything but rats, authorities had found the charred remains of a woman. The skeleton showed evidence of sand erosion, rust, and organic growth. The bones had probably washed out of an old munitions box which was found beside them on the beach. In the remnants of the burned skull, Ubelaker saw what looked like a bullet hole, beveled outward.

In either line of enquiry, the techniques Ubelaker used were similar, the subject matter was the same, and his objectivity was as absolute, whether for science or for the law. But although those lines were parallel, he often felt that they pointed in exactly opposite directions—one toward the light and the other toward darkness.

These were some of the reasons he was not especially looking forward to the trial in Massachusetts. Another was that he knew his testimony there would be more a formality than a revelation. Without a medical X-ray for comparison, Ubelaker would be unable to offer the jury anything more than the sex and approximate age of the victim.

When Paul DeVillers' health had been better, he had been a surgeon at St. Anne's. Now that was behind him. Shaky, ill, in an advanced stage of diabetes, he was no longer able to operate on the living; he had become a medical examiner because that was one of the few avenues left open to him for the practice of his art. Besides, it was interesting work in its way, and it helped take his mind off his condition. He knew well enough what lay ahead.

Two weeks before the trial of Carl Drew, Dr. DeVillers received a telephone call from David Waxler in the DA's office. Although the initial purpose of the call was to discuss DeVillers' testimony about the skull which he and Dr. Keeley had examined several months before, shortly after the conversation began Waxler expressed his frustration that the Commonwealth was not going to be able to offer more positive evidence about the victim's identity.

"Dr. Sturner tells me that a medical X-ray could make all the difference," he said. "Dr. Keeley's been looking for several months, but he hasn't found anything. I'd like to give it one last shot before we go to court."

DeVillers hesitated. The likelihood of finding a comparison radiograph at the eleventh hour seemed remote to begin with, and all the more so if Keeley had already spent several months looking. On the other hand, Keeley had been busy with a lot of other things. "I'll see what I can do," he promised.

When he hung up the phone, he checked the trial date on his calendar, then put his hands to his face to wash away the weariness. Almost as an afterthought, he picked up the telephone and dialed medical records.

Yes, the hospital had treated a patient named Karen Marsden. She had come into the emergency department in November of 1978.

"What was the complaint?"

DeVillers could hear the pages turning while he waited, then the clerk told him, "Sinus headache."

He didn't dare to even smile. "What about X-rays?"

More pages. Then, "There were X-rays." Another pause as the clerk scanned the record. "X-rays of the head. Two views: frontal and lateral."

DeVillers laughed into the telephone.

Dr. Sturner held the radiographs from St. Anne's in one hand and in the other the forensic X-rays of the partial skull which Dr. Keeley had ordered several months before. "They don't match," he said.

Waxler and Fitzgerald stared back at him uncomprehendingly. For months they had been certain the Westport skull was Karen Marsden's. Now, just four days before the start of Carl Drew's trial, the Rhode Island medical examiner seemed to be telling them something that could not possibly be. Neither of them said a word.

"It's the angles," Sturner said, turning the two pictures so both the assistant DA and the state trooper could see as he spoke. "The jury won't know what it's looking at. We've got to reshoot the skull to match the angles of the originals."

Waxler exhaled in relief. "That's simple enough. We have the skull with us."

A half hour later, Sturner shoved the new X-ray onto the frosted-glass viewing box beside the images from the hospital. Even before he pointed out the similarities—in the shape of the nasal cavity, in the pattern of the one-winged butterfly imprinted in the white web work of the forehead—it was apparent to both men that the two sets of pictures were of the same skull.

"Beautiful," Waxler said.

"Just like a fingerprint," Fitzgerald agreed, shaking his head in awe.

*　　*　　*

"That could make a big difference," Ubelaker said when Waxler called with the news.

"It will change the focus of your testimony toward proving that the skulls in the two sets of X-rays are one and the same," Waxler agreed.

"Or proving that they're not."

"We've already compared them, so you don't have to worry about any surprises. And of course you'll have plenty of time to study them in detail before you get to court."

Ubelaker did not ask who had made the comparisons because it did not make any difference; the only comparison that counted was the one he would make himself. Until he had the two sets of radiographs, there was nothing more to talk about.

Waxler also told him that the venue of the trial had been shifted to the city of Fitchburg in the north-central part of the state. Ubelaker agreed to meet Waxler and Paul Fitzgerald at a motel near the city the night before he was scheduled to testify.

When the phone call was over, Ubelaker pressed a finger down on the cradle, then lifted it and dialed a colleague's number. With the discovery of medical X-rays, he knew that the defense was certain to challenge the reliability of his comparison. He was going to need to arm himself with all the precedents he could find for this technique of identification, both in the scientific literature and in the museum's own collection of human skeletal remains.

THIRTY-THREE / PLACE OF JUDGMENT

S tories of the killings of Doreen Levesque, Barbara Raposa, and Karen Marsden had attracted a lot of coverage in southeastern Massachusetts and nearby Rhode Island, and the intensity of that reporting increased with the discovery of the skull in Westport and the growing rumors of satanic rites in the Freetown Reservation. Carl Drew's defense attorney, John A. Birknes, requested a change of venue. It would not be possible, he said, to impanel a jury in Fall River or New Bedford that was untainted by news accounts of the Karen Marsden murder. Superior Court Judge Francis W. Keating agreed, and the case was moved to Worcester County Superior Court in Fitchburg.

Worcester County was a nearly ideal choice. Less than ninety miles northwest of New Bedford, it was near enough to be reached with relative ease by all the participants in the case, including those from out of state; Fitchburg was nearer than either New Bedford or Fall River to Boston and Logan Airport. But in terms of the taint from media coverage, either from the southeastern corner of the state or from Boston, Fitchburg could have been on the other side of Chicago. The county contained a different ethnic mix, relied on different news media, and was a distinctly separate cultural entity from any of the areas surrounding it. Because of this self-containment, Worcester was widely known in the marketing profession as a leading test area for the introduction of new consumer products, a location where campaigns to sell just about anything could be tried and fine-tuned before being taken nationwide.

It was the perfect place to find a group of discerning, intelligent people who knew little or nothing of the Westport Skull Murder, who were still unaware of Robin Murphy's guilty plea, and who had not prejudged Carl Drew.

A reporter from Providence went up to Fitchburg to test the temper of the town about an event that was being described in Rhode Island as the trial of the decade and found a level of indifference just slightly above apathy. A Fitchburg policeman whose beat was near the courthouse told the reporter he didn't know much about the case and didn't care. Local merchants and passers-by repeated the sentiment. They seemed to find a degree of satisfaction in proving that the biggest story in another part of the world was causing hardly a ripple here in Worcester County. In fact, in the week before the trial, for some of the local media, that became the story: not that the murderers, pimps, prostitutes, and Satanists were coming, but that the people of Fitchburg couldn't care less.

In that respect, the new venue was coming to look as if it were almost too good a choice, and shortly after Birknes got his way, he was apparently overtaken by second thoughts. Before the jury was impaneled, he asked Judge Keating to read potential jury members a narrative summary of the murder, so that those who found the crime "repulsive or bizarre" might disqualify themselves.

Judge Keating eyed Birknes sardonically from the bench. "You mean you want a jury that is not repulsed by that sort of thing?"

David Waxler suppressed a smile and rose to his feet from his chair at the prosecution table. "Your Honor, Mr. Birknes may well be undoing what he tried to do by the change of venue."

Keating said he would consider the request, but that there were some obvious liabilities in characterizing to the jury, in advance, the kind of testimony they would be exposed to in the trial. Not the least of these was the possibility that the jury might be required by law to reach its own decision on whether the murder had been committed with "extreme atrocity and cruelty." Surely it would be preemptive for the judge to tell the members, in advance, that it had been.

By Monday, March 2, however, when the jury selection actually got underway, the professed indifference of the city of Fitchburg, whether real or feigned, had evaporated. In addition to more than 130 potential jurors who were called for the selection process, the courthouse was crowded to overflowing by curious spectators and nearly surrounded by a cordon of vehicles, many with microwave relay antennas on their roofs that carried the markings of media from every part of the state.

The 110-year-old courthouse had not seen this much activity or this much drama since Lana Turner and Efrem Zimbalist, Jr., had arrived there with a camera crew some twenty years before to film a trial scene in the movie *By Love Possessed*. It was suggested by more than one spectator that the present proceedings might provide the sequel, to be entitled *By Satan Possessed*.

The ultimate spectator to the high drama was Carl Drew, who was delivered to the courthouse from the Plymouth County House of Correction under heavy guard. Drew was seated behind the defense table at the epicenter of this near seismic activity, wearing a blue three-piece suit, his face smooth-shaven and freshly youthful, his hair carefully trimmed and brushed. David Waxler had expected him to look different from the persona Drew had so carefully cultivated as the Superpimp of Bedford Street, but the extent of the transformation surprised even him.

What had not changed was Drew's laid-back but undeniably power-ful personality. He minutely surveyed each prospective juror, leaning forward intensely to search their faces but still remaining coolly com-posed and oddly passive. As reel one of the process that would deter-mine the entire future course of his life unwound before him, he was taking possession of the courtroom just as he had once ruled Charlie's and Pier 14—at once the heart of the scene and detached from it.

The press had expected the selection of the jury to take as long as a week; it was finished in only four hours. By Monday afternoon, twelve men and four women, chosen after 117 interviews, took their seats in the jury box and were instructed by the judge that they would be sequestered for the duration of the trial.

The following day, while the closely guarded panel was taken to Westport to see the place where the victim had died, the other players in the drama began their journeys to Fitchburg.

Some came to accuse, some with expert testimony, some to pro-vide the details of the police investigation, some to offer character wit-ness, some to offer alibis, and some as incidental players—all of them summoned by the state or the defense to help bring the drama to its conclusion. The witnesses were also sequestered, which meant they were not allowed into the courtroom except when they were sched-uled to testify, so they could not listen to the testimony of others. Theoretically, being sequestered meant they were kept away from each other outside the courtroom as well, but because the case was so big and featured so many players, in large measure what happened outside the courtroom was a matter of chance.

Robin Murphy arrived in a sheriff's car from the state penitentiary in Framingham, where she had already started serving her life sen-tence for the same murder in which she was now to testify against Drew.

The state police met Carol Fletcher at Logan Airport when she arrived from Tacoma and drove her to Fitchburg in an unmarked car, careful for her safety. Like Carl Drew, she had undergone a transformation in the months between the murder and the trial, but she was a changeling of a different kind. It was as though the events which had apparently nourished Drew had drawn from her in the same proportion. She appeared diminished by what had passed and frightened of what was still to come.

George Dean and Brian Field were summoned from Westport. So were Charlie Pierce, the Westport detective, and some of Dean's and Field's neighbors who had participated in the search following the discovery of the skull.

Karen's grandmother. And the other surrogate mother, Elvira Nolin.

Another mother, Maureen Murphy, came to testify—not for her daughter, whose fate had already been decided, but against Carl Drew.

Leah Johnson came. Pam Coady. Cookie Powers.

Margarida Revorido, apparently the only true believer in Carl Drew's innocence, hovered in the vicinity of the courtroom like a phantom, torn between the mandate to distance herself from the others in the case and a desperate appetite for word of what was happening within.

For Alan Silvia, Tom Joaquim, and Paul Carey, Fitchburg meant something else. The trial was the culmination—in their view, the product—of a year and a half of relentless commitment involving one-hundred-hour weeks and superb detective work. This time away from home was a form of compensation at the end of long travail, and they came in a celebratory mood. The state was picking up the cost for everything, and the detectives assumed they would be left pretty much on their own to enjoy the equivalent of a week's paid vacation. The climax would come in the form of a release from a shared obsession, when each of them would be called upon to deliver what he knew to the jury. It was "the biggest case to come out of Fall River since the trial of Lizzie Borden. We'll never be a part of anything like it again," Silvia said to the others, "not in our lifetimes."

As soon as they got to the motel just outside Fitchburg, they asked the desk clerk where Dan Lowney was staying, then went upstairs to leave a message on his door. Their sense of rivalry or enmity with the state police was long behind them, although there was still one major area on which they were deeply divided. The district attorney had chosen to downplay the satanic aspects of the killings: there was plenty of substance to the state's case against Carl Drew without the unnecessary risk and taint of further sensationalism. As a result, the

CPAC detectives had also minimized those aspects, spending relatively little time investigating what was referred to in the press as "cult activities." To the police in Fall River, however, this dimension was at the heart of the case. There were the stories of violent rituals (including persistent but unprovable rumors of mock crucifixions in the state forest) and the discovery of altarlike structures of wood and stone. There was evidence of the killing of cats and other animals and the ritualistic patterns of the stones at the murder site. There were the meetings in Fall River to conjure up the Devil. And there were signs of stoning and ritual disfigurement on the bodies of Doreen Levesque and Karen Marsden. These were more than the esoterica of children playing at evil; they were tangible evidence of evil itself.

Despite the strong feelings of the MCD detectives and the policy position at CPAC, both sides had gone a long way toward accepting their differences and living with them. The relationship between the two factions had become relaxed enough in the several months leading up to the trial that the state police could get away with occasional friendly gibes about the perils of "obsession" with the occult and the Fall River detectives were secure enough that they could accept the banter in good humor, even as a confirmation of their own identities and an acknowledgment of what they had contributed to the solution of the case.

The message Alan Silvia stuck in the motel-room door was a reflection of this new détente. It said, "The Fall River Cult Squad has arrived. We're in the lobby."

When Lowney came looking for them an hour later, he appeared worried. "Which one of you guys left that damned note?"

Silvia glanced at the other two, then said defensively, "C'mon, Dan, where's your sense of humor?"

"It's not my sense of humor you have to worry about. I'm not in that room anymore. Judge Keating thinks you left the note for him."

"You gotta be kidding," Silvia said.

If Alan Silvia was right that the Drew case was the trial of a lifetime, Judge Francis Keating seemed the perfect choice to preside over it. A tough, brilliant jurist, he was equally famous for his Irish wit and incisive command of forensic process. Everybody knew and respected him, and almost everyone in law enforcement or the legal profession had a favorite selection from the large body of Keating apocrypha. While still a young lawyer, one story had it, Keating swore to himself in court and was ordered by the autocratic, Brahmin judge who overheard him to pay a twenty-five-dollar fine for contempt. Instead,

Keating handed the clerk a one-hundred-dollar bill, loudly repeated the profanity three more times, and as the judge fumed apoplectically at the bench, said, "No problem, Your Honor, I've already paid."

No lawyer alive would have dared the same flamboyance—nor would a lawyer have had the same provocation once Keating had ascended to the bench himself. As a judge, his wit became even more of a force to be reckoned with, but always in support of a transcendent respect for the law and the legal process.

When Silvia heard of his reaction to the note intended for Dan Lowney, his first thought was that Keating would interpret it as a deliberate breach, an attempt at familiarity that violated the most basic protocol, and he was scared to death.

The three Fall River detectives followed the state trooper up the stairs. They walked in silence down the hall to the room where the offending message had been wedged an hour earlier, and Lowney opened the door without knocking. The room was filled with smoke. Silvia saw that the beds had been taken away and it was set up as an office. He had testified before Keating in the past, and now he recognized the lean, patrician judge sitting at a table in the center of the room, along with two CPAC detectives, David Waxler, and a couple of other people he assumed were from the DA's office. Lowney stood aside to let the three Fall River miscreants pass into the august presence.

After they had stood there a moment, Keating squinted up at them through the smoke. "Did you leave this note?" He appeared to be asking all three of them as a group.

Silvia's heart sank. "Your Honor, I'm the one who put it there—we thought this was Sergeant Lowney's room, and—"

Keating held up his hand, and Silvia immediately stopped talking. The judge looked them over, lingering longer on Silvia than on the others, pulling thoughtfully at his cigar. "And this is the Fall River Cult Squad?"

Silvia took a deep breath and drew himself up. If that was the way it was going to be, then that was the way it was going to be. "Yes, Your Honor, this is the Fall River Cult Squad."

"Well, in that case," Keating said, "come on in and have a fucking drink."

Half an hour later, Lowney excused himself and left for Boston to bring in an out-of-town witness. David Waxler led Silvia, Joaquim, and Carey to his own room down the hall; they stayed there, working with him on the case, until eleven o'clock that night, going over the next day's events in detail. The three detectives quickly recognized a familiar pattern: Waxler was obsessed—as obsessed as they had been—and there was no way they were going to let down until it was over. That drink with Judge Keating, Silvia realized, was probably the closest the Fall River detectives would ever get to the party they had been hoping for.

Alan Robillard, the FBI's hair and fiber specialist who had been raised in Fall River, had been looking forward to this case for weeks. He knew from his travels on the job that every part of the United States had its own peculiar personality, and although he had not lived in southeastern Massachusetts for several years, he still felt most at home when he was listening to the familiar speech patterns of his childhood in the Flint section of Fall River. He had finally won the opportunity to return there, only to lose it again when the venue of the trial had been shifted to Fitchburg. He would not even have time to take a brief detour into Fall River.

As he drove through the western suburbs of Boston toward Fitchburg, he found himself hoping that his testimony would be over quickly and he could get out of there.

Dr. Douglas Ubelaker arrived at night. He had put in a full day at the Smithsonian, and the sun had already set by the time his flight landed in Boston. He was met at the airport by Dan Lowney, and they drove across the city and out Route 2 through Concord. Ubelaker had serious misgivings about what would be awaiting him when he got to Fitchburg. His briefcase was filled with documentary support of the technique he would use in court to identify the murder victim. But he had still not seen any of the X-rays, either of the calvarium skull taken by the Rhode Island medical examiner or from the hospital that had treated Karen Marsden's sinus headache two years before. Waxler's assurances that the two sets of radiographs were of the same skull did little to relieve his anxiety.

Ubelaker knew that if the two sets of pictures were not taken with the same camera alignment, a comparison in court could be difficult or impossible. He would never testify to something that he himself could not see, but even if the pictures proved to be of marginally fair quality, the documentation he brought with him would be irrelevant unless the jury could see the same thing as well, and clearly.

Matters did not improve when he arrived at the motel where the prosecution had set up its command post. The radiographs were nowhere to be found, and no one could tell him where they were.

*   *   *

When Paul Fitzgerald left the office of the Rhode Island medical examiner, he carried with him a box containing Karen Marsden's skull, the set of X-rays from the hospital in Massachusetts, and a fresh set of companion X-rays of the calvarium which had been taken by Dr. Sturner's lab technician. But there were two problems still to be solved.

First, what was the best way to show the X-rays to the jury so that they could all see the evidence at once and in the same detail? It would not do for the X-rays to be passed from juror to juror; it would be hopelessly confusing, and the Smithsonian's bone man would have to make his point-by-point comparisons as many as sixteen times. On his way out the door, Fitzgerald asked Sturner's receptionist if there were a photo processor nearby that could make slides while he waited. She gave him an address in Providence.

The second problem was how to make effective comparisons between slides. Fitzgerald came upon the solution to that one a few minutes later while he was waiting for the slides to be developed. Both sets of slides would be projected at the same time. This meant two projectors and two screens. He called Information and located an equipment-rental store in Fitchburg.

Ubelaker and Fitzgerald finally met for the first time in a room in the motel near Fitchburg late that evening. They were both scheduled as witnesses in court the following morning, so they wasted little time in amenities. Fitzgerald offered the anthropologist a large manila envelope containing two sets of X-rays. Ubelaker took them into the bathroom and held them up to the light over the sink; while he examined them, the screens were being set up, the projectors were loaded and turned on, and when Ubelaker returned to the room, Fitzgerald flicked off the light.

The first two slides scissored simultaneously into the projection ports. Frontal views of the two skulls—the living Karen Marsden and the unidentified calvarium—appeared side by side; they had been taken from the same angle, and they showed on the screen at the same size. The one-winged butterfly of the frontal sinus was clearly visible in each. Ubelaker silently let out his breath in relief.

He studied the two images for only a moment, to be certain the details were as clear in the slides as in the original X-rays he had just seen in the bathroom. Then he turned to Paul Fitzgerald. "They're the same skull, no doubt about it. You've identified your victim."

In the dark, Fitzgerald nodded. Ubelaker could see he was grinning.

THIRTY-FOUR / **FACE TO FACE**

O n the second day of his trial in Fitchburg for killing Karen Marsden, Carl Drew was indicted by the Bristol County grand jury in New Bedford for the murder of Doreen Levesque.

When Ronald Pina announced the indictment from his office in New Bedford, he named three others involved in Doreen Levesque's murder:

William E. Smith, thirty-one, of Newport, Rhode Island, indicted a few days before Drew.

Robin M. Murphy, eighteen, now serving a life sentence for her participation, with Drew, in a subsequent murder.

And Karen Marsden.

After he had been sworn in as a witness, Ubelaker had a few minutes to look around the courtroom while the projection equipment was being set up in front of the jury box. The first place he glanced was toward the table where the prosecution team was seated.

He had met the prosecutor, David Waxler, the previous evening, right after viewing the slides with Paul Fitzgerald, and they had agreed on the path through which Waxler would lead Ubelaker in today's testimony. Although Ubelaker was appearing in the trial as an expert witness for the Commonwealth, for either him or Waxler to exchange any greeting, or even any open sign of recognition, would not only have been impolitic, it would have violated Ubelaker's personal sense of the neutrality and scientific detachment required by his role in court. He was there only to discuss the interpretation of the evidence. When Waxler happened to glance back at him, both men's expressions were carefully blank, and both quickly looked in another direction.

Ubelaker scanned the defense table. He had not met Drew's attorney and could only assume that the thin, middle-aged man who was studying him from that side of the room was Waxler's opposite number.

Looking beyond him, Ubelaker saw two court officers sitting about fifteen feet away from the attorney, one on either side of a young man who was obviously the accused. The defendant had turned in his chair, his back to the witness box, and was watching the two plainclothes detectives as they set up the screens and projectors.

At that point in his career as an anthropologist, Douglas Ubelaker had already examined the mortal remains of several thousand scientific subjects. But with the exception of the forensic cases on which he reported for the FBI and other agencies of the law—a minuscule proportion of his work—the time since death of nearly all those remains could be counted not in days or weeks, but in centuries. While most of the anthropological specimens in Ubelaker's experience had died of natural causes, there had been a number of obvious exceptions, for example, he had examined remains from the burial rites of a long-vanished kingdom in Ecuador that were clearly human sacrifices. Indeed, his Smithsonian mentor and colleague, Dale Stewart, kept in his office, next door to Ubelaker's, the cast of a body which bore the marks of a murder committed some forty thousand years before the birth of Christ.

For all his experience with victims, or with their remains, this was only the second time in his career that Ubelaker had come into the presence of the other half of the forensic equation: the accused killer.

Until that moment in court, when the defendant turned around and faced him, Ubelaker had given hardly a thought to Carl Drew. There had been no reason to think of him. Ubelaker's forensic examination and his purpose today in court were both limited to establishing the identity of the calvarium skull. He was only vaguely aware of Drew's alleged relationship to the victim; he had heard no evidence and had formed no opinion as to whether Drew was in any way responsible for the murder.

Yet when Drew turned back from the activity behind him and looked across the courtroom toward the witness stand, Ubelaker was not only surprised but mildly taken aback. The defendant appeared to be just a few years younger than Ubelaker himself. Moreover, they were similar in appearance. Drew's dark hair, about the same color as Ubelaker's, was well groomed, and both were dressed for business in dark suits with white shirts and quiet neckties. Drew's features were softer and fuller, but he had a familiar look of quick, concerned intelligence about him. Even his attitude seemed the same, as though he and the prosecution witness were there for the same purpose: the discovery of the truth.

When their eyes met, there was nothing in Drew's expression, no sign of recognition, to suggest that he had noticed the same thing. But to Ubelaker, the similarities produced immediate and unexpected feelings of empathy and unease. He found himself thinking, "We are both someone's children, and we have taken separate ways."

When Ubelaker passed the witness table a moment later, headed for the place between the projectors from where he would give his testimony, he saw further evidence of how separate those ways had been. The word HATE was printed on the four fingers of Drew's left hand. Above it was another tattoo, a small part of which protruded below the end of the shirt cuff—a strip of dark colors with fierce eyes, the cruel caricature of a smile, and the horns of Satan.

The projector motors were turned on, but not the lights. Ubelaker's first task, in response to Waxler's questions, was to lead the members of the jury through a short lesson in physical anthropology.

He started by explaining how the sex and age of a skull could be estimated from its external appearance, pointing to the corresponding places on his own head as he spoke. "There are a number of characteristics on the skull that can be used to determine sex. The supraorbital ridges, the size of the mastoid process, the sharpness of the eye orbits. Males tend to have very blunt supraorbital margins; in females, it's rather pointed, and it's quite a difference."

Because of the location of the screens, Carl Drew and his two guards were allowed to move around to a position of better vantage in viewing Ubelaker's presentation. They stood about six feet to the anthropologist's right, and Drew was following the testimony in much the same way as it was being offered, with a combination of attentive interest and careful reserve. It was as though both the witness and the defendant were each assuming a position of equal distance from responsibility for the horror about to be described and each were equally as detached from its consequences.

"In a young person," Ubelaker said, "the skull is made up of many bones and is not a single bone." He moved his right hand to designate the corresponding sites on his own head as he spoke, beginning with his forehead. "Particularly, the cranial vault is made up of the frontal, the parietals along the sides, the occipital in the back, and the temporal where the ear canal is." He explained how those separate plates eventually knit together in the long thrust toward wholeness which begins before birth and continues on a predictable timetable through to middle age.

The jury watched and listened. Carl Drew watched and listened as well, nodding his head in apparent admiration for the beauty and symmetry of this natural process.

When Ubelaker was finished, Waxler asked for an order to lower the lights. Judge Keating signaled the bailiff who was standing by the switches at the courtroom exit. At the same time, Waxler clicked the remote controls of both projectors, turning on their lamps. The two X-ray images, one of the whole skull and one of the calvarium, appeared beside each other on the two screens and stared blindly out at the somber courtroom.

From where he stood beside the prosecution table, Waxler looked quickly across the room to survey the faces of the jury, trying to measure their reactions. Predictably, when the images first appeared, several of them flinched and looked momentarily away.

The defense attorney shifted his weight in his chair and fidgeted with a pencil. Carl Drew looked briefly at the two images. His expression was impassive, revealing nothing. Then he looked back toward Waxler, who was posing the questions.

"Doctor, is it fair to say that the slide now on the left screen is the one that was identified to you as being that of Karen Marsden, taken in a hospital?"

Ubelaker said it was.

"And the one on the right was identified to you as being from the Rhode Island medical examiner's office?"

"That's correct."

"Doctor, when you had the opportunity to view these slides, did you also have the opportunity to view the X-rays from which these slides were made?"

"Yes, I did."

The prosecutor turned from Ubelaker, pointedly looking over at the jury as he asked his next question. "Now, Doctor, yes or no: in viewing and comparing the skull as shown on the right and the X-rays of Karen Marsden as shown on the left, were you able to reach a conclusion as to whether or not they were from the same person?"

Ubelaker said, "Yes."

Waxler looked back at his witness, then beckoned to him to move closer. "I'm going to ask you to approach the screen." He handed Ubelaker a pointer. "In making this type of identification, what do you look for when you first look at the X-rays?"

Behind Ubelaker, Judge Keating reminded him to keep his voice up so it could be heard by everyone in the room.

"The key to this type of identification is in finding some aspect of the skeletal anatomy that is unique to the individual. It has to be a characteristic that is shared, of course, by the known and the object of the inquiry." He placed the tip of the pointer on the screen at the left. "We all have orbits. We all have nasal structures. But there are elements within all of us that are absolutely unique to us, and there are a lot of them. If one can pinpoint these in a comparison, it is convincing evidence that it did come from the same individual."

Waxler asked him to point out such a unique feature in the medical X-ray on the left screen.

"One very obvious one is right here," he said, laying the tip of the pointer on the upper center of the screen. "Right behind our supraorbital ridges in the upper nasal area there are air pockets, which we all have, which are called sinuses. We all know that because they occasionally lead to nasal congestion. In this individual, on this left side it extends up above the normal area where these sinuses occur—and not on the right. It's a variant of the normal pattern: not just a slight variation, but one that extends high up on the left side."

Waxler asked if this particular abnormality could have been associated with severe sinusitis. Before Ubelaker could answer, Drew's attorney, John Birknes, objected and the judge disallowed the question. It was known that sinusitis was the condition for which Karen Marsden had sought help at the hospital where her medical X-ray was taken, but that was too flimsy a bridge to support the jury's possible assumption that the two skulls were therefore the same.

Waxler shifted his focus. "Doctor, having identified that particular abnormality, would you turn to the skull and tell me whether or not you can point out the same sinus cavity."

Ubelaker walked over to the second screen. Standing in the light of the first projector, he said, "The same sinus cavity appears right here also. The shape is a rather exact match."

Waxler gestured toward the screen on the left. "In the X-ray of Karen Marsden, were you able to find a second characteristic that was also unique?"

"Right up here," Ubelaker said, laying the tip on the top of the image. "It looks like it's on the forehead; in reality it's on the back of the skull. The X-ray looks completely through, and we're getting an image of all sides."

With the pointer, he indicated the ragged thread of a suture line where two of the plates of the skull had begun growing together, the tracings of a riverbed in the satellite photograph of a dead planet. "This is the sagittal suture. We all have one, but its exact course varies with every individual. Most sutures do not have this troughlike depression in the bone."

In response to further questions from Waxler, the anthropologist moved back to the image projected on the right, identifying the exact same characteristics of shape and grooving.

Waxler asked if Ubelaker had found a third common point for comparison.

"Yes," he answered, pointing to the medical X-ray of the whole skull. "In the upper portion of the right eye orbit, there is an area of density; this apparently reflects a buildup of bone around a tiny hole which goes through the orbit at that point." He shifted to the other screen. "That same characteristic is present right here in the same position on the right orbit."

"I ask you to return to the X-ray of Karen Marsden," the prosecutor said, speaking to the witness, but looking at the jury. "Were you able to find a fourth characteristic?"

"There is a fourth characteristic," Ubelaker stated. He pointed to the sphenoid bone, which was visible through the orbit. "There is a very hard bone that is U-shaped, comes up along the sides, goes through the inside of our heads, and comes up on the other side. The lateral wings of that bone extend out beyond the orbits and can vary in their appearance and position." Using the pointer, he indicated the ways in which the unique shape of that particular sphenoid bone was the same in both X-rays.

Waxler clicked both remote control buttons. New X-ray views of the skull appeared on the two screens, this time taken from the side. He asked the witness if there were characteristics in these pictures that could corroborate the earlier comparisons.

Ubelaker said there were and pointed to the center of the picture on the left. "This is called the sella turcica. And this saddle right here is where the pituitary gland is attached to the base of the brain. There is some variation in the appearance of this little horn." He pointed across to the other slide. "The same characteristic is here."

The court recessed for lunch. When Ubelaker returned to the stand an hour later, the prosecutor had just one more question. "Doctor, based on your expertise and your observations, what is your opinion on whether or not the Karen Marsden X-rays and the skull X-rays came from the same person?"

It was the most important question Waxler had asked up to that point in the trial. No matter how many witnesses the prosecution would be able to offer, until it was answered, the death of Karen Marsden would remain either an enigma or an abstraction.

"In my opinion," Ubelaker said, mindful of keeping his voice loud enough to be heard by the judge behind him as well as the jury, "both sets of X-rays come from the same individual."

He remained on the stand another fifteen minutes for cross-examination. From the prosecutor's table, Waxler watched the jury as Birknes attacked the anthropologist's credentials, his qualification to interpret X-rays, and the scientific basis for reading bones in the same way that other specialists read fingerprints. But Ubelaker stood up to it without any sign of annoyance, impatience, or insecurity; he was a professional. And by the time the cross-examination was over, Waxler was convinced that Ubelaker's testimony had held up as well.

The prosecution's last two witnesses for the day were Robillard and another scientist named Mark Babyak from the FBI laboratory. When they were finished, Waxler stood beside his desk and watched the jury file from the courtroom. So far, he had made a successful case. Today's testimony should have eliminated any stain of uncertainty; the hair and clothing found in the woods, as well as the skull, all had been positively identified.

Karen Marsden was dead.

Now, in order to prove Carl Drew had killed her, Waxler knew his next witnesses would have to bring her temporarily back to life.

THIRTY-FIVE / **DEVOL POND**

S uccess in trial law, in common with success in any other form of theater, depends on the creation of an environment for the willing suspension of disbelief. In law, that disbelief is called reasonable doubt. As with any sacred trust, reasonable doubt is a heavy burden, and the average juror is grateful for the opportunity to give it up—but only with the assurance that his responsibility can be set down evenly and righteously on the scales of justice. On the day after the courtroom identification of the mortal remains of Karen Marsden, David Waxler could sense that a place had been cleared on the scales by the testimony of Dr. Ubelaker, the FBI, the Fall River detectives, and the state troopers and that the jury had perceptibly set down an important portion of its collective disbelief—it had surrendered any reasonable doubts about the identity of the victim.

But if the police and scientific testimony had allowed the calvarium skull to tell its story, this was only a prologue: the full eloquence of any cry for justice would depend on the words of others. Over the next three days of the trial, Waxler systematically, painstakingly, laid down a tapestry of testimony by people who had known the victim, not as an X-ray from a hospital's archives or as a skull that had been found in the woods, but as a living person, a girl named Karen Marsden. Her friend, Cookie Powers. Her grandmother. Her son's foster mother, Elvira Nolin. Another friend, Carol Fletcher. Her lover, Robin Murphy.

As he laid down these strands, Waxler just as methodically cleared another resting place on the scales, a much larger one, upon which the jury was invited to lay down the remainder of its doubts about Karen Marsden's final hours and, once freed of them, to become, with the participants, witnesses to the events of her terrible death.

And as he continued to weave, the tapestry came to life.*

Karen still could not stop the tears. As soon as the two girls stepped back into the cold street outside the Nolins' apartment, her eyes welled up again, her nose began to run, and she wiped at her cheeks with the sleeve of her coat. Robin looked at her furtively with a combination of concern and disdain, unwilling to acknowledge her friend's grief, but equally unable to ignore it. As they walked toward South Main, Robin moved slightly to the lead—a way of changing the subject before Karen could put it into words.

Maybe the tears were because of saying goodbye to JJ—not just because of how Karen felt about her son, but because of how leaving him again made her feel about herself. When the court had first given the boy to the Nolins, she had not wanted to see him at all. Even though the Nolins were fulfilling their parental role by court decree, they were doing it more successfully than Karen had ever been able to do from the natural impulses of motherhood, and the pain of her failure had been stronger, at least at first, than the joy of reunion.

Eventually, when she was able to force herself through the first few, reluctant visits, the Nolins became unacknowledged foster parents, if only partially and intermittently, to Karen as well as to her son. Her anger and regret at her own failure were still there, but instead of confirming Karen's judgment against herself, the visits eventually began to admit of acceptance and even of forgiveness. The Nolins were nice people. They were good for JJ. If Karen were some other person than what she was, her son would never have met them. Whenever God closes one door, He opens another.

Still sniffling and wiping at her eyes with the sleeve, she quickened her step and closed the space between herself and Robin. "You're being mean," she said. "You didn't have to say that stuff."

Robin quickened her own pace to stay ahead. "You make your choice, I make mine. You're going to Florida, I'm going to Rhode Island. At least I'll be back later tonight."

The evening before, Karen had told Robin and Carol Fletcher that she intended to leave Fall River with a friend named Richie Thomas who was going to Florida. They had fought about it off and on all that

The description of the events on the night of Karen Marsden's murder contained in this chapter has been reconstructed from transcripts of the testimony given at Carl Drew's murder trial and from statements made by participants and others to the police prior to trial. Most of the description is based on testimony and statements of Robin Murphy and Carol Fletcher.

afternoon. The rancor had culminated a few minutes earlier in the Nolins' apartment, when Robin had told Karen she was going out of town that night and didn't want anything to do with her. "C'mon," Karen said now, skipping to catch up, "I don't know if it's for real. We're just talking."

"Fine. I'm going to Rhode Island," Robin repeated. "That's for real."

"Can I come?"

"No."

Karen didn't press further, and as they got nearer to South Main they both slowed their pace. Robin allowed Karen to catch up with her and, looking sideways at her, asked, "So what are your plans?"

Still looking teary and puffy, still fighting the impulse to weep aloud, Karen said, "The Hub, I guess."

"Smart," Robin said, sarcastically.

"Why are you being this way?" Karen asked. "Smart what?"

"Smart stupid," she answered. "Carl Drew, Carl Davis—"

Karen's sorrow at being left out of Robin's plans quickly seesawed into anger. "Will you stop it?" she yelled. Then, in a slightly more controlled voice, "For one thing, they hang out on Bedford, where they can sit indoors and drink. For another, there's people all over the place up there. Nobody's going to hurt me if everyone's watching. It's as safe as anywhere."

"Safe as anywhere," Robin mimicked, making Karen sound like an idiot.

When they got as far as the Cottage Mill Bar, the two girls left the sidewalk, walking between the parked cars and out onto the street. Robin held out her thumb. The first vehicle that came along, a pickup truck driven by a man of about thirty, stopped and the two girls got in.

A few blocks later it stopped long enough for Robin to get out. She headed up toward Harbor Terrace on foot. Despite what she had said to Karen, Robin had no intention of going to Rhode Island that night. She was going to see Sonny Sparda, who was expecting her for dinner in her apartment, and then she was heading back downtown.

Carol Fletcher drove slowly down Bedford Street in her rental car, a yellow, two-door 1978 Oldsmobile with a brown vinyl top. The evening had not started, and she was already tired. She had driven to Taunton early that morning to pick up some friends of her pimp, Carl Davis, and had brought them back down to Fall River to retrieve a car they had left there a day or two earlier. It turned out not to be ready, and the friends had hung around with her and Davis until six o'clock. As soon as they were gone, Carol left the apartment and headed to work; she and Davis lived together, and he was in his own car just a few lengths ahead.

It was raw and the sky was threatening, not quite cold enough to snow—a good night to work from the car. When she got to Pier 14, she parked at the sidewalk and went inside for a look around. There was no one there she knew. She ordered a sombrero—a warming drink with coffee, brandy, and cream—at the bar. When she finished, she ordered another one. She left part of the second drink on the bar and went back outside. She drove down the street to Charlie's and saw Karen Marsden standing on the sidewalk.

There was no place to park, so she pulled as close to the curb as she could, and Karen came over to the car. Carol rolled down the window and said, "They warned me against hanging with you." She was referring to Carl Davis and Carl Drew.

Karen shrugged it off. She knew it already. "I got something really important—I want to talk with you. It won't take long." Somebody behind them blew his horn. Karen opened the door of Carol's car and got in.

Karen was shaking with the cold, and as usual her eyes were red, as though she were coming down with something. Carol drove around the block and pulled up in front of the liquor store next to Pier 14. "I'm getting some beer," she said. "Want anything else?"

Karen shook her head to indicate no, then said, "Yeah, get me some gum."

Carol closed the door and walked around the car. Karen rolled down her window and called over to her, "And a pack of cigarettes."

When Carol returned, she passed a small bag to Karen and put the beer bottle on the seat between them. She started up the car and drove another few blocks, this time pulling into the parking lot in front of the Hub Pool Room. They sat there, facing the street, and Carol opened the bottle.

"You don't drink beer," Karen said.

"It's for you," she said, passing the bottle to the passenger side.

Karen took the bottle and started to talk, wandering from topic to topic. She told Carol where she and Robin had been earlier in the evening and where Robin was now, back at Sonny's house. "She told me she's going to Rhode Island. I don't think she is. I think she said it because she's pissed at me talking about Florida." Karen took a long pull at the bottle of beer. "I was thinking—"

Carol was not surprised that Karen was wired; it seemed as though she had not come down for weeks. As she rambled on, Carol nodded perfunctory encouragement and scanned the street ahead of them for passing tricks.

"I was thinking about JJ," she said. "About if something happens to me, you know?"

"Yeah," Carol said, distractedly. She had heard all this before, and she knew where it was going. "Nothing's going to happen to you, but if it does, he'll be great. Everybody loves him. He's a sweetie."

"You wouldn't let anything bad come to him, would you?" Karen asked.

Carol looked over at her, but just briefly. For a long time, Karen had been Carl Drew's first lady, and she'd made him a lot of money. But in the past few weeks—ever since she'd started talking to the cops back before Christmas—she had gotten more and more stretched and desperate-looking and strung further and further out on drugs. Carl Drew was always saying the Devil would take his toll, and Karen looked as if he was right. Carol smiled reassuringly and continued scanning the passing cars. "Of course not. Nothing's going to happen to either one of you."

Karen took another pull from the bottle of beer. "You and me have been friends a long time—" she said.

Carol nodded and looked further down the street. They really had not been friends for all that long.

"What I mean is," she continued, sounding plaintive, "if I've been bossy sometimes—"

Carol glanced toward the far sidewalk, away from Karen.

"I didn't mean anything bad by it, you know? I had to do the things I did. When I was working for Carl, he made me say and do a lot of things I hated."

"That's the life," Carol said quickly, dismissing it. The street was a constant battlefield of dominance and submission—of tricks over girls, of girls over tricks, of pimps over other pimps, of pimps over everyone around them. Sometimes the pimps used their fists, and sometimes they waged their battles by proxy. Carol was not interested in a confession, much less an act of contrition, for something every one of them did every day of their lives.

Karen pushed in the lighter beside the radio, then fished in the paper bag Carol had given her and brought out the soft pack of Marlboros. She peeled off the cellophane ring, tore a corner of foil, and thumped out a single cigarette.

"The thing is, about Florida—" she said, her face glowing briefly from the hot coil as she lit up, "I think Robin's more pissed because it's with Richie Thomas, you know? Not that I'm necessarily going to do it. But it would get me away from Carl, that's for sure."

Richie Thomas had suggested the trip just the night before, and Robin had been angry because Karen had responded so quickly. Later that same night, when Karen had told the two girls of her new plans, such as they were, she inadvertently had gotten Carol Fletcher into trouble with Carl Davis; both he and Carl Drew had warned Carol to stay away from Karen Marsden and Robin Murphy—and in that few minutes Carol had talked to them on the street, Davis had come out of Pigeon's Cafe and asked her what she was doing hanging around with people he had told her to avoid.

Now, sitting in her car with Karen, Carol shrugged and said, "Yeah, well, I guess everything comes down to who's in charge."

A Duster pulled up opposite the parking lot, and the man behind the wheel peered at the two girls in the yellow Olds. He pointed to Karen and pantomimed through the window, "How much?"

Karen leaned the bottle on the seat and sized him up. She held up three fingers of her left hand and five of her right, silently mouthing "Thirty-five."

The man nodded, and signaled for her to come over.

"I got one," Karen said. "I'll be right back." She got out of the car and ran over to the Duster, then stopped abruptly and ran back to scoop the cigarettes off the front seat of Carol's car. "I'll be right back," she said again. She got into the Duster with the trick and they drove off.

Before the Duster was out of sight, Carol backed the Olds out of the parking lot and headed in the other direction.

Despite Sonny Sparda's invitation to supper, Robin had only stayed at Harbor Terrace for a few minutes before deciding to walk back down to Bedford Street. She had gone less than a block before Carol Fletcher pulled up beside her. Robin looked in and saw that Carol was alone. She got into the front seat, and they pulled out into the traffic.

At the corner next to the Hub, they stopped and went inside to look for Karen. She was not there, and they waited for her in the parking lot across the street. After about ten minutes more, the Duster returned, and Karen got out.

When Karen walked over to the Olds, she looked at Robin, who was standing outside the car, and asked, "What are you doing with Carol?"

"We came up to get you."

Karen and Robin got in the front seat, and Carol turned back out of the parking lot. She said she was going to check with Carl Davis to see if he was still mad about the night before; she did not mention that she had been with him for almost the entire day. Once more, the yellow Olds headed up toward Bedford Street.

Friday night was always busy in that part of town. This particular night, because the weather was threatening, many of the prostitutes were sitting in parked cars rather than standing on corners, and there was even more congestion than usual. Directly ahead of the Olds was a Barracuda with two men in their twenties; it slowed at each corner as they checked out the prospects. When they came to the corner in front of Pier 14, the Barracuda pulled diagonally toward the curb and stopped, blocking Carol's car and the other traffic behind it.

Carl Drew and Carl Davis were standing on that corner. They walked over and got into Carol's car without saying anything. Drew got into the back seat. Davis indicated he was going to sit in the front, so Karen got in back, and Robin slid in beside her, putting Karen in the middle. There was a moment of quiet before Drew, from the other side, said, "You've been talking too much."

Karen looked straight ahead, not answering. She knew what was coming. She had been through it all before, when it was someone else's turn. And in her mind, she had been through it about herself as well.

In the front seat, Carl Davis turned up the volume on the radio and said to Carol Fletcher, "Move."

She pulled the car out into the traffic again. Davis pointed where to drive. She turned left and headed back down Bedford. At the Hub Pool Room, Davis told her to turn left again, onto Pleasant. They drove east on Pleasant for a few blocks, then took the westbound exit onto 195. Carol was aware of some conversation in the back seat, but most of the words were lost in the blare of music. A few minutes later they were out of Fall River. There was no conversation about where they were going, but it was obvious that both Davis and Drew had a destination in mind. They got off 195 at Sanford Road.

Carol had had a conversation with Carl Drew a week before. Drew, referring to himself as Satan and saying that Satan must be paid his toll, had told her he was going to kill Karen Marsden—it was just a matter of finding the right time and the right place. Carol continued following Davis's instructions, and a minute later they turned again. They drove slowly by a freshwater pond, and she realized they were at Family Beach, in Westport.

Carol looked around in the darkness; she realized that she had been there before, in the daytime. Just a month earlier, Robin had directed her over the same route to this same destination, and Karen had been with them. When they had gotten to Family Beach that time, Robin told Karen, "If something happens to you because you can't keep your mouth shut, it will be Carl Drew that does it, and this is where it will be." Now, in the starlight, they drove by the recreation area and Carol saw the dark water of Sawdy Pond, patched in places with a thin laminate of rotting ice. Davis indicated three more turns, this time down unpaved roads, and finally he showed her where to park, in an area of deep woods.

She turned off the lights and then the engine. The car radio died as soon as she turned the key, and the car was embraced for a moment by the silence and darkness. Davis reached over and removed the key from the ignition.

Then, in the back seat, Carl Drew said, "I warned you Satan would have his toll."

Karen's answer was nearly inaudible. "I'm not afraid of Satan."

"I told you if you said anything about Doreen Levesque, you'd die. But you couldn't keep your fucking mouth shut," he said, his voice rasping and cold.

"I'm not afraid of you either," Karen said.

"You should be." From the front seat, Davis opened the door on the passenger side and the overhead light came on. In the rearview mirror, Carol could see the tears in Karen's eyes and the whiteness of her face, like a mask. Drew told her, "Your time has come."

From the other side, Robin said, "You shouldn't have told anyone you were going to Florida."

In the same small voice, Karen answered, "God is going to help me."

"God isn't going to help you," Drew said. "God can't help you. The only one here is Satan."

Davis stood outside the car and held the seat forward for Robin. When she was outside, Drew pushed Karen across the seat toward her and said, "Take her."

Robin reached back into the car and grabbed Karen by one arm and the hair on the back of her head. Karen's head bent back. Although Robin was only slightly taller, she was far more powerful.

Karen looked desperately at Carol Fletcher as she was being pulled from the back seat. "Don't let anything happen to JJ. Please. Please don't let anything happen to him." She cried out with the pain of

Robin's grip on her hair. Carol got out the driver's side, looking away without answering.

There were patches of old snow on the road and in the woods, and although the night was cold, the temperature was above freezing and the ground beneath their feet was slush. Robin was wearing hiking boots, but Karen had on a pair of open-toed high-heeled clogs of wood and leather.

Carl Drew was the last to get out of the car. He was wearing black motorcycle boots and his black leather jacket.

Suddenly, Karen twisted out from under Robin's grasp and began to run. She only got a few feet away before Robin caught her by her hair and pulled her violently backward; her feet ran out from under her and she fell heavily to the ground. Drew watched as Robin subdued her, then he said, "Hit her."

Robin punched Karen in the face. Karen screamed, and Robin punched her a second time. Drew said to hit her yet again, and Robin did.

"This is just the start of it," Drew said, kneeling down beside the fallen girl. "You're going to suffer, to feel pain."

Terrified but still defiant, her face bloodied, Karen said, "God is with me. You can't hurt me. God is going to help me, no matter what you do."

When Karen said God would help her, Carol Fletcher flinched and stepped back. It was obvious now that Karen did not expect to live, that she was calling upon God to help her through her death. Both girls had been brought up as Catholics and now, in her last minutes on earth, Karen was seizing upon the offer Christ had made to the thief on the cross: in return for believing, immortal life.

The words had exactly the opposite effect on Robin. She yelled something incoherent back at Karen and punched her again, then pulled her by her hair until the helpless girl was standing, frantic and off balance, and clamped her windpipe with an arm around her neck from behind. Karen's face was pointed toward the sky. With Robin still pulling on her hair as well as cutting off her breath, they left the road and started into the woods. Karen could not keep on her feet in that position, and because she was being dragged, she quickly lost her clogs. Drew picked them up and carried them. Davis and Carol Fletcher followed along behind.

After a time, when Robin became so exhausted from her exertions she could not continue, Drew let her rest. He tore at Karen's coat, held his buck knife under her eyes, then stabbed the blade repeatedly into the fabric, just missing her neck and chest as he did. She was still being held around the throat by Robin from behind, and although Karen followed the blade with her eyes, the only sounds she could make were choked, breathless sobs. Drew finally pulled off the coat and threw it onto the forest floor. They continued on.

When Robin became exhausted again, a further distance into the woods, they stopped a second time. Carl Drew said, "Just let her go." Robin pushed her away, and when Karen fell to her knees Drew pulled at the next layer of her clothing. He peeled the two sweaters over her head and threw them to the ground. He tore at her shirt, and where it did not give way by ripping, he slashed the fabric with his knife. Karen was still conscious, but something apparently had happened to her throat from the pressure of Robin's armhold, and she coughed, gasping for air. Robin grabbed at her hair again, and a large clump of it came loose in her hand. She threw it aside and renewed her hammerlock around her neck.

Robin and Drew carried her that way across a low stone wall and to a small clearing. Finally, Robin said, "I can't. I can't anymore."

Drew said one final time, "Let her go."

Then he said to the others, "Pick up rocks." They looked around in the snow. Carl Davis and Carol Fletcher each found a small stone and threw it. Drew and Robin found rocks as well and hit Karen with them in their hands, and she fell. Karen's face was bloody, and she was half naked, lying on the ground on her back, groaning softly in pain.

Drew knelt beside her, and Robin was behind her, at her head. He took Karen's hand in his, studying her anguished face in the darkness, then looked down at her rings. "You won't be needing these where you're going." And finding the joint in her wrist, he sawed with his buck knife between the bones, severing the hand. Karen tried screaming, but blocked, feral, choking noises came out instead. Drew continued using the knife on the severed hand to remove the rings, then passed the knife to Davis and hit Karen in the face to make her stop the noises. He pointed to Karen's gold earring and looked up at Robin. "Tear that off," he said, and Robin did.

Drew undid Karen's jeans, roughly pulled them off, with the underpants, and threw them into the darkness. They fell across the branches of a small scrub oak at the side of the clearing. Drew looked up at Robin again and said, "Get down on her."

Robin hesitated at first, but before he had to say it again they changed places, and she moved past Drew to where he had just been kneeling. Drew held Karen's upper body still and watched as Robin did as she was told. Standing a few feet away, Carol Fletcher could see very little motion from Karen, but she knew she was still conscious because she could hear the sounds of her tortured breathing and muffled moans.

After he had been watching this for less than a minute, Drew began to cough, and then he averted his face and gagged. Turning obliquely back, he told Robin to stop what she was doing and get away from Karen. When she did stop, he said, "You lezzies make me sick." Robin moved further back, perhaps to demonstrate obedience to his command or in fear of being included in his rage.

From his new position behind her head, Drew raised the upper portion of Karen's body with both his arms around her neck and shook her fiercely. She had raised her own arms in the vaguest gesture of resistance, probably more to protect her mutilated wrist than to defend against the new assault. When Drew stopped, Carol Fletcher could still hear the small, breathless sounds of whimpering in the dark.

Drew then looked over to Davis and indicated he was to hand Robin his buck knife. When Robin took it, Drew said, "Cut her throat."

Robin said nothing. Holding the knife in her left hand, without hesitation she leaned across the white body and drew the blade across the side of the neck. There was a warm spurt, and blood the color of ink gushed from the stroke of the blade, covering both her hand and the knife.

There was one last, muted rustling of breath. The arm with the hand dropped quietly from its posture of defense and lay at repose beside the pale body.

Drew turned his head as though to gag again, but then turned back. Glowering in the darkness at Robin, he said, "Deeper."

Now using the knife as she had seen Drew use it minutes before, like a saw, Robin began cutting into the muscles and tendons of the neck. After a couple of minutes, she stopped and leaned back. There was no flesh left to cut. She offered the knife to Drew in surrender.

Once more, Drew put his powerful arms around what remained of the neck. He strained, there was a sound of snapping cartilage, and the head fell off the body. His jacket was glistening with blood, but the leather and the darkness hid the color. He used his knife to disconnect the last of the tissue holding the head to the neck.

Drew passed the head to Robin. He told her to tear out the hair. She placed the head on the ground and leaned down on it with her right hand. She began pulling out the hair and strips of the scalp with the other.

Drew told her to take out the eyes.

She said, "I don't know how."

Drew stood up and kicked the head into the darkness. He ran after it and kicked it back toward the body. He kicked it again.

Carol Fletcher and Carl Davis watched in the dark for a few minutes, then moved toward each other, and together they started walking back through the woods to the car.

Drew and Robin did not notice they had gone. They knelt beside the body in the darkness, one at her left and one at her right. With his buck knife, Drew carved a line diagonally across from one of Karen's shoulders, across the ribs, to her opposing hip. Then he crossed it with another long incision from the other side. As he made the X, he spoke in tongues, his voice a low, rasping, satanic chant.

Robin had heard that sound before, at services in the Freetown Reservation, in ceremonies with skulls and candles on Seabury Street where Drew had once lived, and under the bleachers the night that Doreen Levesque had died. It was the language Drew used to conjure up Satan, to summon his presence. And as he chanted, he would use blood—sometimes his own, sometimes from animals—to induct others into the cult. Robin had imitated this same language herself, when she had been at Sonny's. But she did not imitate it now. She sat silently in the dark as Carl Drew prayed beside the body and offered Karen Marsden's soul to Satan.

When Drew finished the incantation, he looked down at the body in silence for a time, then dipped his thumb into the blood on her chest. Like a priest applying the chrism, he laid his fingers on the top of Robin's head and made an X on her forehead with the thumb. He said to her, "Now you are one of us."

Eventually, they returned through the woods to the car.

Carol Fletcher was sitting behind the wheel, and Davis waited beside her. They saw Drew and Murphy walk around to the back of the car, and they heard one of them open the trunk. Then the lid was closed. They opened the door on Davis's side of the car and got into the back seat.

As he had told her two hours before in Fall River, Davis waited until the door was shut, then turned to Carol and again said, "Move."

When she turned the key, the radio came on again at full volume. Carol reached over and turned it off. She backed the car out of the place where she had parked and turned onto Robert Street.

A minute or two later, while they were still on the unpaved road, Drew told her to stop. He reached across the back of the seat and took the keys from the ignition, then got out and walked to the trunk. He opened the lid a second time and a moment later closed it again. When he got back into the car, he said, "The body won't be found in one piece."

Carol drove back toward Fall River. From the rear seat, she heard fragments of comments from Robin—about having to do what she did because of Carl Drew—but she was not listening. Drew laughed once or twice, but otherwise he did not answer. Most of the trip home was in silence.

When they got back to the city, Drew and Robin got out at the same place, just below Harbor Terrace. As the yellow car pulled away, Drew asked Robin where she was going. She told him Sonny's. He said, "You're not going to say anything to anyone about what happened tonight." She said she wasn't. They were alone on the sidewalk. Laying his hand on her head a final time and using the same thumb with which he had anointed her, he wiped the blood off her forehead. Then he turned away, not so much in dismissal but as though Robin had never been there. His hands jammed into the pockets of his leather jacket, his head thrown back as he slipped into his familiar jog, the steam of his breath preceding him, Drew headed back down toward Bedford Street.

Robin walked into Sonny Sparda's apartment. Sonny and David Roche were the only ones there. Sonny asked if she were sick or if something were wrong. Robin looked at herself and saw that she was wet from the thighs down, from where she had been kneeling in the slush and snow in the woods. She said she had been running. She quickly went into the bathroom to wash the blood off her hands before anyone noticed and peered carefully into the mirror to make certain Drew had removed all the blood that he had put on her face.

As Robin Murphy told her story in court, she said that she had not been in control of her own body or her mind through the whole experience, not even an hour later, when she returned to Sonny's apartment.

But she also said that when she walked out of the bathroom there, she was hungry and sat down to the supper that had been waiting for her since six that evening. It was chicken, and it had become cold. Robin ate it anyway. She drank a beer. And when she was finished with the food and drink, she told the jury, she pushed back the plate and smoked a joint.

THIRTY-SIX / **FRIDAY THE 13TH**

Although none of the witnesses in the Drew trial was allowed in the courtroom to hear the testimony of those who came before, that safeguard insulated only those who were next in line to testify. For the rest, reliable summaries and critiques of earlier testimony were available at every hand. For the rare witness who did not have friends in the audience, local radio stations offered the highlights on the hour and a half-dozen newspapers reported the details the morning after. The day after Robin's testimony, the Providence *Journal-Bulletin* carried a detailed account under the headline, "Souls of slain women 'given to Satan,' Miss Murphy tells packed courtroom."

Witnesses who were represented by counsel were kept particularly well informed of the turns in Carl Drew's prospects. In at least one instance, the testimony by the forensic experts and then by Carol Fletcher and Robin Murphy may have had an impact on defense strategy. Carl Davis had been scheduled to lead off the final day of testimony. Despite his decision to go for a separate trial, Davis had appeared, more than anyone else in the case, to share a common bond with the defendant: he was Carl Drew's principal alibi, and Carl Drew was his. But that was before.

Before the medical X-rays had been admitted into evidence and the jury had been able to see for itself that Karen Marsden was really dead. Before they heard the victim's last words, spoken when her death was certain: that she was unafraid and that God would help her. Before they learned of the cutting of her throat. Before the offering of her soul, the praying in tongues, the mutilation, the anointing with blood.

But by the time Davis arrived in the courtroom, all these things had been revealed or had come to pass and a sense of resolution—the deceptive tranquillity of unreleased rage—lay over everything. Whoever followed that testimony was not only an anticlimax but a detriment to justice, standing between a terrible, unanswered guilt and the rising hammer of righteous retribution. It was not where Davis wanted to be. He invoked his Fifth Amendment right against self-incrimination and refused to testify. Neither Drew nor the jury was in the courtroom when Davis appeared before Judge Keating, but by the time he was removed and they returned, the sense of inevitability was palpable.

The remaining witnesses for Carl Drew's defense seemed dispirited and even reluctant. They appeared in rapid succession, performed their duty, and were soon finished.

A woman named Linda Riley testified that she had dated Drew briefly in 1978; she had never heard him speak in a low raspy voice or a strange language, and he had never spoken to her of Satanism or cults.

Attorney John Birknes questioned Richard Guinen about what he and Maureen Murphy had heard from Robin after the Levesque murder. The questions seemed pointless, and Guinen's answers added nothing to what the jury had already been told.

Birknes questioned Robin's mother as well. Yes, Robin had talked about the Levesque killing, but the conversation was confused, Robin was upset, and her mother had told her to "just go to bed and get some sleep."

Nancy Numan, Sonny Sparda's neighbor in Harbor Terrace who had told the police she had a vision of where they would find Karen's body, testified that she had known Sonny and Drew for several years and had never seen any evidence of Satanism or of cult activities. When Waxler cross-examined for the prosecution, he asked if she had ever noticed the wall-sized mural of Satan in Sonny's apartment. She said she had. Judge Keating instructed the jury to disregard the question and the response as irrelevant.

Carl Drew's stepmother testified that he believed in God.

Robert Bohun, Sonny Sparda's young neighbor, testified that on February 8, 1980, he had heard Robin Murphy say that Karen was going to be killed and Carl Drew would be framed for it. In cross-examination, Bohun decided what Robin had said was not "framed" but "blamed." He was excused.

Carol Dias told of an argument she had once witnessed between Carl Drew and Robin Murphy, and she said that Robin had hinted at revenge.

Margarida Revorido gave Drew his alibi for the night of the murder.

The bartender at Pier 14 stopped far short of the same alibi. He said Friday nights were too busy for him to keep track of people, and that particular Friday night was a long time ago. In apparent desperation, Birknes asked for his "best estimate as to the likelihood" that Drew had been there all that particular evening. When Waxler objected, Judge Keating quickly said, "Absolutely excluded."

Pamela Coady testified on the overheard telephone conversation between Robin in Texas and Sonny in Fall River. When she was shown the police report on that call, she said, "There's a lot of lies in here." Keating dismissed the jury and asked Pam if she had taken any drugs prior to coming to court. She said she had taken Tranxene for her nerves, on the advice of her physician. Keating told her that if she did not conduct herself properly, she would be held in contempt and locked up. When the jury returned, Pam held herself together for another couple of questions, faltered, then lost it completely. She held onto the rail in front of the witness stand, weeping, and shouted up to Keating, "I don't want to talk, all right? Send me to jail." Keating allowed a few more questions, but she broke down a second time, yelling, "I don't even remember. I put this all out of my mind. I don't want to remember nothing, don't you understand?" The judge excused her and ordered her to be taken from the courtroom.

David Roche testified to the same argument witnessed by Carol Dias and of a subsequent threat by Robin to frame Carl Drew. In cross-examination, Waxler asked him if he ever said anything of that threat to the Fall River police. Roche first said he did not, then said he did, then said he did not, then said he did, reversing himself a total of six times on that single point.

While the jury was out, Sonny Sparda was called. She had just spoken with a court-appointed lawyer, and she told Judge Keating that she was going to follow his advice against self-incrimination and plead the Fifth Amendment.

The last witness for the defense was Carl Drew.

In his first few minutes on the stand, Birknes guided Drew swiftly through the long chain of events that had brought him from New Hampshire to Fall River and ultimately to this courtroom. Drew next told the jury how each of the people in the case had come into his life.

Sonny Sparda was a friend of Drew's stepmother, and Carl had met her first in New Hampshire.

Karen Marsden was introduced to Drew by a mutual friend, and after they had dated once or twice, she asked Drew to show her how to make a living on the streets. She worked for him only two nights and then went on her own, with no recriminations and no threats.

Karen brought him Cookie Powers. After Drew helped recover her car, she worked for him for two months, then she too went her way, just as amicably.

Drew and Margarida Revorido were lovers. When she worked the streets for him, he had no other women.

Drew and Robin Murphy never got along from the day they met.

He had never heard of Doreen Levesque, never seen her or met her, and knew nothing of her existence until the police showed him her picture one day, three months after she had been murdered.

He admitted to having slapped Robin once in an argument. He said she had threatened to get even. But the last time he had seen Robin prior to the trial was in Sonny Sparda's apartment at Harbor Terrace, back in February of 1980. Robin had been sitting on the washing machine. Sonny was sitting on the kitchen table. Drew was sitting on the refrigerator. It was a nice, friendly visit. Nothing unusual had happened, and he had no reason to think she still carried a grudge from the incident involving the slap.

Carl Drew had never belonged to a satanic cult, had never attended anything like a cult ritual, had never even heard of a satanic language.

He had a tattoo on his chest. It was the American eagle.

Drew did not know if Robin Murphy had ever engaged in any cult activity.

Birknes led him through the events of the evening of February 8, 1980. They were precisely the same events described by Margarida Revorido. He talked and drank with her at Charlie's and the Pier, and she left him now and then to check the traffic or turn a trick. Drew and Carl Davis smoked a joint in front of the Pier; they saw Karen drive by, a passenger in Carol Fletcher's car; the girls did not speak to Drew or Davis, and Drew never saw Karen again. He and Margarida were not out of each other's company for more than twenty minutes at a time all night. Drew did not hear that Karen was missing for another two days, when he was told by Sonny—who had heard from Robin.

The same night he heard about Karen, Drew said, he was warned the cops were looking for him in connection with her murder. They picked him up the next night and took him to the station, where he cooperated with them in every way.

He said that Margarida had been arrested for prostitution and sentenced to a term in Framingham. A few nights later, Drew met Leah Johnson in a bar and she asked him for a place to stay. He took her in, and she was with him for the next four weeks, right up to the time of his arrest. He and Leah used to take mescaline and T (a codeine-based form of Tylenol) at Sonny Sparda's apartment. Leah asked him what he knew about the girls who had been murdered; she said the word was going around that he had done some of the killings. Drew looked at the jury and quoted his answer: "I could never do what they're try-ing to say that I've been doing."

He did give Leah a ring, but only after finding it was glass. He gave her his knife to protect herself.

Drew was not present at the murder of Karen Marsden. He was not involved in its planning. He knew nothing about it. And he repeated that he knew nothing about the death of Doreen Levesque.

Birknes turned back to the bench. "That's all I have."

Nothing was ever said about the lie detector test which the court in Bristol County had authorized seven months earlier. The test was given, but it was never offered in evidence, and the results were never made public.

Judge Keating called the luncheon recess.

Things did not go quite as smoothly that afternoon, when David Waxler questioned Drew.

Several months after Karen Marsden had stopped working for Drew, he had argued with her and struck her. Drew characterized the incident as a disagreement that he had settled by hitting her in the face—nothing serious.

Waxler also took Drew through the events of the night Karen Marsden died. Drew said Margarida had given him $200 that night. The prosecutor pointed out that he had testified just a few minutes earlier that the most he ever took in during a single night was $150. Drew repeated that she had taken in $200; he did not seem to be bothered by the inconsistency.

Waxler asked Drew if the Fall River police had taken a photograph of him at the time of his arrest. Drew said they had. Waxler asked, "Is it fair to say that you looked a little different on that night than you do today?"

Drew nodded reasonably. "You could say that."

"You had a little pointed goatee and a little thicker mustache? Wore your hair further back?"

With the slightest of smiles, Drew nodded again. "Yes."

Waxler looked over at the jury. There were no projection screens in the courtroom and no comparisons of Drew before and after the killing as there had been of the victim. But he was hoping the contrasting images would form as effectively in their minds and to the same end.

"Mr. Drew, would you take off your jacket and roll up your right sleeve?"

Birknes objected, but after a brief bench conference the judge permitted the question.

Waxler approached the witness stand. "Now, you have a few tattoos on that arm, is that right? One is a cross with a heart on it, and your name?" Drew nodded, and Waxler pointed to another one just below it. "Would you tell us, what is that a picture of?"

Drew said, "Tattoo of a devil's head." His reply was so soft that Keating looked down from the bench and made him repeat it.

"And what does it say right above it?" Waxler asked.

"Avengers," Drew answered.

"Avengers," Waxler echoed. "What did it used to say above the word Avengers?"

Drew looked back at him under lowered eyebrows, his voice even and controlled. "It said Satan."

"Did you have that taken off?"

"I took it off, yes."

Waxler looked back at the jury. "Sonny Sparda has one just like it, doesn't she?" When Waxler turned again to the witness, he saw that Drew had not taken his eyes off him.

"Yes," Drew said, "she does."

Birknes rose at the defense table and appealed to the judge. "If it would please the court—" When Keating looked down at him, Birknes gestured toward Waxler and the witness. "If it please the court, he has him standing there without his jacket on."

"I don't detect a chill, Mr. Birknes," Keating replied. "He may have further questions. When he hasn't, he will put it back on."

Birknes persisted, a lawyer's device for breaking the continuity of his opponent's presentation. "Will he instruct us when he is finished with that line of questioning?"

"No," Keating answered. "We will let him run his cross-examination as you ran yours—uninhibited, relatively."

But Waxler had nothing more to ask about tattoos. A few minutes later, Keating told Drew he could replace the jacket.

Then Waxler led Drew through the items of evidence recovered at the murder site. He had him pick up the sweaters, the jewelry, the coat. He identified the coat. Waxler asked him if he had seen it the night of February 8, in the car. Drew said he had not. Birknes objected to his client being made to touch each of the items, but the judge permitted it. The jury watched, and it was apparent that some of them, at least, were recalling the testimony they had heard from Carol Fletcher and Robin Murphy about the last time Carl Drew had held those same items of clothing in his hands.

Waxler read Drew's criminal history into the record: the armed robbery of Mary Sahadi with a handgun on February 19, 1975; the armed robbery of Edward Fisher with a handgun on December 26, 1974; the armed robbery of Nancy Frazier with a handgun on Christmas Day of that same year.

That was the end of Waxler's cross-examination and the end of the evidence. The two attorneys each presented his summation—first Birknes, then Waxler.

Because it was late afternoon by the time the lawyers were finished, Judge Keating thanked the jury and told them he would charge them in the morning, in both first- and second-degree murder.

The next day was Friday, the 13th of March, 1981.

David Waxler was nervous. He expected to win—he had expected to win from the time he was assigned to the case, months before, even prior to the discovery of the medical X-rays and the positive identification of Karen Marsden's skull. But he was nervous anyway. Despite the testimony and the evidence, there was no guarantee the jury would convict Drew on first-degree, and Waxler considered that anything less would be a disaster. After the judge's charge to the jury, Waxler had gone across the street for lunch, and an hour later he wandered back to the courthouse. Shortly after he got there, he was invited into Keating's chambers. The judge was at his desk, smoking a cigar. The prosecutor lighted a cigar of his own and seated himself in a red leather chair.

David Waxler was only thirty years old at the time the Murphy and Drew cases came to court. He had worked in Pina's office for two years, and although this was his sixth murder case, it was only the third to reach trial. The other two were a New Bedford stabbing case that had gone to manslaughter and an insanity-defense first-degree murder case where a young man stabbed his girlfriend repeatedly and left her impaled to the floor of her apartment with a knife through the neck. Waxler had won a conviction in that as well.

The Marsden murder was the most complex because there were so many interrelated cases. It had been Waxler's principal responsibility to develop the strategy for determining the order for having those cases heard so that the maximum pressure was brought to bear on each defendant at exactly the most vulnerable times, starting in the fall of 1980, in order to knock down the largest number of dominoes. It was the strategy, and not just his performance in the courtroom, that he considered the most crucial and best-managed part of his job as prosecutor.

Born and bred in New Bedford, Waxler had done twelve years of public schools and then gone on to Brandeis. When he got his degree, he took off for Iran, Afghanistan, and ultimately the Himalayas, where he lived and traveled for several months before returning for law school.

He did not believe that Carl Drew was truly a Satanist, at least not in the sense that he was really speaking in tongues and was consciously taken over by the Devil in order to allow evil energies to pass through him into this world. It was Waxler's view that Drew simply recognized that this was a good and effective tool when used on the generally weak, immature, impressionable, and not terribly intelligent people who came within his orbit. He thought that what Drew and his followers had in common was their view of themselves as being in the middle of some B movie, perhaps *The Mephisto Waltz* or *The Creature from the Black Lagoon.* The difference was that Drew was the director, and everyone else was an extra.

In fact, models for the kind of activity Drew had imitated were everywhere. Since the midsixties, it had been possible for anyone, including children, to go into a store in almost any part of the country and find hundreds of books on witchery and satanic ritual. One of the things Waxler thought about a lot during the trial was the movie *Rosemary's Baby,* and he decided that what had made it such a frightening film was the matter-of-fact way in which the evil was played out against the viewers' expectations for that kind of activity. People played Scrabble and shopped in supermarkets and did other day-to-day things, all the while they were plotting to give birth, in a midtown New York apartment, to the Antichrist.

Waxler had taken only a few puffs on his new cigar when Keating told him that the jury had just returned with a question. John Birknes was across the street. "I thought you ought to hear about this, David, because I know how nervous you are about this whole thing."

"I'm not nervous," Waxler lied. "John's the one who should be nervous."

Keating eyed him through the smoke, showing his sharpest, most sardonic smile. "Well, I guess I can tell you what the question is. They want to know if they can find Drew guilty of manslaughter or if they just have to acquit him, based on my charge." He turned around and picked up the telephone. "I'll be with you in a minute."

The cigar dropped from Waxler's mouth, bounced off his lap, and fell onto the floor. In that instant, he was virtually in tears. He said, "How—" The news was so devastating, so far beyond his worst imagining, that he could not even think of what to ask. The judge continued on the telephone for another thirty seconds, and when he turned back to Waxler, his nose was wrinkling in a combination of curiosity and distaste. Waxler followed the judge's gaze down to where the cigar lay at his feet and saw that the rug was beginning to burn.

Keating could not control himself any longer; he hung up the telephone and started to laugh. "That'll teach you, you cocky little punk."

Waxler was still uncertain what had really happened, but he realized instantly that what Keating had told him a moment earlier was a hoax. He sat back in the chair with an overwhelming sense of relief, although still too shaken to fully appreciate the judge's joke.

Keating laughed so hard he had a coughing fit, but finally collected himself. "Don't you want to know what the jury really asked?" he wheezed.

Waxler was still so dazed, the best he could manage was a nod of his head.

Keating imitated the voice of the foreman. "'Do we have to find cruel and unusual conduct as well as premeditation?'"

"My God," Waxler said.

Just a few minutes later, at three-ten in the afternoon, the jury returned again. An officer ran across to find Birknes, the press and spectators filled the courtroom, and Judge Keating gaveled the trial back into session.

The foreman delivered the verdict slip to the assistant clerk of the court. The clerk passed the slip to Judge Keating, who read it in silence.

Carl Drew was instructed to rise and face those who had judged him.

"Has the jury agreed upon a verdict?" the clerk asked the foreman.

"We have."

"On Bristol County Indictment 6298, do you find the defendant, Carl H. Drew, guilty or not guilty?"

"Guilty."

"Guilty of what?"

"Of first-degree murder."

Flash bulbs popped all over the courtroom as the press recorded the moment at which Carl Drew received the verdict.

Drew gave away nothing. There was a guard on either side of him and one behind. He looked over the heads of the jury, his arms hanging by his sides. It was hard to see any sign of the Satanist whose biography was written on his skin. For some reason, at that moment, Drew looked younger than he had looked at any time in the trial.

As Margarida Revorido wept a few feet away, Judge Keating finished the ritual of justice.

"The court, having considered the offense for which you stand convicted, orders that you be punished, therefore, by commitment to the Massachusetts Correctional Institution at Walpole for the term of your natural life, and that you stand committed until you be removed in execution of this sentence. You have the right to file an appeal within twenty days. Mr. Sheriff, the defendant Carl H. Drew is in your custody for this sentence."

The verdict meant that there would never be any possibility of parole. Drew lowered his head and looked at the floor. The guards led him from the courtroom through the door by which the jury had just entered.

Margarida, still weeping, ran across to the door used by the public and continued running until she was out of the building.

THIRTY-SEVEN / **CROSSES**

There are certain rare times in life where habit and ethics and circumstance—and sometimes the law and even science—converge for an instant to illuminate the pure truth. The last words of a dying man or woman, for example, are held by the law to be sworn before God. Flashes of insight or heroism or cowardice frequently accompany great danger.

The last day of a murder trial, especially when the trial ends in conviction, often provides the appearance of such an intersection. The crime is great. The truth is proven. The punishment is absolute. The just are destined for reward.

Carl Drew was without freedom, without power, without hope. He could appeal his conviction, but in continuing to deny his guilt, he was bound by a dreadful paradox: without confession there is no atonement, and without atonement there is no redemption. When the King of Bedford Street was led into the sherrif's car for the return to prison, the life he had imagined for himself seemed gone forever.

By contrast, the departure from Fitchburg of the three Fall River detectives who had brought Carl Drew to justice was filled with all the hope and happiness of the newly blessed who step exuberantly forward to claim the promises of God. No longer constrained from speaking with the press, they would be awash with fame. Kaegael had told them there would be a commendation by the mayor before the city council. Alan Silvia and Tom Joaquim, still in their twenties, had freed themselves from the anchor of their origins, rising up within the system that had tried so long to keep them down and now looked forward to the gratitude of their city and long, successful police careers. Even greater rewards seemed in store for Paul Carey; he had been keeping a careful record of their collective role in solving the crime, with the intention of turning the story into a bestseller.

Not even the pragmatic professionalism of Paul Fitzgerald or Dan Lowney was immune from the gratifying sense of symmetry. Unlike the Nighters or Carey, they had no expectation of special recognition, and the death of Karen Marsden was only one of twenty-three murders they had investigated in Bristol County that year. But the case was an unusual one: they had both known the victim, the truth had been complicated and deeply buried, and proving the identity of the skull required, in Fitzgerald's words, "the kind of spectacular luck that we like to think of as great police work." They had played crucial roles in helping the DA and the prosecutor engineer the delicate chain of dominoes that so far had produced two convictions, a guilty plea, and three life sentences. With the same key witnesses and essentially the same testimony against the remaining two defendants, they looked forward to a clean sweep.

But just as surely as contrition is necessary for salvation, so is great hope the one absolute requisite to terrible disappointment.

Fall River had other plans for everyone.

THIRTY-EIGHT / NATURAL LIVES

From the shores of Bristol, Rhode Island, the view across the two miles of Mount Hope Bay to neighboring Massachusetts is a step back in time. The city of Fall River appears unreal, a perfect diorama of a nineteenth-century New England town nestled in a green-plush jewel box of ancient trees and farmland, its tranquil homes and churches processing neatly up the gentle slope above the deep, silver waters between the Taunton River and the tidal reaches of the Sakonnet. At dusk, the lights of the city send out winking signals of warmth and comfort against the descending darkness.

The only real anachronism is the long green ribbon of the Braga Bridge to the north, but even that helps with the illusion; it hides the battleship *Massachusetts,* which lies at anchor beneath its eastern end, and it also shields the remains of the Harbor Terrace apartments, now abandoned, boarded up, and partially demolished, in the bridge's shadows on the side of the hill.

From the Rhode Island side of the water, there is no sense at all of Fall River's century-long slide into decay. At that distance, the gray stone mill buildings are merely picturesque. The barrooms of Bedford Street where Carl Drew once held court are mostly boarded up—Pier 14 is now an appliance storehouse, and Charlie's is an empty shell— but they were never visible from the water side of the city anyway.

The nightly convoy of pimpmobiles and cruising tricks, and all but a few stragglers from the former small army of hustlers, are gone as well. In the ten years since the chain of murders, much of the commercial sex and dope trades has shifted to neighboring New Bedford. Twelve New Bedford–area prostitutes have disappeared in the past two years, and the murdered remains of ten of them have been found by the roadsides just outside the city. CPAC detectives in Bristol County estimate that some one hundred thousand pounds of marijuana, cocaine, and heroin are now landed every year through New Bedford's deepwater port.

Cities continue to evolve even when they are dying.

After the trial of Carl Drew, Carol Fletcher was allowed to return to the West Coast. She never testified in the trials of any of the other defendants. Nor did Robin Murphy. Both Andy Maltais and Carl Drew, on the other hand, were quickly back in court. The feeling of closure, of finality, that comes with a guilty verdict, especially in a murder trial, is as deceptive as the waterside view of Fall River.

A week after Drew's conviction, Willie Smith's attorney notified the court that his defense would be based in part on the means by which Smith had been identified in the murder of Doreen Levesque; Robin had picked him out of a mug book and not in person. Robin's credibility would come under increased attack as the case moved nearer to trial.

As Willie Smith's attorney worked on discrediting Robin, he was also trying to disconnect his client from Carl Drew. Drew denied any role in the Levesque killing when he was arraigned in Bristol County Superior Court on May 13, and he and Smith were subsequently scheduled to be tried together for the crime. It took six months for Smith's lawyer to succeed in splitting the case into two trials.

David Waxler had left the district attorney's office within a few days of winning Drew's conviction in the Marsden murder. The Levesque case was assigned to another assistant DA. In November, the new prosecutor announced plans to postpone the case against Drew, saying that prosecuting him for the Levesque killing would cost the state as much as one hundred thousand dollars and would be "an exercise in futility," in that it was likely to result, at best, in a meaningless second life sentence.

Because that decision conflicted with Drew's constitutional right to a speedy trial, fourteen months later, in January of 1983, the charges against him in the Levesque case were quietly dropped. But the week before that happened, a more material cause for dismissal was offered in the Bristol County Superior Court.

Robin Murphy was brought down in handcuffs from Framingham State Prison and placed on the stand as the prospective lead witness in the trial of Willie Smith, scheduled for the following Monday. She told the court she had not been present at the Diman School when Levesque was killed. She said she had lied about everything. She said her attorney had made her do it. She said her knowledge of the

Levesque case was entirely hearsay, from her friend Karen Marsden. The judge reminded her that perjury under immunity in a capital trial was punishable by life imprisonment. Robin raised her manacled hands to her face and wept. On Monday, the day he was scheduled to stand trial for murder, Willie Smith was released.

As soon as Smith heard the news, he told reporters, "I think this was a joke. I never knew any of those people. I never knew Robin Murphy."

On the basis of Robin's new testimony, both Carl Drew and Andy Maltais appealed their previous convictions. It was decided in the subsequent hearings, however, that Robin Murphy had been lying when she recanted. Both convictions were upheld.

But the case against Carl Davis disintegrated. He never came to trial for his involvement in the murder of Karen Marsden. In 1982 he was convicted for assault and battery and an attack with a dangerous weapon on another Fall River prostitute and sentenced to prison for seven to ten years. His victim was Sonny Sparda.

Charges of intimidating a witness were not pressed. Davis served the minimum required time and is now free.

Fall River had grown weary of the murder trials. Nobody wanted to be reminded of the stories of Satanism and dark rituals in the forest from a time that now seemed long ago.

When Carol Fletcher had been brought to Seattle for extradition prior to testifying in the Drew trial, she had jumped from the courthouse window. Once Drew's trial was over, she was allowed to return to the West Coast, and the DA never called on her again. Pina told the press that he was unable to locate her. Paul Fitzgerald or Dan Lowney could have found Carol Fletcher in a minute, but when the Smith and Davis cases came to a head, Pina didn't ask them to. He'd had a falling-out with Fitzgerald and Lowney and had transferred both of them out of the Bristol County CPAC unit shortly after Drew was convicted.

Even today, although she has changed her name and lives in another city, Carol Fletcher is still very easy to find. Ten years after the murder of Karen Marsden, she says, "I don't remember half the things that night. They talked to me and told me what I knew and what I didn't know, and they told me it was impossible for me not to have been there. But I sit there and I say, 'But, I don't think I was,' you know? When you're doing drugs, it's kind of hard to tell the reality from the nonreality, you know?"

Carol has given up drugs and prostitution and works at a straight job. She thinks of Karen often and feels that if she had been given the chance she would have had a different life now as well. "It was a phase. We weren't always like that, and she wouldn't have stayed like that forever. She was trying to get out of it, but Robin and Carl kept bringing her down. Robin used to say to us, if she goes down, everybody goes down with her."

Almost as frequently, Carol thinks of Karen's little boy, JJ. It haunts her that he will have to live the rest of his life without his mother. Karen's last wish—please don't let anything happen to JJ— haunts her as well; she has not seen JJ since his mother's death.

Carol lived in Europe for a while, then went back to Washington State and eventually married a man she met out there. If the earlier time in her life is hard to remember, it is also hard for Carol to talk about it. Her husband has been told nothing about how she lived as a young woman, about the murders, about her past.

The last time she was in Fall River was 1984. She says she'll never return.

David Waxler returned to a brief celebrity a short time after going into private practice when he handled the defense in the notorious Big Dan's case, the trial of four Portuguese immigrants for gang rape on the pool table in a New Bedford bar. But if the Big Dan's case had many of the elements of his previous triumph, this time he may have been the victim of his earlier success. Bristol County was sick and tired of having the world's attention invited to the spectacle of public sex and crime within its boundaries, and all four defendants were convicted. Today he spends almost all of his time on personal injury work.

"The Marsden murder drove me into retirement as a prosecutor," he says, and it's only partly a joke. "After the Drew trial, I went home and looked at myself in the mirror and said I can't keep doing this. The day-in, day-out involvement was really taking a toll on me. The reason I got out of the DA's office was that after a while you begin to get overwhelmed by the human wreckage that litters the roadside of the criminal justice system, whether it's victims or witnesses or defendants or families; it's all dented and bumped and totaled people instead of cars. And I think it does catch up with you after a while.

"These days, I'm dealing with people who have been seriously hurt or family members of people who have been killed in accidents. There's a little more satisfaction because even though you can throw money at those things and say it doesn't help, it really does help. So you're not working for some philosophical ideal of society. You can say, 'This person was hurt. They were damaged physically and financially and psychically, and you're going to have to compensate them for it.' If you're able to do that, it's satisfying. I don't do very much criminal work at all."

It is a widely held belief, especially in America's prisons, that the defendants with the worst cases are usually also the ones with the worst lawyers, and that the sentence is the price such defendents are forced to pay, because they have no money, for offenses committed in the courtroom by their attorneys. There can be some truth to this belief: court-appointed defenders are notorious for ignoring their clients, missing dates and deadlines, shirking their obligations, and often for simple incompetence. At the outset, on the face of it, Carl Drew may have had some reason to be nervous about the lawyer appointed to represent him in the trial for his life.

Although John Birknes had been an attorney for several years, he had been in active practice for only three of the ten years prior to the trial; the other seven were spent in Boston as a United States marshal. He was glad to get the assignment of defending Drew. At the time he accepted the case, his practice was small and relatively prosaic, certainly not the kind that got his name on the front pages with the same regularity as either his client or his prospective adversaries. He was quiet and methodical, wore three-piece suits, and had the intelligent, attentive, but understated manner one might associate more with a country doctor than with the defense attorney in a spectacular murder trial.

There was nothing understated in the defense John Birknes gave Carl Drew. "The case generated a tremendous amount of pressure simply because of its nature," he recalled ten years later. "On top of that was all the publicity, which was relentless. There wasn't any room for error or for oversight. I gave it everything I had." The police and the other attorneys in the case agree. Birknes was thorough, he was on time, he was tenacious, and he did not give up an inch of ground without an honorable battle. But when the trial was over, he resigned as Carl Drew's attorney.

"We agreed in advance Carl would get another attorney if we lost. I don't consider myself an appellate lawyer. I had taken it as far as I could go," he says. Today Birknes conducts a primarily civil practice in New Bedford and serves as town counsel for Dartmouth, Massachusetts.

*   *   *

Alan Silvia still has strong feelings about the events of ten years ago, and not all of them are positive. "In the end, nobody came up and patted us on the back and told us we did a good job. We worked like hell; our motivation was the exhilaration of knowing we were doing the right thing—and I guess we also had to settle for that as our reward. But a part of me was lost in the process. I was drained. I'll never have the intensity I had then; it's just not there anymore. There should be a big payoff for a thing like that—you put a lot into it, and there should be a big result. We were all put in for commendations for the case, but they never made it out of the police station."

Paul Carey felt the same way. "We solved the case. Kaegael told us we were supposed to get a commendation before the City Council; we got nothing. I can see the mayor's point: he didn't want Satanism brought up in the city of Fall River. The DA didn't want us to get credit for what we did; he took it all. Nothing came of it. It was the biggest case that ever came out of Fall River in my twenty-four years as a cop. Nothing."

Both Carey and Silvia stayed on with the Fall River Police Department. But there are no longer any Nighters in the Major Crimes Division. Carey moved into the Tactical Unit. Silvia is in Sexual Abuse. They work the same hours as everyone else.

Tom Joaquim remained a detective with the Major Crimes Division for another seven years, and then he quit. He is now a game warden.

For a long time, Paul Fitzgerald continued to serve in North Dartmouth. In late 1989 he became a lieutenant and is now assigned to the State Police Barracks in Middleboro, Massachusetts.

Dan Lowney is now retired and living in Florida.

Ted Kaegael retired as a captain.

Captain Andrade died of cancer in the late winter of 1989. He worked as a policeman until just before the end.

Judge Keating is dead as well.

Dr. William Sturner is still chief medical examiner for Rhode Island.

Dr. Paul DeVillers succumbed to diabetes and heart disease. His colleague, Dr. Ambrose Keeley, has also died.

Dr. Douglas Ubelaker is still curator of anthropology at the Smithsonian and continues in his parallel role as consultant in forensic anthropology to the FBI. His forensic assignments since the Drew trial now number in the hundreds.

Andy Maltais served out his life sentence. He died in prison, following a series of strokes, six years after his conviction. He maintained his innocence and was still appealing his case at the time of his death.

Cookie Powers left Fall River. The police have no idea of her present location.

Sonny Sparda has been in and out of jail for drugs and other charges, but still lives in Fall River. Silvia saw her a few months ago by chance and they grinned at each other in recollection of their shared adventure, and continued on their separate ways.

Brian Field sold the lot in Westport back to George Dean. "He really gave it back to me, at the same price he'd paid for it," Dean said, "although it was worth a lot more by then. I guess maybe the property had been spoiled for him because of what happened there."

George Dean retired as chief of the Westport Fire Department. He still lives in the town. In 1988, he was a witness in a case of groundwater pollution, and he sent out a roll of film to develop pictures he had taken in support of his testimony. When the prints came back, they included the pictures he had taken years before—of the skull in the woods, the clothing, and Karen Marsden's hair.

Carl Drew exhausted the appeal process in his own case the year after Maltais died. He is now in Norfolk Prison. He looks a lot better today than in his photos from ten years ago. His brown hair is cut relatively short, in the style of the 1950s, and seems lighter than 10 years ago. He is clean-shaven, and there is no trace of the puffiness or flab he had accumulated at the time of his trial. His arms and chest are powerful, the product of seven hours a day pumping iron in the prison gym, and he carries himself like an athlete in the peak of condition.

"When I first got into the joint, my life was hell, not only from inmates but from the cops. I was put into a small room, on the floor, and kept there all that first weekend like an animal. They'd come every half hour and beat the door or bring the food and say, 'The Devil sent this up.' I had twenty cops outside the door at one time.

"What the cops were really mad about—I mean mad at me—is, here's a new guy that's moving into town, and I just moved right into Bedford Street and started taking over. If I did these crimes, sure I deserve to be in jail. But I never took a life—anybody's life. I don't see how I could—I would think I'd be in Bridgewater [the Massachusetts correctional institution for the criminally insane] today, at this point, if I did do that. I don't see how a person can live with themselves if they did what they say I did to this broad."

But Carl Drew is not in Bridgewater, and he does not appear to be insane. His father, who never communicated with him after his arrest, died in the summer of 1989. Drew says, "He has a lot to answer for." Sonny Sparda wrote to him for a while, and he is still visited occasionally by one brother, one sister, and his mother. He says Margarida Revorido comes to see him every week, faithfully, and that they plan to be married "within the next few months." She works in a mill in Fall River and leads a straight life. Carl says she is still beautiful.

Although there were several attempts on Drew's life during his first years in prison, he says, "No one ever managed to knock me off my feet." Today those attempts have ended. He leads a relatively uneventful life, but not an unpleasant one. He works in the kitchen. His cell is equipped with a television, bookshelves, and a foot locker. "If you saw my room, you wouldn't think it was a cell."

In some ways, Drew's life today is better than it was on Bedford Street. He has made a home for himself, he carries himself with the old authority, and a full decade after the murders that caused the newspapers to call him "Son of Satan," he retains the one quality that escaped almost everyone else in the case except the DA, Ron Pina.

Although he says he never expects to get out of prison, he is still a force to be reckoned with. He is a celebrity.

In that respect, Carl Drew may prove more durable than his old nemesis. Ronald Pina was defeated in the Democratic primaries in the fall of 1990 and left office the following January.

As of this writing, Robin Murphy is being held in the prison at Lancaster, in north-central Massachusetts. It is a matter of record that she made a bargain with the DA to testify at subsequent murder trials in exchange for immunity in the two other killings and the chance for eventual parole in the murder of Karen Marsden. It is also a matter of record that she did not keep her end of the bargain.

But even if Ron Pina, who struck the bargain, had held onto his job, the district attorney's office does not have the final power to decide whether the Commonwealth of Massachusetts will keep its side of that same promise. The parole board is an authority in its own right, and its control of any prisoner's future, up to the full term of the sentence, is nearly absolute.

Although theoretically Robin is in jail until at least 1996, in fact she is eligible for a parole review in another few months. The prison at Lancaster is a pre-release center.

*   *   *

Unknown to all the participants except the prosecution team, Karen Marsden's skull had been present at the trial of Carl Drew in Fitchburg—but it was kept in a box under the witness table and never introduced in evidence. Eventually, the box with the skull wound up back in the Evidence Room in the state police barracks in North Dartmouth. It stayed there for eight years.

From time to time, Paul Fitzgerald, who was in charge of North Dartmouth during that period, would call over to New Bedford and ask for permission to dispose of the skull for burial. His persistence eventually paid off. In early January of 1989, Fitzgerald got a call from a funeral home.

When the undertaker arrived at the barracks, it was at the same time a state police captain was giving an interview to a newspaper reporter. It was about the roadside murders of the summer before—all involving drugs and prostitution. That fall and winter the skeletal remains of nine of the victims had been found by the side of highways in the New Bedford area. The captain was in charge of the dogs that had been used to search out the bodies. When the reporter heard about yet another skull, she thought at first it was a new victim of the latest series.

On January 3, 1989, the only part of Karen Marsden's body that was ever recovered—the calvarium skull—was finally buried at Oak Grove Cemetery, just two blocks north of Bedford Street in the center of Fall River.

The day was sunny but windy and bitter cold. The arrangements had been made by a minister acting on behalf of Karen Marsden's grandmother, but no family or friends were present at the burial. According to the minister, there was no funeral service for Karen Marsden "because of the circumstances." The only witnesses were some cemetery workers, the man from the funeral home, and the reporter who'd followed from the barracks. The grave is unmarked.

SOURCE NOTES

INTERVIEWS WITH AUTHOR

John A. Birknes, Jr., Esq., attorney, New Bedford, Mass.; Chester Blythe, special agent and forensics expert, Federal Bureau of Investigation, Washington, D.C.; Sgt. Paul Carey, detective, Major Crimes Division, Fall River Police Department, Fall River, Mass.; Margaret Charig, reporter, *Standard Times*, New Bedford, Mass.; Robert Courey, M.D., radiologist, St. Anne's Hospital, Fall River, Mass.; George Dean, Chief (retired), Fire Department, Westport, Mass.; John Doherty, Esq., attorney, Brockton, Mass.; Carl Drew, Norfolk, Mass.; Lt. Paul Fitzgerald, detective, D Troop, Massachusetts State Police, Middleboro, Mass.; Carol Fletcher; Arthur (Tom) Joaquim, detective (retired), Major Crimes Division, Fall River Police Department, Fall River, Mass.; Capt. Theodore Kaegael, detective (retired), Major Crimes Division, Fall River Police Department, Fall River, Mass.; Sgt. Daniel Lowney, detective (retired), Massachusetts State Police; James F. Lyons, former administrator, St. Anne's Hospital, Fall River, Mass.; Stephen Marquart, Office of Public Affairs, Federal Bureau of Investigation, Washington, D.C.; Kenneth Martin, detective, Bristol Country Crime Prevention and Control Unit, Massachusetts State Police, New Bedford, Mass.; Rev. Hubert Morden, minister, First Baptist Church, Fall River, Mass.; Robin Marie Murphy, Lancaster, Mass. (just long enough for her to decline a meeting); Alan Robillard, special agent and forensics expert, Federal Bureau of Investigation, Washington, D.C.; Alan Silvia, detective, Major Crimes Division, Fall River Police Department, Fall River, Mass.; T. Dale Stewart, M.D., Curator of Anthropology Emeritus, National Museum of Natural History, Smithsonian Institution, Washington, D.C.; William Sturner, M.D., Chief Medical Examiner, State of Rhode Island, Providence, R.I.; Douglas H. Ubelaker, Ph.D., Curator of Anthropology, National Museum of Natural History, Smithsonian Institution, Washington, D.C.; David H. Waxler, Esq., attorney, New Bedford, Mass.

TRANSCRIPTS

Andre Maltais interview with Ronald Pina et al. District Attorney's Office, New Bedford, Mass., February 5, 1980, to 12:40 P.M., 1–19.

Andre Maltais interview with Ronald Pina et al. Fall River, Mass., February 5, 1980, afternoon, 1–10.

Robin Murphy interview with Joseph Macy, Esq. District Attorney's Office, New Bedford, Mass., April 9, 1980, 8:30 P.M. to 9:10 P.M., 1–43.

Robin Murphy interview with Trooper Robert St. Jean et al. District Attorney's Office, New Bedford, Mass., April 29, 1980, 9:10 P.M. to 10:30 P.M., 1–83.

Robin Murphy interview with Trooper Robert St. Jean et al. District Attorney's Office, New Bedford, Mass., April 29, 1980, 9:10 P.M. to 10:30 P.M., 1–55.

Robin Murphy interview with Trooper Brian McMahon et al. District Attorney's Office, New Bedford, Mass., May 1, 1980, 1–26.

Defendant's guilty plea in murder and grant of immunity in related cases. Proceedings of January 14, 1981, 24–34.

Robin Murphy testimony. Trial on Case 5803.

Carol Fletcher grand jury testimony. January 8, 1981, 3–48.

Carol Fletcher interview with Detective Arthur (Tom) Joaquim. Fall River Police Department, Fall River, Mass., February 17, 1980, 1–23.

Paul Fitzgerald grand jury testimony. May 9, 1980, 1–18.

Alan Silvia grand jury testimony. May 9, 1980, 19–23.

Daniel Lowney grand jury testimony. May 9, 1980, 24–33.

Brian McMahon grand jury testimony. May 9, 1980, 34–48.

Margarida Revorido interview with Sgt. Daniel Lowney. Plymouth County House of Correction, Plymouth, Mass., May 24, 1980, 1–14.

Mildred (Cookie) Jukes interview with Sgt. Daniel Lowney et al. District Attorney's Office, New Bedford, Mass., June 16, 1980, 1–45.

Nancy Braga interview with Sgt. Daniel Lowney. Plymouth County House of Correction, Plymouth, Mass., November 12, 1980, 1–10.

Leah Johnson deposition by David Waxler and John Birknes. District Attorney's Office, New Bedford, Mass., January, 1981, 1–88.

TESTIMONY FROM THE TRIAL OF CASE 6298:

Francis W. Keating; David H. Waxler; John A. Birknes, Jr.; the jurors; Brian Field; George Dean; Charles Pierce; Martin Fay; Donna Wheelock; Paul Fitzgerald; Daniel Lowney; Carolyn Guilmette; Paul Bedard; Douglas Ubelaker; Alan Robillard; Mark Babyak; Michael Baretto; Mildred Powers; Anne Gabbour; Donna Murphy; Elvira Nolin; Robin Murphy; Carol Fletcher; Leah Johnson; William Sturner; Alan Silvia; Paul Carey; Maureen Sparda; Linda Riley; Henry Rose; Pamela Coady; David Roche; Debra Skarpos; Carl Drew.

POLICE REPORTS

Fall River Police Department (hereafter cited as FRPD), *Homicide of Barbara Raposa Case #80-956, Det. Joaquim,* interview, site visit with Carol Fletcher, Karen Marsden, et al., January 30, 1980.

FRPD, *Homicide of Barbara Raposa Case #80-956, Det. St. Pierre,* telephone call and two meetings with Robin Murphy, February 9, 1980.

FRPD, *Missing Person Case #80-1476, Officer Janssen,* call from subject's relative, February 10, 1980.

FRPD, *Missing Person Case #80-1476, Det. Silvia,* Drew interview; photographs; hair sample; examination of buck knife, February 10, 1980.

FRPD, *Missing Person Case #80-1476, Det. Silvia,* Cowen interview, February 10, 1980.

FRPD, *Missing Person Case #80-1476, Det. Silvia,* Murphy interview, February 10, 1980.

FRPD, *Missing Person Case #80-1476, Det. Silvia,* Sparda interview, February 10, 1980.

FRPD, *Missing Person Case #80-1476, Det. Silvia,* Fletcher interview, February 10, 1980.

FRPD, *Missing Person Case #80-1476, Det. Silvia,* call from CPAC Det. Lowney re Leah Johnson, February 10, 1980.

FRPD, *Missing Person Case #80-1476, Det. Carey,* Sparda interview, February 11, 1980.

FRPD, *Missing Person Case #80-1476, Det. Joaquim,* Officer Bruce McCabe re Donna Murphy, February 11, 1980.

FRPD, *Missing Person Case #80-1476, Det. Phelan*, Powers interview, February 11, 1980.

FRPD, *Missing Person Case #80-1476, Det. Silvia*, Nancy Marsden interview, February 14, 1980.

FRPD, *Statement Det. Saucier*, call from Nooman [Numan], February 15, 1980.

FRPD, *Missing Person Case #80-1476, Det. Joaquim*, follow-up at Dave's Beach, February 15, 1980.

FRPD, *Missing Person Case #80-1476, Det. Joaquim*, call from Nancy Marsden, February 15, 1980.

FRPD *Missing Person Case #80-1476, Det. Joaquim*, Numan interview, February 15, 1980.

FRPD, *Missing Person Case #80-1476*, Det. Joaquim, search for car reported by Fletcher, February 16, 1980.

FRPD, *Missing Person Case #80-1476 (Confidential Report), Det. Silvia*, Fletcher descriptions of two white males; site visit; February 16, 1980.

FRPD, *Missing Person Case #80-1476, Det. Silvia*, car search in State Forest, February 17, 1980.

FRPD, *Missing Person Case #80-1476 Det. Carey*, contents of car trunk; Fletcher interview, February 17, 1980.

FRPD, *Missing Person Case #80-1476 (cont. investigation), Det. Joaquim*, Fletcher ID of two suspects, February 17, 1980.

FRPD, *Supplementary Report, Missing Person Case #80-1476, Det. Phelan*, Jones interview, February 18, 1980.

FRPD, *Missing Person Case #80-1476, Det. Joaquim*, Jennings interview, February 20, 1980.

FRPD, *Missing Person Case #80-1476, Det. Carey*, interviews with Bohun, Deschenes, Murphy, Sparda, February 22, 1980.

FRPD, *Missing Person Case #80-1476, Det. Carey*, Deschenes interview, February 23, 1980.

FRPD, *Vehicle Check — Central St. F[all] R[iver], Det. Carey*, Jennings interview, February 23, 1980.

FRPD, *Missing Person Case #80-1476, Det. Joaquim*, Deschenes interview, February 24, 1980.

FRPD, *Missing Person Case #80-1476, Det. Joaquim*, Maureen Murphy, Richard Guinen interviews, February 29, 1980.

FRPD, *Missing Person Case #80-1476, Det. Silvia*, Nolins interview, February 29, 1980.

FRPD, *Missing Person Case #80-1476, Det. Silvia*, Sparda interview, February 29, 1980.

FRPD, *Missing Person Case #80-1476, Det. Silvia*, Sparda interview, March 2, 1980.

Massachusetts State Police, Bristol County Crime Prevention and Control Unit, *Tpr. Dusoe*, discovery in Westport, April 13, 1980.

Bristol CPAC, *Homicide Case #80-0066, Tpr. Fitzgerald*, search for body, April 14, 1980.

FRPD, *Missing Person Case #80-1476, Det. Joaquim*, query from missing person's relative re Westport skull, April 15, 1980.

FRPD, *Missing Person Case #80-1476, Det. Phelan*, call from relative, April 15, 1980.

Bristol CPAC, *Homicide Case #80-0066, Tpr. Fitzgerald*, skull autopsy, April 15, 1980.

Bristol CPAC, *Homicide Case #80-0066, Tpr. Fitzgerald*, search with dogs, April 16, 1980.

FRPD, *Missing Person Case #80-1476, Det. Silvia*, Sparda interview, April 17, 1980.

FRPD, *Missing Person Case #80-1476, Det. Silvia*, Sparda interview, April 22, 1980.

FRPD, *Missing Person Case #80-1476, Det. Carey*, Alves interview, April 22, 1980.

FRPD, *Missing Person Case #80-1476, Det. Silvia*, Sparda interview, April 23, 1980.

FRPD, *suspicious person complaint, Officer Mroz*, Barbara Lewis, Complainant, April 23, 1980.

Bristol CPAC, *Homicide Case #80-0066, Tpr. Fitzgerald*, Sparda, Maureen Murphy interviews, April 24, 1980.

Bristol CPAC, *Homicide Case #80-0066, Tpr. Fitzgerald*, Fletcher telephone call, April 24, 1980.

FRPD, *Articles removed from auto rented by Carol Fletcher, Det. Phelan*, April 25, 1980.

Bristol CPAC, *Homicide Case #80-0066, Tpr. Fitzgerald*, further search of Westport area with divers, April 25, 1980.

Bristol CPAC, *Homicide Case #80-0066, Tpr. Fitzgerald*, grid pattern search in Westport, April 27, 1980.

Bristol CPAC, *Homicide Case #80-0066, Tpr. Fitzgerald*, meet suspect at airport, April 29, 1980.

Bristol CPAC, *Homicide Case #80-0066, Tpr. Fitzgerald*, visit second suspect on West Coast, May 1, 1980.

FRPD, *Doreen Levesque (Possible Suspect William Smith Case #79-9911), Det. Silvia*, search for William Smith, May 4, 1980.

FRPD, *Missing Person Case #80-1476, Det. Joaquim*, investigation of bloodstained jacket, boots, May 4, 1980.

FRPD, *Missing Person Case #80-1476, Identification of jewelry, Det. Silvia*, May 5, 1980.

FRPD, *Missing Person Case #80-1476, Det. Carey*, interviews with relative, Hinote, May 5, 1980.

Bristol CPAC, *Homicide Case #80-0066, Tpr. Fitzgerald*, Coady interview, May 7, 1980.

Bristol CPAC, *Homicide Case #80-0066, Tpr. Lowney*, Leah Johnson interview, May 7, 1980.

Bristol CPAC, *Homicide Case #80-0066, Tpr. Fitzgerald*, arrest in Westport murder, May 8, 1980.

Department of Anthropology, American Museum of Natural History, *FBI Case No. 00417015, Dartmouth, Massachusetts, Ubelaker*, sex and age of Westport skull, May 9, 1980.

Bristol CPAC, *Homicide Case #80-0066, Tpr. Lowney*, Drew interview, May 9, 1980.

Bristol CPAC, *Homicide Case #80-0066, Tpr. Lowney*, search and seizure warrant, May 9, 1980.

Bristol CPAC, *Homicide Case #80-0066, Tpr. Lowney*, Johnson interview, May 12, 1980.

Bristol CPAC, *Homicide Case #80-0066, Tpr. Lowney*, recovery of ring, May 15, 1980.

Report of the FBI Laboratory, Spec. Agt. Wallace, skull, clothing, hair, comb, portions of brain, blood, rocks, buck knife, dirt, and bottles collected at murder site, May 29, 1980.

Report of the FBI Laboratory, Senior Chemist Drew Richardson, blood matching and brain chemistry, June 19, 1980.

Letter to District Attorney Pina from Medical Examiner, Third Bristol District, Paul R. DeVillers, M.D., probable identity of Westport skull, July 7, 1980.

Bristol CPAC, *Homicide Case #80-0066, Tpr. Fitzgerald*, Uretsky interview, November 13, 1980.

Office of the Bristol County District Attorney, *Summary of an interview with Carol Fletcher, Assistant District Attorney Waxler*, November 21, 1980.

Bristol CPAC, *Homicide Case #80-0066, Tpr. Lowney*, Fletcher interview, November 24, 1980.

EVIDENCE AND OTHER DOCUMENTS

Defendant Carl Drew's answer concerning alibi defense, January 28, 1981.
Consent search authorization, February 10, 1980.
Psychiatric evaluation by Salvador Jacobs, M.D., March 3, 1980.
Autopsy report on calvarium skull, April 13, 1980.
Fletcher interview report, May 7, 1980.

Affidavit in support of request for warrant, May 9, 1980.
Psychiatric evaluation by John E. Snell, M.D., June 7, 1980.
Memorandum in opposition to defendant's motion to vacate, September 12, 1980.
Findings and rulings on defendant's motion to suppress, November 19, 1980.
Discovery, December 8, 1980.
Chronology on Case 5803, Commonwealth of Massachusetts *v.* Andre Maltais.
Application for grant of immunity, Robin Murphy.
Application for grant of immunity, Carol Fletcher.
Witness lists for Case 6298, Commonwealth of Massachusetts *v.* Carl Drew.
Witness lists for Case 5803.
Verdict slip, Case 6298, March 13, 1981.
Appeal Review, Case 6298.
Curriculum vitae, William Sturner.
1979 Annual Report, Douglas Ubelaker, Department of Anthropology, National Museum of Natural History.
1980 Annual Report, Office of Chief Medical Examiner, Rhode Island Department of Health.
1980 Annual Report, Douglas Ubelaker, Department of Anthropology, National Museum of Natural History.
1985 Annual Report, Office of Chief Medical Examiner, Rhode Island Department of Health.
Motion by author for vacating of impoundment order in Case 6298, August 1, 1989.
Allowance of motion to vacate, August 7, 1989.

NEWSPAPER REPORTS

"Third robbery suspect charged," New Bedford *Standard-Times*, January 2, 1975.

"Three held in holiday thefts," New Bedford *Standard-Times*, January 9, 1975.

"Girl found murdered in Fall River," New Bedford *Standard-Times*, October 14, 1979.

"Father; Slain girl faced harsh world," New Bedford *Standard-Times*, October 16, 1979.

"Eulogist quotes slain girl's letter to Jesus," New Bedford *Standard-Times*, October 18, 1979.

"At 17, she had 'lived a lifetime,' was looking for help," New Bedford *Standard-Times*, October 21, 1979.

"Witness saw suspect over body; Murder hearing witness tells horror story," New Bedford *Standard-Times*, February 16, 1980.

"Murder suspect released on bail," New Bedford *Standard-Times*, April 9, 1980.

"3 deaths possibly came from hands of 'satanic cult'; Cult, skull link probed," New Bedford *Standard-Times*, April 17, 1980.

"Cult members 'witnessed' deaths—police," New Bedford *Standard-Times*, April 18, 1980.

"Search party finds slacks but no body at Westport pond," New Bedford *Standard-Times*, April 28, 1980.

"Murder charged in Westport skull case," New Bedford *Standard-Times*, May 9, 1980.

"'Satanic cult' linked to Fall River slayings," *Providence Journal*, May 9, 1980.

"2 arraigned in Westport skull case," New Bedford *Standard-Times*, May 10, 1980.

"Third suspect arraigned in Westport skull case," New Bedford *Standard-Times*, May 14, 1980.

"3rd suspect held in girl's slaying," Fall River *Herald*, May 15, 1980.

"3rd District Court action," New Bedford *Standard-Times*, May 17, 1980.

"DA presents reports on 3 murder suspects," New Bedford *Standard-Times*, June 3, 1980.

"Murder defendant's report withheld," New Bedford *Standard-Times,* July 3, 1980.

"Judge denies release of evaluation," New Bedford *Standard-Times,* July 4, 1980.

"Bail set for murder suspect," New Bedford *Standard-Times,* July 24, 1980.

"Judge rules defense may talk to witness of murder," New Bedford *Standard-Times,* August 8, 1980.

"Psychiatric test conducted," New Bedford *Standard-Times,* September 16, 1980.

"Murder defendant wins separate trial," New Bedford *Standard-Times,* September 27, 1980.

"DA may ask death penalties," New Bedford *Standard-Times,* October 1, 1980.

"Suspect's insanity plea is revoked," New Bedford *Standard-Times,* October 9, 1980.

"Judge denies bail to 2 men charged with slaying woman," New Bedford *Standard-Times,* October 17, 1980.

"Judge to hear plea for withholding suspect's statement," New Bedford *Standard-Times,* January 3, 1981.

"Jury selection in murder trial to begin," New Bedford *Standard-Times,* January 11, 1981.

"Murder lawyer: Duo controlled client's will," New Bedford *Standard-Times,* January 13, 1981.

"Illness interrupts testimony," *Providence Journal,* January 15, 1981.

"Fall River teen admits guilt in killing," New Bedford *Standard-Times,* January 15 1981.

"Woman, 18, admits role in brutal 'execution'," *Providence Journal,* January 15, 1981.

"Star witness tells of actions before Raposa died," New Bedford *Standard-Times,* January 20, 1981.

"Witness tells jury she knows details of Levesque killing," New Bedford *Standard-Times,* January 21, 1981.

"Judge separates pair's murder trial," New Bedford *Standard-Times,* February 3, 1981.

"Fall River murder trial transferred to Worcester," New Bedford *Standard-Times,* February 4, 1981.

"Murder trial moved," New Bedford *Standard-Times,* February 5, 1981.

"Jury selection in murder case," *Fitchburg Sentinel & Enterprise,* March 2, 1981.

"Marsden murder trial begins," New Bedford *Standard-Times,* March 2, 1981.

"'Cult slaying' of girl described in court," Brockton *Enterprise & Times,* March 3, 1981.

"Defendant indicted in second murder," New Bedford *Standard-Times,* March 3, 1981.

"Escape plan alleged; Under constant guard," *Fitchburg Sentinel & Enterprise,* March 3 1981.

"Murder jury picked; to see Westport site today," New Bedford *Standard-Times,* March 3, 1981.

"Grand jury indicts in second slaying," *Fitchburg Sentinel & Enterprise,* March 4, 1981.

"Murder jury visits Westport," New Bedford *Standard-Times,* March 4, 1981.

"Prosecutor opens state's case with ghastly murder account," *Fitchburg Sentinel & Enterprise,* March 5, 1981.

"Witness to offer alibi," New Bedford *Standard-Times,* March 5, 1981.

"Expert says skull part was murder victim's," *Fitchburg Sentinel & Enterprise,* March 6, 1981.

"Experts match hair to victim," New Bedford *Standard-Times,* March 6, 1981

"Trial raises possibility body set afire," Fall River *Herald,* March 6, 1981.

"Key witness struck deal with Bristol County DA," *Fitchburg Sentinel & Enterprise,* March 7, 1981.

"Prostitute: Defendant called himself 'Satan', made threats," New Bedford *Standard-Times*, March 7, 1981.

"Threatened life of girl, witness says," *Fitchburg Sentinel & Enterprise*, March 7, 1981.

"Cult murder trial told defendant ordered slaying," *Associated Press*, March 10, 1981.

"Gruesome cult murder told," *United Press International*, March 10, 1981.

"'Possessed' witness says she cut lover's throat under orders," New Bedford *Standard-Times*, March 10, 1981.

"Slaying involved satanic rite," *Fitchburg Sentinel & Enterprise*, March 10, 1981.

"Souls of slain women 'given to Satan'," *Providence Journal*, March 10, 1981.

"Told of torture-killing," *Fitchburg Sentinel & Enterprise*, March 11, 1981.

"Victim warned at murder scene 2 weeks earlier," New Bedford *Standard-Times*, March 11, 1981.

"Prostitute gives murder suspect an alibi," New Bedford *Standard-Times*, March 12, 1981.

"Defendant denies cult killing," *Associated Press*, March 13, 1981.

"Jury to get murder case today," New Bedford *Standard-Times*, March 13, 1981.

"Murder trial goes to jury today," *Fitchburg Sentinel & Enterprise*, March 13, 1981.

"Tales of pimps and Satan turn Fitchburg on its ear," New Bedford *Standard-Times*, March 13, 1981.

"Friday 13th verdict: 'Guilty!'," *Fitchburg Sentinel & Enterprise*, March 14, 1981.

"Killer gets life term," New Bedford *Standard-Times*, March 14, 1981.

"Murder suspect bases defense on misidentification," New Bedford *Standard-Times*, March 20, 1981.

"Lawyer files motion for new trial in murder case," New Bedford *Standard-Times*, April 1, 1981.

"Judge to hear plea for new murder trial," New Bedford *Standard-Times*, April 8, 1981.

"Murderer reportedly threatened," New Bedford *Standard-Times*, April 8, 1981.

"Hearing on new trial delayed," New Bedford *Standard-Times*, April 10, 1981.

"Killer seeks new trial," New Bedford *Standard-Times*, April 15, 1981.

"Judge denies new murder trial," New Bedford *Standard-Times*, April 24, 1981.

"Killer faces 2nd charge of murder," New Bedford *Standard-Times*, May 5, 1981

"Judge appoints lawyer for murder suspect," New Bedford *Standard-Times*, May 9, 1981.

"Denies second murder," New Bedford *Standard-Times*, May 13, 1981.

"Arraigned in 2nd murder," *United Press International*, May 14, 1981

"New man to press murder charges," New Bedford *Standard-Times*, May 19, 1981.

"Murder trial witness gets a new lawyer," New Bedford *Standard-Times*, August 1, 1981.

"Co-defendant's attorney challenges combined trial for woman's slaying," New Bedford *Standard-Times*, September 15, 1981.

"Murder witness immunity argued," New Bedford *Standard-Times*, September 24, 1981.

"Trial judge forbids mention of 'satanic cult'," New Bedford *Standard-Times*, September 25, 1981.

"Judge won't repeal witness's immunity," New Bedford *Standard-Times*, September 29, 1981.

"Judge splits Levesque murder case," New Bedford *Standard-Times*, November 7, 1981.

"Murder suspect out on bail after 19 months," New Bedford *Standard-Times*, December 11, 1981.

"Slayer seeks trial for 2nd murder," New Bedford *Standard-Times*, January 9, 1982.

"Accused killer sought on charges of intimidating, hitting witness," *Providence Sunday Journal*, January 24, 1982.

"Judge delays ruling on speedy trial," New Bedford *Standard-Times*, January 28, 1982.

"Murder suspect to appeal witness' immunity status," New Bedford *Standard-Times*, February 4, 1982.

"Convict requests speedy trial in second murder," New Bedford *Standard-Times*, May 5, 1982.

"Murder suspect seeks dismissal of charges," New Bedford *Standard-Times*, May 19, 1982.

"Courts clear way for more 'cult' trials," New Bedford *Standard-Times*, May 29, 1982.

"Testimony allowed in cult murder trial; High court to let participant talk in Fall River case," *Journal Bulletin Wire Reports*, May 29, 1982.

"R.I. man again linked to Fall River murder," New Bedford *Standard-Times*, July 9, 1982.

"Judge upholds photo identification of suspect in Fall River murder," New Bedford *Standard-Times*, August 6, 1982.

"Witness: I lied about 'cult' murders," New Bedford *Standard-Times*, December 30, 1982.

"DA Pina drops 'cult' murder case; Suspect free after 22 months in jail," New Bedford *Standard-Times*, January 4, 1983.

"Roofer cleared of Satan cult killing; Witness admitted that she 'lied' to grand jury," Fall River *Herald*, January 4, 1983.

"Lawyers for convicted slayers seek their release," New Bedford *Standard-Times*, January 8, 1983.

"DA quietly drops 2nd murder charge," New Bedford *Standard-Times*, January 14, 1983.

"Former assistant DA to fight bid for new cult murder trial," New Bedford *Standard-Times*, February 16, 1983.

"Slayer's attorney asks more time to review recanted story," New Bedford *Standard-Times*, March 1, 1983.

"Lawyer: Prosecution may have allowed lies," New Bedford *Standard-Times*, March 3, 1983.

"Lawyer is silent on claim that prosecution knew witness lied," New Bedford *Standard-Times*, March 4, 1983.

"Cult murder witness says she was told to lie, lawyer says," New Bedford *Standard-Times*, July 16, 1983.

"With 2 witnesses missing, state may drop murder charge," *Providence Journal*, October 21, 1983.

"High court mulls hearing on another trial for cult killer," New Bedford *Standard-Times*, December 12, 1983.

"Judge says convicted murderer is entitled to hearing on new trial," New Bedford *Standard-Times*, December 16, 1983.

"Different judge to hear killer's plea for new trial," New Bedford *Standard-Times*, April 20, 1984.

"Witness says she lied rather than 'rot in jail'; New trial is sought in murder of prostitute," New Bedford *Standard-Times*, July 17, 1984.

"Reputations at stake: Killer's motion for new trial raises questions about lawyers' integrity," New Bedford *Standard-Times*, July 18, 1984.

"Judge rejects bid for new trial in 1980 murder of prostitute," New Bedford *Standard-Times*, August 10, 1984

"Killer's appeal rejected," New Bedford *Standard-Times*, March 16, 1986.